Serverless Security

Understand, Assess, and Implement Secure and Reliable Applications in AWS, Microsoft Azure, and Google Cloud

Miguel A. Calles

Apress®

Serverless Security: Understand, Assess, and Implement Secure and Reliable Applications in AWS, Microsoft Azure, and Google Cloud

Miguel A. Calles
La Habra, CA, USA

ISBN-13 (pbk): 978-1-4842-6099-9   ISBN-13 (electronic): 978-1-4842-6100-2
https://doi.org/10.1007/978-1-4842-6100-2

Managing Director, Apress Media LLC: Welmoed Spahr
Acquisitions Editor: Susan McDermott
Development Editor: Laura Berendson
Coordinating Editor: Jessica Vakili

Distributed to the book trade worldwide by Springer Science+Business Media New York, 1 NY Plaza, New York NY 10004. Phone 1-800-SPRINGER, fax (201) 348-4505, e-mail orders-ny@springer-sbm.com, or visit www.springeronline.com. Apress Media, LLC is a California LLC and the sole member (owner) is Springer Science + Business Media Finance Inc (SSBM Finance Inc). SSBM Finance Inc is a **Delaware** corporation.

For information on translations, please e-mail booktranslations@springernature.com; for reprint, paperback, or audio rights, please e-mail bookpermissions@springernature.com.

Apress titles may be purchased in bulk for academic, corporate, or promotional use. eBook versions and licenses are also available for most titles. For more information, reference our Print and eBook Bulk Sales web page at http://www.apress.com/bulk-sales.

Any source code or other supplementary material referenced by the author in this book is available to readers on GitHub via the book's product page, located at www.apress.com/978-1-4842-6099-9. For more detailed information, please visit http://www.apress.com/source-code.

Printed on acid-free paper

Table of Contents

About the Author

Miguel A. Calles is a certified Cybersecurity engineer, works on cloud computing projects, and writes about Cybersecurity. He has worked on multiple serverless projects as a developer and security engineer, contributed to open source serverless projects, and worked on large military systems in various engineering roles. He started in Cybersecurity in 2016 for a US government contract, has been doing technical writing since 2007, and has worked in multiple engineering roles since 2004. Miguel started to gain interest in Cybersecurity when he was in middle school and was trying to reverse engineer websites.

Miguel is a Principal Solutions and Security Engineer at VeriToll, LLC. He has a Bachelor of Science degree in Material Science and Engineering from the Massachusetts Institute of Technology, a Master of Business Administrator degree from the University of Florida, a Cloud Security Alliance's Certificate of Cloud Security Knowledge certification, and a CompTIA A+ certification.

About the Technical Reviewer

David A. Gershman is a Cybersecurity engineer for a government contractor and has the CISSP certification. He has also taught Computer Science at California Polytechnic University, Pomona, on topics ranging from introduction programming to computer networking and Cybersecurity for over 20 years. In his spare time, David enjoys restoring and programming retro 8-bit computers.

Acknowledgments

I would like to express thanks to the following persons and organizations:

- My wife and kids for supporting me in this endeavor.

- My mentor J.R. Richardson for helping me in my professional development and encouraging me to explore new ways to grow.

- David Gershman for introducing me to the field of Cybersecurity and throughly reviewing this book.

- Guise Bule for inviting me to join Secjuice (a blog site that promotes writing about Cybersecurity and information security), where I first started writing about Cybersecurity and serverless computing topics.

- David Huang from Paradigm Sift for his friendship since my college days and helping me troubleshoot a topic in Chapter 8.

- VeriToll (my employer at the time of this writing) for allowing me to write this book and introducing me to the world of serverless computing.

- Raytheon, before they became Raytheon Technologies, for the several years of writing technical manuals and design documents that prepared me for writing my first published book.

- Several teachers that had a lasting impact on my education – Ms. Mary Lang, Mr. Michael Swatek, and Professor Fiona Barnes.

- Apress for allowing me to share what I have learned about Cybersecurity in serverless computing.

- Last but not least, my Creator for helping me achieve a life goal and His provision.

Introduction

When I started working with the Serverless Framework, I was curious about the security aspect. I was transitioning to a project for a mobile app with a serverless back end. Previously, I was an information assurance (IA) engineer working on Cybersecurity for US Government military systems. I had become accustomed to using well-defined processes and requirements in my role as an IA engineer. The systems we were securing were part of a vast network of other systems with strict IA requirements. The threats seemed limited; and implementing Cybersecurity, in many cases, was following a list of checklists and requirements. But, Cybersecurity in the world of serverless development was a new frontier.

The more I worked with serverless, the more I wondered about its Cybersecurity. Cybersecurity with serverless projects seemed to lack the oversight that I experienced in the IA world. The team could release a serverless application without addressing security. I searched for serverless security and found limited information. I did find some helpful documents on the top serverless security risks and well-written blog posts about specific topics. I was looking for a book that provided an overview of serverless security and guidance on approaching it.

I decided to write this book with the intent to fill that void and provide a resource that addressed multiple aspects of serverless security. I leveraged my IA and Cybersecurity experience, my hands-on experience with serverless, and my research to write this book. In one perspective, this book provides an overview of serverless security. You could be new to serverless and learn how to approach serverless security by performing a risk assessment. From another perspective, this book provides practical ways to address serverless security. You could be looking for examples and recommendations to implement in your serverless projects. I am excited to share this book with you because I believe it will guide you in identifying areas of consideration when securing your serverless application.

## CHAPTER 1

Introduction to Cloud Computing Security

In this chapter, we will review cloud computing and how its security evolved. We will learn how serverless computing relates to cloud computing and how securing serverless computing differs from the typical cloud computing Cybersecurity. We will review Cybersecurity, how it applies to cloud computing, and why it is needed. This chapter will set the foundation for Cybersecurity in serverless computing by putting it in the context of cloud computing and its security.

Cloud Computing Service Models

Cloud computing is a service offering where a client rents computing resources, physically located in an offsite location, from a provider. The resources are available on demand, and the client accesses them using the Internet. A client can rent resources from networking and storage equipment to fully developed software applications. Five major service models define how providers make cloud computing resources available to their clients: Infrastructure as a Service (IaaS), Container as a Service (CaaS), Platform as a Service (PaaS), Function as a Service (FaaS), and Software as a Service (SaaS). Table 1-1 depicts how the responsibility of the resource varies among the cloud computing types and compares to the traditional on-premise computing. We will briefly review each cloud computing service model.

1

© Miguel A. Calles 2020
M. Calles, *Serverless Security*, https://doi.org/10.1007/978-1-4842-6100-2_1

Table 1-1. *Comparison of Cloud Computing Service Models and On-Premise Computing*

Resource	IaaS	CaaS	PaaS	FaaS	SaaS	On-Premise
Application	C	C	C	C	VR	C
Data	C	C	C	C	V	C
Functions	C	C	C	VR	V	C
Runtime	C	C	VR	V	V	C
Security†	C	C	VR	V	V	C
Middleware	C	C	VR	V	V	C
Databases	C	C	VR	V	V	C
Operating Systems	C	C	VR	V	V	C
Containers	C	VR	V	V	V	C
Virtualization	VR	V	V	V	V	C
Servers/Workstations	VR	V	V	V	V	C
Storage	VR	V	V	V	V	C
Networking	VR	V	V	V	V	C
Data Centers	V	V	V	V	V	C

V = Vendor managed, R = Rentable resource, C = Client managed

†Security resources typically includes security software and appliances. Cybersecurity is essential for each resource type.

Infrastructure as a Service (IaaS)

Infrastructure as a Service (IaaS) is a service offering where a provider makes infrastructure (e.g., networking equipment and computing equipment) available for a client to use. IaaS enables a client to rent infrastructure without having to procure it. The client is responsible for configuring and fine-tuning the different infrastructure components. The provider is responsible for maintaining the infrastructure, making it accessible, and ensuring a minimum level of reliability and availability. This type of cloud computing is the closest to an on-premise model of buying, storing, powering, configuring, maintaining, and administering the infrastructure components, but with the simplified configuration and reduced maintenance and administration.

Container as a Service (CaaS)

Container as a Service (CaaS) is a service offering where a provider makes software container creation and orchestration (e.g., Docker[1] and Kubernetes[2]) available for a client to use. CaaS enables a client to compile all the software packages (needed by an application) into a container without having to set up the infrastructure. The client is responsible for configuring the container and defining the orchestration. The provider is responsible for maintaining the infrastructure, the container virtualization, and the orchestration software. This type of cloud computing provides the benefit of running a lightweight platform without having to set up the infrastructure nor install the orchestration software.

Platform as a Service (PaaS)

Platform as a Service (PaaS) is a service offering where a provider makes a specific platform (e.g., an operating system, a database, and a web server) available for a client to use. PaaS enables a client to rent a platform without having to set up the infrastructure. The client is responsible for configuring and fine-tuning the platform to meet the specific need. The provider is responsible for maintaining the infrastructure, keeping the platform software up to date, and ensuring a minimum level of reliability and availability. This type of cloud computing provides the benefit of defining the computational need without having to determine what kind of infrastructure is needed to power the platform.

Function as a Service (FaaS)

Function as a Service (FaaS) (typically associated with serverless computing) is a service offering where a provider enables a client to run individual software functions and interconnect them to make an application. FaaS allows a client to rent computing

---

[1]Docker is a registered trademark of Docker, Inc.
[2]Kubernetes is a registered trademark of The Linux Foundation.

time needed to execute the functions without needing to maintain any supporting software and hardware. The client is responsible for writing all the software functions and defining the orchestration among them. The provider is responsible for properly configuring and maintaining the infrastructure and platforms needed to execute the functions. This type of cloud computing provides similar benefits as PaaS and CaaS offerings, but without having to configure the platforms and containers, and enables the client to develop a SaaS offering.

Software as a Service (SaaS)

Software as a Service (SaaS) is a service offering where a provider makes a specific piece of software (e.g., a web application) available for a client to use. SaaS enables a client to rent a piece of software without needing any hardware other than an Internet-connected computing device. The client is responsible for customizing any software settings provided by the application. The provider is responsible for ensuring the web application is available and preventing others from accessing the client's account data. This type of cloud computing provides the benefits of using the software without having to perform maintenance.

Cloud Computing Deployment Models

Cybersecurity was a big concern in cloud computing in its infancy and continues to be one. Cloud computing disrupted the traditional on-premise Cybersecurity model. This new model required different strategies to implement Cybersecurity, and it shared responsibilities with a third-party provider, which reserves the right to secure the system differently than the client desires. Furthermore, the provider not only has to implement Cybersecurity to establish trust with its clients. The provider also needs to secure its offering to protect itself from external threats, which also includes its clients. New models were birthed to accommodate the differing levels of adoption of cloud computing.

The Private or Enterprise Cloud

An enterprise uses a private cloud to have on-premise computing equipment interconnected to on-premise networking equipment. This configuration is referred to as a cloud because the computing equipment interconnects over an intranet (i.e., an internal Internet). Ideally, the data is only accessible within the physical premises of the enterprise for the highest Cybersecurity benefit; see Figure 1-1. An enterprise might choose a private cloud to protect sensitive data.

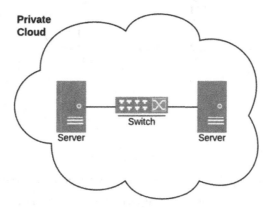

Figure 1-1. *Private Cloud*

A private cloud can have the lowest Cybersecurity risk, assuming proper Cybersecurity measures are in place. The enterprise is mostly or entirely responsible for the Cybersecurity risk. It, therefore, results in higher costs because it must procure, configure, and maintain all the networking and computing equipment and configure and maintain any Cybersecurity measures. The enterprise may favor the private cloud because the higher costs might be lower than those of a Cybersecurity breach, and it has greater control over the Cybersecurity measures.

The Public Cloud

A provider establishes and provides a public cloud to make computing resources available for rent over the Internet. This configuration enables an enterprise to put data in the public cloud and have it accessible from any Internet-connected device; see Figure 1-2. Ideally, Cybersecurity measures protect data by limiting access to only specific parties. An enterprise might choose a public cloud to lower costs, increase accessibility and availability, and offset risk.

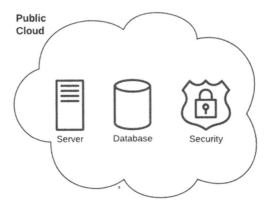

Figure 1-2. *Public Cloud*

A public cloud might have higher Cybersecurity risks because there is no direct purview over the infrastructure and Cybersecurity measures. The provider and the enterprise share the Cybersecurity risk. The enterprise must have the expertise to adequately configure the cloud's Cybersecurity measures and protect its data. The enterprise might favor the shared Cybersecurity risk because it cannot afford to set up and maintain a private cloud, lacks the expertise to secure a private cloud, or prefers faster development and deployment.

The Hybrid Cloud

An enterprise adopts a hybrid cloud to set up private and public clouds to work together. This configuration enables an enterprise to use a private cloud for its more sensitive data and a public cloud for its less sensitive data; see Figure 1-3. It further allows taking advantage of both sets of features and computing capabilities of both clouds. An enterprise might choose a hybrid cloud to meet legal and contractual requirements, lower costs, and configure varying levels of Cybersecurity measures.

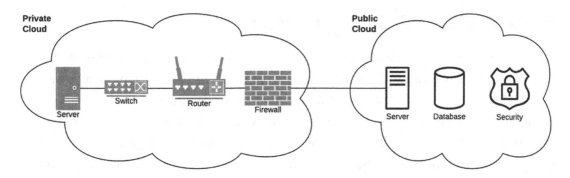

Figure 1-3. *Hybrid Cloud*

The hybrid cloud might be the best of both worlds in some situations. Still, it potentially has a higher Cybersecurity risk than a private cloud and not necessarily a lower risk than a public cloud. We should use properly configured private cloud security equipment (e.g., firewall systems, intrusion detection/prevention systems, and security information and event management systems) to establish a connection between the public and private clouds. The connectivity between the private and public clouds presents an opportunity for the bypassing of security equipment and exposing the data within the private cloud. The enterprise might favor the increased Cybersecurity risk for several reasons: it wants to take advantage of features within the public cloud; it has several layers of Cybersecurity measures to mitigate the risk of the external connection; it has multiple private clouds; the public cloud only has access to a limited set of private clouds.

Applying a Cloud Computing Model to FaaS

FaaS can support all three deployment models. FaaS was initially introduced as a public cloud solution because it reduces most of the configuration and maintenance effort. As the FaaS offering matured, providers added the ability to access a private cloud from a FaaS solution. The industry realized the need for having FaaS within a private cloud, and it created a FaaS solution that runs on software containers installed on servers within a private cloud. In this book, we will mostly explore Cybersecurity in the public cloud.

An Overview on Cybersecurity

Cybersecurity, or security for short, is the practice of identifying the assets that need protecting, the threats against those assets, and the defenses needed to protect those assets. Many engineers, developers, and managers have become accustomed to implementing security in traditional on-premise systems: desktop computers, laptops, servers, networking equipment, operating systems, and so on. The cloud computing era disrupted how companies and individuals view their assets. Consequently, the practice of security had to evolve to work in this new computational method. Now that the assets and infrastructure are provided by a third party, the cloud computing provider and the client share the responsibility for implementing security.

We can summarize security and its implementation in three words: confidentiality, integrity, and availability. Using the confidentiality, integrity, and availability (CIA) model (sometimes referred to as the CIA triad) is one way to identify the security risks and security measures needed to mitigate those risks. We will explore each element.

Confidentiality

Applying confidentiality to a piece of data is giving access only to the intended recipients. Said another way, confidentiality is preventing unauthorized access from unintended recipients. A common term in recent news is "privacy." An enterprise may choose to implement confidentiality using encryption and access control.

Data has no encryption by default. Applying encryption to data prevents access to it. The data is encrypted using a key, and only that key can decrypt the file to return it to its original state. The key can be a password, file, or certificate. The encryption should happen while the data is at rest (i.e., while it sits in the file system) or while it is in transit (e.g., being transferred over the Internet).

Data has no access control by default, but modern operating systems do implement some level of access control. Access control defines which data is accessible to others and how that data is used. In an operating system that supports it, the access control determines whether the current user can read, modify, or execute the data and also defines whether other users can have similar privileges. It might also allow specifying a subset of users that can read, modify, or execute the data.

FaaS solutions provide encryption and access control. The account owner needs to enable shared access or public access; the account owner is the person or entity that manages the account on the public cloud. The data owner can assign read, modify, and delete privileges to the data; the data owner is the person or entity that manages the data stores in the public cloud. The account owner is responsible for configuring the cloud infrastructure to set the desired level of confidentiality. The cloud infrastructure provides encryption for data in transit, data at rest, and access control to the data owner and others. The provider's cloud infrastructure only gives the account owner access to the data. Cloud infrastructure supports encryption in transit and at rest.

Integrity

Ensuring integrity for a piece of data is giving confidence the data someone sent you is the same data you received. Said another way, integrity is making sure there are no unintended modifications to the data, and the intended recipient has trust they received the expected data. The enterprise may choose to implement integrity using checksums, version control, or logging.

A checksum is a representation of the data and is used to determine whether the file has changed since it was last accessed. For example, when a user creates a file, the system records its checksum. When the user modifies the file, the checksum also changes. The user or file system can use the checksum to determine whether the file has changed.

Whenever a user creates, modifies, or deletes a file, a version control system or a logging system captures the change. The version control system saves a copy of the file for each version (and sometimes a checksum). In contrast, a logging system records the type of change, the user who invoked the change, the time the change occurred, and other relevant information.

FaaS solutions provide integrity solutions natively and as an add-on feature. The account owner is responsible for configuring the cloud infrastructure to set the desired level of integrity. The owner can also enable logging systems to capture changes to the file and add checksums to the different versions of the data. The cloud infrastructure supports version control of files. The cloud infrastructure natively does file replication at the hardware level while maintaining the data integrity.

Availability

Providing availability for a piece of data is using measures to ensure intended recipients can use the data. Said another way, availability is making sure the intended recipient can access the data at any time. The enterprise may increase availability through maintenance, replication, and redundancy.

Performing maintenance ensures the hardware hosting the data continues operating as long as possible without interruption. For example, if a user stores a piece of data on one piece of equipment, and it stops functioning, that data is no longer available for a user to access. Had that unit been adequately maintained, it could have continued operating longer, or the maintainer could have observed symptoms of imminent failure. Therefore, it is essential to maintain hardware to keep it running to increase availability.

Replication and redundancy create replicas of data on other pieces of hardware. For example, in the event one unit fails, others make the data available for a user to access. An enterprise will use hardware components (e.g., Redundant Arrays of Independent Disks, or RAIDs) to provide local, built-in redundancy and data backup software to achieve geographical (offsite) redundancy.

FaaS solutions provide availability natively when storing data in the public cloud, which has a minimum level of guaranteed availability. The account owner is responsible for selecting a cloud infrastructure with the desired minimum availability and configuring any additional availability features. For increased availability, the data owner can choose to replicate the data across multiple geographic locations within the public cloud infrastructure. Using cloud infrastructure eliminates the need to perform routine hardware maintenance. However, regular checks of the account configuration and data access are still warranted.

The Need for Cloud Computing Cybersecurity

Approaching Cybersecurity is similar, yet different, in public and hybrid clouds vs. a private cloud. The enterprise has more control and influence of the security measures in a private cloud. The security measures are implemented based on the risks identified in an assessment. The enterprise should assess public and hybrid clouds similar to a private cloud, but with the understanding that the threats vary.

Examples of Threats

Threats exist in the three cloud computing models and manifest themselves in several ways. We will explore a few examples of how threats manifest.

Data Breaches from Insecure Data Storage

Since cloud storage configurations support private, shared, and public access, it is probable public access was set unintentionally.[3] For example, an attacker can use an improperly configured cloud storage system to access highly sensitive data. An inexperienced user may accidentally grant public access while attempting to limit sharing to a small group. A user may also temporarily give public access to transfer data to other parties, but forget to revert to private access. Data breaches can result from an improperly configured cloud storage system.

Data Breaches from Identity and Access Management Misconfiguration

Someone can access another person's account if the Identity and Access Management (IAM) system has a misconfiguration. The data owner might use an IAM system to share data access with multiple users. Shared access should be limited to the users that require the data and no one else. For example, the finance team should only have access to confidential financial records, and not the engineering team or suppliers. Data breaches have occurred because a supplier had access to a network where sensitive data was processed.[4] Data breaches can result when one account is compromised, and it has access to data it should not.

Denial of Service Attack Due To Software Vulnerabilities

Any application exposed to the Internet is vulnerable to Denial of Service (DoS) or Distributed Denial of Service (DDoS) attacks. Cloud services limit how much computing power a client can use at any given time. An attacker hopes to exploit a weakness in the application by sending multiple simultaneous requests and making the application unavailable to the users. This downtime can result in financial loss and lost productivity.

Weaknesses can exist at any level. For example, an attacker can exploit a software library with a known vulnerability by sending a large piece of data such that the

---

[3]"100GB of secret NSA data found on unsecured AWS S3 bucket. 29 November 2017. Adam Shepard. IT Pro. www.itpro.co.uk/security/30060/100gb-of-secret-nsa-data-found-on-unsecured-aws-s3-bucket

[4]"What Retailers Need to Learn from the Target Breach to Protect against Similar Attacks." January 31, 2014. Chris Poulin. Security Intelligence. https://securityintelligence.com/target-breach-protect-against-similar-attacks-retailers

application takes a significant time to process the entire data or eventually times out.[5] If thousands or millions of requests are sent simultaneously to a vulnerable software function, the application may stop responding for all users and result in a DoS to the user base.

Identifying Threats

The three previous examples illustrate the realization of threats. Your understanding of the threats to your application will help you determine how to protect against them. We will explore how to identify threats in the next chapter.

Key Takeaways

In this chapter, we reviewed cloud computing and Cybersecurity. This chapter aimed to provide a foundation for the remainder of this book. We established concepts and terminology in cloud computing. We will briefly review these concepts and terms.

We explored cloud computing service models:

- **Infrastructure as a Service (IaaS)** is using infrastructure (e.g., computing and networking equipment) over the Internet.

- **Container as a Service (CaaS)** is using a software container (e.g., Docker) over the Internet.

- **Platform as a Service (PaaS)** is using a configured platform (e.g., a database) over the Internet.

- **Function as a Service (FaaS)** is running and orchestrating functions (e.g., an email subscription function) over the Internet.

- **Software as a Service (SaaS)** is using an application (e.g., a web-based email) over the Internet.

We covered cloud computing deployment models and how FaaS supports them:

---

[5]"Serverless Security & The Weakest Link (Avoiding App DoS)." 8 February 2019. Ory Segal. PureSec Blog. www.puresec.io/blog/serverless-security-and-the-weakest-link-or-how-not-to-get-nuked-by-app-dos

- **Private cloud** is where an enterprise uses computing equipment it acquired and accesses it over an internal network. An enterprise can set up an internal FaaS solution on its hardware.

- **Public cloud** is where an enterprise uses computing equipment from a third party and accesses it over the Internet. An enterprise can use a provider's FaaS solution.

- **Hybrid cloud** is where an enterprise uses private and public clouds for different purposes and uses security equipment to interconnect them to minimize risk. An enterprise may configure a private FaaS solution to access data from a public cloud and vice versa, given the security equipment on both sides are configured to enable access.

We learned the confidentiality, integrity, and availability model in Cybersecurity and how FaaS supports all three.

- **Confidentiality** is ensuring only the desired recipients can access a piece of data. FaaS ensures confidentiality by limiting data access to the account owner with access control systems and by using encryption.

- **Integrity** is ensuring the data was unchanged and uncorrupted from the last time it was accessed. FaaS provides integrity with version control systems and logging systems.

- **Availability** is ensuring the intended recipient can access the data without disruption. FaaS provides a minimum level of availability and increases with replication across geographical regions.

We reviewed examples of Cybersecurity threats to depict the need for Cybersecurity in cloud computing.

In the next chapter, we will examine how to assess a FaaS application and perform a security risk assessment.

CHAPTER 2

Performing a Risk Assessment

In this chapter, we will learn how to perform a risk assessment for a serverless application. We will explore how to understand how the application works, which includes reviewing documentation, source code, and system accounts and using the application. We will discuss why we scope the risk assessment. We will learn how to develop a threat model and how to use it to start creating the risk assessment.

Conventions

We will review the conventions used throughout this book. For clarity, we will use one example application throughout. We might deviate from this example application at times when it makes sense to explain a concept better. We will use one FaaS framework (or typically referred to as a serverless framework) for consistency, except where it lacks support for a security configuration we are learning or when we can better learn a principle by directly modifying the configuration. For simplicity, we will use one programming language in the examples because it may become overwhelming to cover the same principle in all programming languages supported by the serverless provider and framework. The goal is to ensure an optimal experience in learning security concepts with less focus on prescriptive approaches for implementing them.

Example Serverless Application

Throughout this book, we will use a fictitious ecommerce mobile app in the examples. This app allows users to buy and sell goods using a mobile app. The app brokers the transactions to ensure both buyer and seller are protected. The mobile app communicates to an Application Programming Interface (API) to execute the transactions.

15

© Miguel A. Calles 2020
M. Calles, *Serverless Security*, https://doi.org/10.1007/978-1-4842-6100-2_2

The serverless framework will create the API. The serverless application will integrate with other third-party services, which provide additional capabilities. The examples and exercises reference this fictitious application but do not provide a fully functioning system.

Serverless Frameworks

The three major FaaS and serverless providers are Amazon Web Services (AWS), Microsoft Azure,[1] and Google Cloud.[2] You can manually set up functions using their web-based consoles. You can choose an automated way to deploy the functions by leveraging FaaS or serverless frameworks. There are several serverless frameworks, which support different programming languages and multiple providers. We will focus on a framework that supports AWS, Azure, and Google Cloud.

We will use the Serverless Framework[3] in this book, not to be confused with the term "serverless framework." Serverless, Inc. created a serverless framework that supports AWS, Azure, Google Cloud, and other serverless providers. The Serverless Framework is written in Node.js[4] JavaScript and has open source and paid versions. At the time of this writing, the open source project has over 30,000 stars, forked over 3000 times, and is actively maintained.[5] For these reasons, we will use the Serverless Framework throughout this book.

Programming Language

The Serverless Framework was built using Node.js and exists as a package in the npm[6] package manager. npm is arguably the fastest growing package repository with at least one million packages at the time of this writing.[7] The popularity is probably a result of JavaScript being one of the easiest programming languages to learn.[8] We will use Node.js

---

[1]Azure is a registered trademark of Microsoft Corporation.

[2]Google and Google Cloud are registered trademarks of Google LLC.

[3]Serverless Framework is a registered trademark of Serverless, Inc.

[4]Node.js is a trademark of Joyent, Inc.

[5]Serverless GitHub repository. https://github.com/serverless/serverless

[6]npm is a registered trademark of npm, Inc.

[7]Module Counts website. www.modulecounts.com

[8]"The 10 easiest programming languages to learn." 17 July, 2017. Alison DeNisco Rayome. TechRepublic. www.techrepublic.com/article/the-10-easiest-programming-languages-to-learn

in the examples for ease of understanding, compatibility with the Serverless Framework, and the runtime engine support from AWS, Azure, and Google Cloud.

Terms, Keywords, and Acronyms

This book will use different terms, keywords, and acronyms throughout this book. They are defined in their first use and may be defined again if it aids in understanding and helps avoid confusion. Table 2-1 lists terms, keywords, and acronyms repeatedly used throughout the book.

Table 2-1. *Terms, Keywords, and Acronyms Used Throughout the Book*

Term, Keyword, or Acronym	Definition
API	Application Programming Interface
AWS	Amazon Web Services, a serverless platform
Azure	Microsoft Azure, a serverless platform
CLI	Command-Line Interface
Google Cloud	A serverless platform
HTTP	HyperText Transfer Protocol
HTTPS	HyperText Transfer Protocol Secure
JavaScript	A programming language
Node.js	A JavaScript runtime environment
npm	A package manager for Node.js
OS	An acronym for operating system
Serverless	Short for Serverless Framework, a serverless framework
serverless	Another term for Function as a Service
serverless.yml	A configuration file used in the Serverless Framework
sls	A CLI command for the Serverless Framework

Understanding the Application

It is essential to understand the application when performing a risk assessment because each application is unique in its requirements, purpose, and capabilities. Not all application designs are the same, even if multiple applications perform similar functions. For example, the Microsoft Office[9] suite has word processing, presentation, and spreadsheet capabilities. The open source equivalent of Microsoft Office is The Document Foundation LibreOffice[10] suite, which also has word processing, presentation, and spreadsheet capabilities. Microsoft Office mostly uses C++, whereas LibreOffice uses C++, Extensible Markup Language (XML), and Java. Both Microsoft Office and LibreOffice prefer different XML file formats, though they do provide limited support for both file formats. Microsoft Office integrates well with the Microsoft Windows operating system (OS), Microsoft Office 365 online editor, and Microsoft SharePoint cloud-based file sharing.

In contrast, LibreOffice is a cross-platform desktop application. These two office suites are different though they provide similar capabilities. Therefore, the assessor should view each application as unique and avoid applying preconceived security measures to it.

Reviewing Documentation

Reviewing the documentation is one way to begin understanding how the developers designed an application. The documentation captures the design decisions. There is an inherent divergence from the latest version of the documentation and the latest version of the application for several reasons:

- The documentation is no longer maintained.

- Design decisions were made based on discovery while creating and updating the app.

- The documentation updates are in progress and not yet released.

---

[9]Office, Office 365, SharePoint, and Windows are registered trademarks of Microsoft Corporation.
[10]"LibreOffice" and "The Document Foundation" are registered trademarks of their corresponding registered owners or are in actual use as trademarks in one or more countries.

- The documentation only captures specific software releases.

- The current team members may be unaware that documentation exists and need updating.

In either situation, reading and understanding the documentation provides insight and prompts to inquire for additional information. There are different types of documents to review:

- **Architecture and design diagrams** give visual depictions about how the application integrates various components to operate and execute its intended purpose. There are different types of diagrams, each with a different viewpoint or perspective of the system.

- **Requirement documents** state the functionality and objectives the application is required to achieve. These requirements may be contractual or technical.

- **Manuals** provide instruction for configuring and using the application and are written for developers, technical support, or users.

Each document type provides insight into the application about its intended design, objective, or use. There might be a plethora of documentation to review and a limited time to review it. Therefore, it is imperative to select the documents you and the development team agree are the most important to review and to choose a sample of other documents as cost and schedule permit.

The architecture and design diagrams are likely to be the most helpful in becoming acquainted with the application, especially if you are asked to review an application of which you were not involved in its development. There are different types of diagrams of which some include

- **Architecture diagrams** are higher-level views of the application. These include

  - **System architecture diagrams** depict the relationship among all the system components (e.g., hardware and software) and external systems and how they communicate.

- **Software architecture diagrams** depict the relationship among the different software elements (e.g., modules, functions) and how they integrate.

- **Application architecture diagrams** depict the relationship among the different aspects of the objects of the application (technical requirements, operational needs, and functionality).

- **Enterprise architecture diagrams** depict the organizational impact and stakeholder interaction.

- **Security architecture diagrams** depict the security components used to mitigate risks.

- **Design diagrams** are lower-level views of the application, such as

  - **Activity diagrams** depict the different activities the application performs.

  - **Use case diagrams** depict how actors use the application.

  - **Timing diagrams** depict the timing among different interactions within the application.

  - **Sequence diagrams** depict the sequence of events in the application.

  - **Class diagrams** depict how software classes are defined and relate.

Each gives insight into the application and may highlight security weaknesses. For example, you might consider noting a potential area of concern if a diagram shows an authorization function that does not communicate with an identity and access management system because the function might be vulnerable to granting unauthorized access to data. Even if potential security weaknesses are not evident by reviewing the diagrams, it will allow you to determine focus areas for your assessment.

EXERCISE 2-1: PERFORMING A DOCUMENT REVIEW

Objective:

In this exercise, you will practice reviewing architecture and design diagrams and identify potential security concerns.

Relevant Information:

The ecommerce mobile app team has provided you with a set of documents:

- A system architecture diagram in Figure 2-1

- An application architecture diagram in Figure 2-2

- A use case diagram in Figure 2-3

- An activity diagram in Figure 2-4

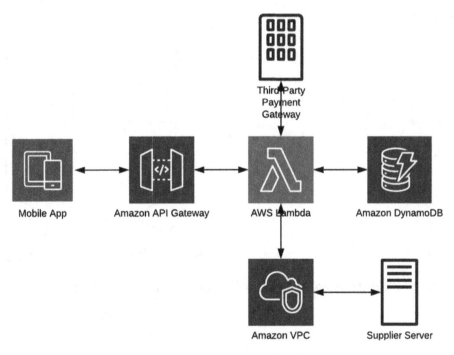

Figure 2-1. *System Architecture Diagram for the eCommerce Application*

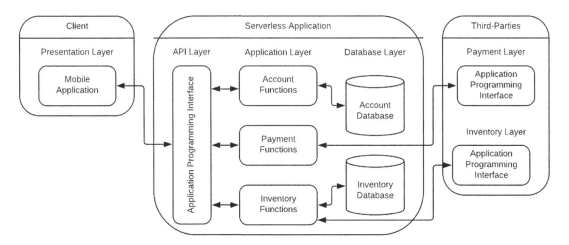

Figure 2-2. *Application Architecture Diagram for the eCommerce Application*

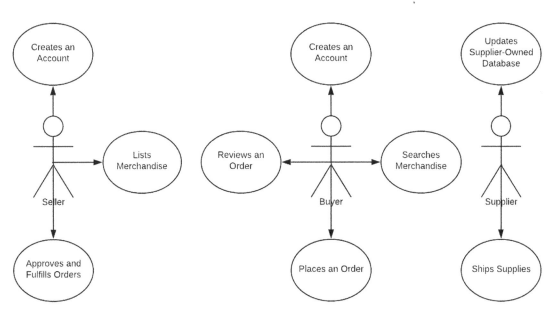

Figure 2-3. *Use Case Diagram for the eCommerce Application*

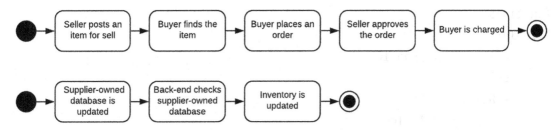

Figure 2-4. *Activity Diagram for the eCommerce Mobile Application*

Instructions:

Review each diagram to understand how the application works and identify how they relate.

Create a document highlighting areas of concern. Include a list of follow-up questions to inquire of the team.

Reviewing Source Code

Reviewing the source code will allow you to assess how the developers implemented the design and where the implementation diverged from the design. Several automated tools analyze source code. Using these tools will systematically find flaws in the code. In Chapter 3, we will explore how to secure the code. Time permitting, you should perform a manual investigation of the code in addition to using automated tools.

Listing all the source code files used in the application allows you to enumerate the functions used in the application. You can depict how each function interacts by creating a flow diagram, or you can assess the divergence of an existing diagram. Having the function list allows you to list all the inputs, event triggers, outputs, and any other relevant information. The Serverless Framework simplifies the function listing; see the example in Listing 2-1.

Listing 2-1. Sample Serverless Framework Configuration File

```
service: eCommerceAuthentication

provider:
  name: aws
  runtime: nodejs10.x
```

```
functions:
  login:
    handler: login.handler
    events:
      - http:
          path: auth/login
          method: post
  verifyMfa:
    handler: verifyMfa.handler
    events:
      - http:
          path: auth/verifyMfa
          method: post
```

The Serverless configuration file (named "serverless.yml") identifies the following information:

- **The service** has a name of "eCommerceAuthentication." The name and the naming convention do the following:

  - Lists the application name "eCommerce" to differentiate this group of serverless functions from another application

  - Describes the functions as supporting "Authentication" and differentiates this group from others in the "eCommerce" application

- **The provider is AWS.**

- **The programming language runtime** engine is Node.js version 10. Each function can use a different runtime as needed.

- **The functions** are "login" and "verifyMfa." The function names are named to describe their purpose.

- **The file information** is listed in the "handler" key and describes the following:

  - The files are located in the root level of the Serverless project directory because there is no directory specified in the "handler" value.

- The filenames are "login" and "verifyMfa" and are the same as the function name (i.e., the name before the ".handler" part of the path).

- The entry points into the function are the "handler" method within the source code because ".handler" is the second part of path. Note: The actual file extension is ".js" because we are using Node.js.

- **The event triggers** are HyperText Transfer Protocol (HTTP) events. Sending an HTTP request to the web address of service appended with the "path" value will trigger the function.

You can use this information to build a spreadsheet to document all the functions; see Table 2-2.

Table 2-2. *Sample Function Listing*

Service	Function Name	Runtime	File Paths	Entry Point	Event Trigger(s)
eCommerceAuthentication	login	Node.js 10	login.js	handler	HTTP
eCommerceAuthentication	verifyMfa	Node.js 10	verifyMfa.js	handler	HTTP

The table lists all the information extracted from the Serverless configuration file. You can expand it as needed to support your assessment and also add other columns (e.g., description, imported modules, external interfaces, internal interfaces, etc.). This table consolidates information to simplify your assessment as you automatically and manually review the source code.

Reviewing Accounts

Your security assessment should include a review of the system accounts used in the application. The account used to run the serverless application should be part of the assessment. You should also consider reviewing the accounts for any third-party services and integrations. You may need to log in to the system accounts to perform your assessment. The application team might have some hesitation in providing you with administrator credentials. Still, they may grant you access to an account with read-only or limited permissions. We will explore how to secure your serverless provider account in Chapter 6.

You should have a standard set of questions to ask when reviewing the different accounts:

- Is there an account for each application environment (e.g., development, test, and production), or does the account support having different environments?

- Does the team avoid using shared accounts whenever possible?

- Does the application have an account with restricted access?

- Are account credentials (i.e., username and password) stored securely?

- Is multi-factor authentication supported and enabled?

- Are logins rate limited and locked out after too many attempts?

- Are access controls used to restrict the modification of the serverless application and its data?

You can use these sample questions as a starting point in your review or to ask the development team to investigate in the situation they give you no access to the accounts. The goal is to ensure the accounts have measures in place to protect the accounts from external threats and from it being a threat to the application.

Using the Application

Using the application is a tangible way of learning how it works. By interacting with the front end, you can see how the front end calls the back end. You will need a tool to capture the network traffic. Note the times as you take actions on the front end, and you can correlate the network calls made to the back end.

You will benefit greatly in using a network analyzer to record the traffic. Wireshark[11] is a free and open source traffic analyzer that runs on Microsoft Windows, Apple

---

[11]Wireshark is a registered trademark of the Wireshark Foundation.

macOS,[12] and Linux[13] operating systems. It allows you to see all the network traffic sent and received on the network connection of the computer running Wireshark; see Figure 2-5. You might want to see additional network traffic. To see all the data in the network, you will need to set that network connection as a switched port analyzer (or port mirror) to allow Wireshark to see all the network traffic. Wireshark is a powerful network analyzer, but you may need support from a network engineer to allow it to receive all the necessary traffic.

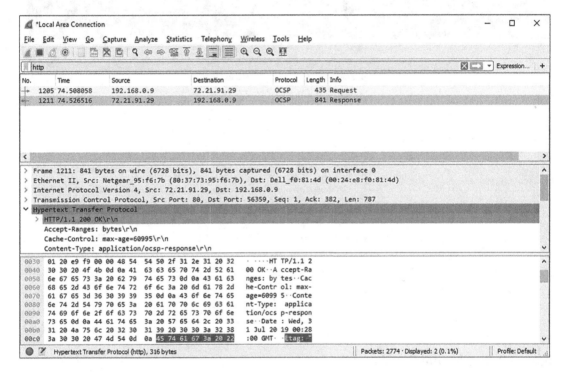

Figure 2-5. *Wireshark Network Capture*

Developer tools exist that help simplify the network analysis when using the application. For a web-based application, you can use the developer tools on Google Chrome and Mozilla Firefox[14] web browsers, which have built-in network analyzers; see

---

[12]Apple and macOS are trademarks of Apple, Inc., registered in the United States and other countries.

[13]Linux is a registered trademark of Linus Torvalds.

[14]Mozilla and Firefox are trademarks of the Mozilla Foundation in the United States and other countries.

Figures 2-6 and 2-7. For a mobile application, you can use Apple Xcode for Apple iOS[15] applications and Google Android Studio[16] for Android applications. Both allow you to build the application, run it on a simulated or emulated device, respectively, and view the application logs. You will need the source code to use Xcode and Android Studio, and you will have a limited network analysis by viewing the logs. The developer tools can help you correlate front-end actions with back-end requests.

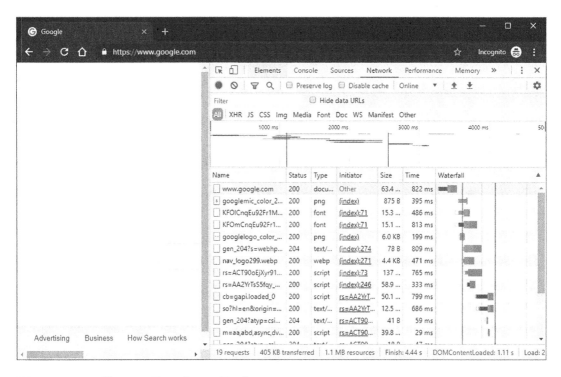

Figure 2-6. *Chrome Developer Tools*

---

[15]Apple, iOS, and Xcode are trademarks of Apple, Inc., registered in the United States and other countries.

[16]The "Android" name and other Google trademarks are property of Google LLC.

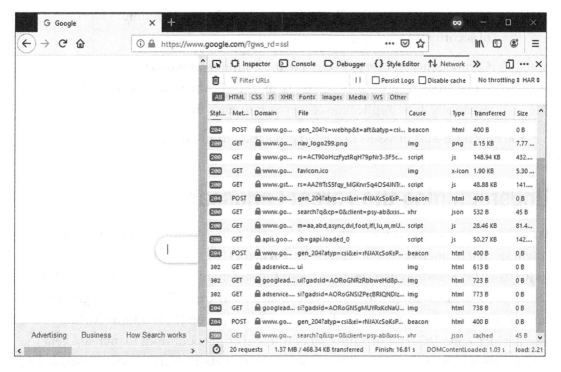

Figure 2-7. *Firefox Developer Tools*

Scoping the Security Assessment

You should limit your assessment to the scope you were assigned. Said another way, you might only have the permission to assess the serverless application, but not the mobile app, the third-party services, and any interfaces. You could draw a dotted line enclosing all the components you are responsible for assessing. This line is called a security enclave or a trust boundary.

The boundary defines what components need a thorough assessment. In general, you will use these guidelines:

- The edges of the boundary should have a security measure enabled to protect against external threats.

- The components within the boundary should meet a minimum level of security.

- Components and services outside the boundary might have no required security level. Still, there can be recommendations for them, especially if the application team can influence them.

You now have a list of assets that need protection from threats.

Understanding the Threat Landscape

With the numerous security breaches and Internet crimes reported in the news, it might seem it happens every other day. Threat actors (e.g., hackers) see Internet crime as lucrative because they can steal money or sell stolen information on the Dark Web. Other threat actors want to buy stolen information and are willing to pay a significant amount of money for it. The Federal Bureau of Investigation (FBI) Internet Crime Complaint Center (IC3) reports the cost of Internet crime continues to increase year over year; see Figure 2-8.[17] From 2012 to 2018, the reported annual loss increased from $581.4 million[18] to $2706.4 million, which is a 465.5% increase. Given the significant increase in less than a decade, it is imperative to understand and protect against threat actors and their threats.

---

[17]"2018 Internet Crime Report." Federal Bureau of Investigation Internet Crime Complaint Center. https://pdf.ic3.gov/2018_IC3Report.pdf

[18]"2013 Internet Crime Report." Federal Bureau of Investigation Internet Crime Complaint Center. https://pdf.ic3.gov/2013_IC3Report.pdf

IC3 Complaint Statistics
2014-2018

2014 269,422	2014 $800.5M
2015 288,012	2015 $1,070.7M
2016 298,728	2016 $1,450.7M
2017 301,580	2017 $1,418.7M
2018 351,937	2018 $2,706.4M

1,509,679 TOTAL COMPLAINTS $7.45 Billion TOTAL LOSSES

Figure 2-8. *FBI IC3 Complaint Statistics 2014–2018*

Threat Actors

Threat actors are the individuals or groups that are a threat to your application. There are different groups of threat actors, each with varying levels of skill and motivation, including

- **Script kiddies** lack skills to orchestrate their attacks, and their motivation varies from curiosity on hacking, embarrassing their target, or malicious intent. They use open source hacking tools or scripts to run against their target. Their attacks lack sophistication, but they can still inflict damage. Implementing standard security measures (e.g., enabling firewalls and keeping systems up to date with software patches) will typically protect your application from script kiddies.

- **Cybercriminals** can strategically orchestrate their attacks, and their motivation is typically financial gain. They use a variety of tools like script kiddies, leverage social engineering to fool individuals to disclose sensitive information, and deploy malicious software (e.g., ransomware). They are less likely to perform an attack if costs exceed the value of the target. Implementing training and detection tools, in addition to standard security measures, will help detect and prevent an attack.

- **Hacktivists** can strategically orchestrate their attacks, and their motivation is to support a cause or fulfill a mission. They use any means to accomplish their mission because they are unmotivated by financial gain and returns on their investments. Understanding their motivations, agendas, and attack patterns can help in implementing custom defenses against their attacks.

- **State-sponsored attackers** can strategically orchestrate their attacks, and their state sponsor governs their motivation. They benefit from leveraging their sponsor's resources, threat intelligence, and personnel to help them achieve their goals. They can solicit support from other hackers when needed. Understanding the political interests of the different states can help in implementing custom defenses against their attacks.

- **Insider threats** have varying skill levels, and their motivations vary from inadvertent to intentional. Some insiders accidentally or unknowingly are threats. Providing training on social engineering, other predatory techniques, and cyber hygiene will help protect against these inside attacks. Other insiders are disgruntled and want to inflict damage, but may or may not have the skill level to achieve an attack successfully. Ensuring a single person only has the access and privileges to accomplish their job responsibility will minimize the extent of damage an insider can inflict. Providing training on detecting and reporting insiders will also help protect against these threats. In all cases, securing systems assuming there are malicious actors inside the organization will mitigate the risk of an attack.

Now that we have an understanding of the different threat actors and their motivations, we can explore the attack surface they might use to accomplish their goals.

Attack Surface

A threat actor, or attacker, can exploit a vulnerability to execute an attack. A vulnerability is a weakness in the security caused by an error in software, a misconfiguration, or an omission. The attack becomes more powerful and effective with the increasing number of vulnerabilities the attacker discovers. The collection of all known and unknown vulnerabilities is considered the attack surface.

Imagine you have a set of darts and a dartboard. The dartboard is the attack surface, the darts are your attacks, and your throwing precision is your attack skill. The more vulnerabilities you have, the wider the dartboard becomes. You are extremely likely to hit a dartboard the size of a person. However, you need an exceptional skill and precision to hit a dartboard the size of a quarter. Our goal as the defender is to shrink the attack surface and keep it small as long as possible.

The attack surface in a serverless application is similar to a web application.[19] It differs due to the differences in deployment and administration. Table 2-3 highlights some of the differences between a typical web application and a typical serverless application.

Table 2-3. *Attack Surface Differences Between Typical Web and Serverless Applications*

Focus Area	Typical Web Application	Typical Serverless Application
Code platform/engine	Web server	Function service
Code deployment	Upload to server	Upload to service
Configuration settings	Web server configuration	Function service settings
Data inputs/requests	HTTP, database, local storage	HTTP, database, event triggers
Security configuration	Web server platform and OS	System account/service settings
Security patching	Web server platform and OS, software packages	Software packages

---

[19]The OWASP Foundation published an Attack Surface Analysis Cheat Sheet to their GitHub page. https://github.com/OWASP/CheatSheetSeries/blob/master/cheatsheets/Attack_Surface_Analysis_Cheat_Sheet.md

Start with the typical set of focus areas when quantifying the attack surface. Vulnerability scanners and other tools can systematically generate the list of vulnerabilities that comprise the attack surface. Continue your assessment by assessing the deployment resources, the event triggers, and system account settings. You can use your discovery of the attack surface to create a threat model.

Creating a Threat Model

Up to this point in your assessment, you will have

- Acquired knowledge of the application and its design

- Identified the trust boundaries and assets

- Determined the potential threat actors and motivations

- Enumerated potential vulnerabilities

With this information, you have sufficient data to create a threat model.[20] You can use a diagram or a matrix to document the threat model.

In its simplest form, a threat model shows the defenses used to protect assets from threats and threat actors. A threat is an action or event that exploits a vulnerability or weakness in a system. A threat actor is a person or organization that exercises the threat. The threat model may or may not include threat actors depending on whether they are relevant to understanding the threats. The threat model for our example application might look like Figure 2-9 in a pictorial form.

---

[20]The OWASP Foundation published a Threat Modeling Control Cheat Sheet to their GitHub page. `https://github.com/OWASP/CheatSheetSeries/blob/master/cheatsheets/Threat_Modeling_Cheat_Sheet.md`

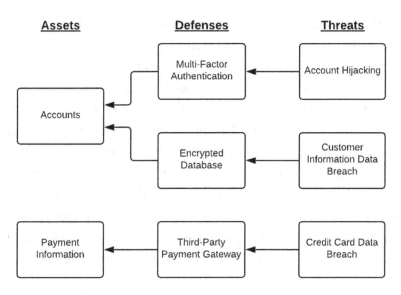

Figure 2-9. *Sample Threat Model Diagram*

The threat model for our example application might look like Table 2-4 in a matrix form.

Table 2-4. *Sample Threat Model Matrix*

Asset	Threat	Mitigation
Accounts (system)	Account hijacking	Multi-factor authentication
Accounts (application)	Customer data exposed	Encrypted database
Payment information	Credit card data exposed	Third-party payment gateway

Your threat model becomes the start of the risk assessment you present to your stakeholders.

Preparing the Risk Assessment

You will use the risk assessment to inform your stakeholders about the risk level present in their application. You should determine the risk level based on the negative impact to the business if risks are realized. For example, you might find a vulnerability in a computer system that shows announcements in the displays in a lobby. You might classify it as a critical vulnerability if the computer uses business logic or data. The business might deem it as unimportant and having a low risk if it runs in a network with no Internet connectivity and has no access to business data.

There is always a risk, even if it might seem insignificant. You might determine the risks are a failure to disseminate information to guests and employees and an unplanned expenditure to replace the equipment. The business might classify this as low risk because there are other means to distribute information, and there is a buffer built into the budget for unplanned replacements. The security professional might present a different risk level based on findings. The risk level might change to high or critical risk if the lobby system uses a static username and password to log in to a serverless application, and it can escalate privileges to access customer data. Using the threat model and your knowledge of the business will help you classify the risk levels; see Table 2-5.

Table 2-5. *Sample Risk Assessment*

Asset	Threat	Risk	Likelihood	Impact	Mitigation
Accounts (system)	Account hijacking	Medium	Probable	Minor	Multi-factor authentication
Accounts (application)	Customer data exposed	Medium	Remote	Serious	Encrypted database
Payment information	Credit card data exposed	Medium	Remote	Serious	Third-party payment gateway

In addition to presenting the risk level (i.e., low, medium, high), you should present the likelihood a risk is to manifest and the impact it will have. The business will have increased interest in critical risks and how likely they are to impact their business operations and profits. For example, as an extreme, there is a threat the entire Internet stops working. Your business may lose thousands of dollars for every minute the application is down. The likelihood this will happen is extremely rare. You can further reduce the business' concern by presenting mitigation using caching and offline capabilities that will resynchronize upon the restoration of Internet connectivity.

You may have a threat that is extremely likely to happen, and it will cost thousands of dollars for every day the application is degraded. Although the impact is low in comparison, if the threat is realized easily and often, it results in having a significant cumulative impact. The goal is to have the most of the risks results in moderate business impact or lower by staying within the desired range of impact and likelihood; see Table 2-6.

Table 2-6. *Risk Matrix*

Likelihood	Impact				
	Minimal	**Minor**	**Major**	**Serious**	**Catastrophic**
Improbable	Low	Low	Low	Low	Medium
Remote	Low	Low	Low	Medium	Medium
Occasional	Low	Medium	Medium	Medium	High
Probable	Low	Medium	Medium	High	High
Frequent	Medium	Medium	High	High	High

Your goal is to portray the risk to the business accurately. Ideally, the majority of your findings have low risk, some have medium risk, and little to none have high risk. Your assessment will include the mitigations currently used and mitigations to put into effect to reduce the risk level. You will learn mitigation techniques in the coming chapters for protecting a serverless application and reducing risk. The last chapter will help you to finalize your risk assessment.

Key Takeaways

In this chapter, we reviewed the steps for performing a risk assessment. Understanding how one prepares a risk assessment provides us with the items we will want to investigate as part of our assessment.

We established the setup we will use throughout this book:

- **A fictitious ecommerce mobile app** is the example application under evaluation.

- **The Serverless Framework** is used to deploy the functions to the FaaS provider.

- **Node.js** is the programming language used in the function code.

- Several **terms, keywords, and acronyms** were defined.

We explored different ways to understand the application, which include

- **Reviewing different types of documentation** (e.g., architecture and design diagrams, requirement documents, and manuals) to learn how the developers designed the application and its intended purpose

- **Reviewing the source code** to enumerate the different functions, runtime engine, entry points, and event triggers

- **Reviewing the system accounts** to identify external and internal threats

- **Using the application** to capture the application network traffic as a tangible way of understanding its design

We can use this knowledge to perform a risk assessment by

- **Determining and defining the trust boundaries** to scope the security assessment

- **Understanding the threat actors**, which might include script kiddies, cybercriminals, hacktivists, state-sponsored attackers, and insider threats, and their motivations

- **Quantifying the attack surface** by discovering vulnerabilities

- **Creating a threat model** that captures the assets, threats, and mitigations

Finally, we used the assessment to quantify the risks, their likelihood, and impact on the stakeholders.

The following chapters will focus on specific aspects of serverless security. You may use each chapter as a guide to compile a risk assessment. In the next chapter, we will explore how to reduce risk by securing the application code.

CHAPTER 3

Securing the Code

In this chapter, we will review the importance of securing the application code. We will learn how to choose the runtime and version for our serverless functions and how to assess any libraries and dependencies they use. We will discuss static code analysis tools, unit tests, and regression tests and how they help secure our application code. Finally, we will learn how multiple events can trigger serverless functions and review examples on performing input validation on those events.

Importance of Securing the Application Code

The following chapters focus on practical approaches in securing the application. The security strategy may seem different when compared to a typical system that uses servers and operating systems. In these systems, it may seem there is more emphasis on securing the infrastructure and platforms that run the application. Though it may appear these security focus areas are more important, the topics discussed in the following chapters are also important. This chapter focuses on securing the application code.

We have abstracted the infrastructure and platform when we deploy our application to a serverless environment. We have little influence over the security posture of the operating system (OS), code platform, and the other mechanisms used to run the serverless application. But we can secure the application code. In other systems, we could take advantage of the security implementation for the OS and platform to mitigate risks in the code. But in a serverless environment, we cannot secure the OS and platform. Therefore, it is imperative to secure the code we deploy to our serverless platform.

Choosing a Runtime Engine and Version

Your serverless provider might support multiple runtime engines (e.g., Node.js, Python, Java, etc.) and different versions. For example, Amazon Web Services (AWS) supports

M. Calles, *Serverless Security*, https://doi.org/10.1007/978-1-4842-6100-2_3

various runtime engines and the ability to create a custom runtime; see Figure 3-1. You must determine which runtime engine to use based on how it will support the application and its security.

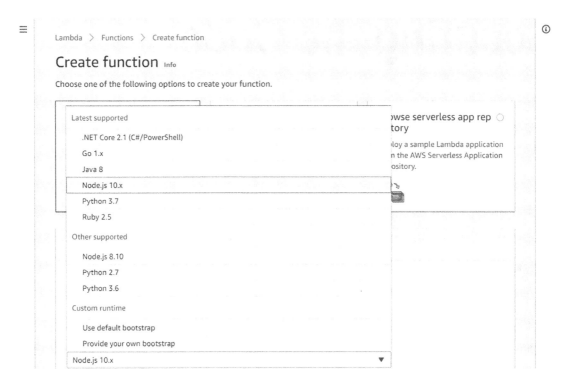

Figure 3-1. *AWS Lambda Runtime Options*

This book focuses on security and will not give you guidance on how to choose between Java, Node.js, Python, Ruby, and so on to meet the functional requirements for your application. In the situation where only one runtime meets those requirements, choosing the latest runtime version typically has the least number of vulnerabilities, and it is considered the most secure version to adopt. You may also have the ability to select a different runtime engine per function, thus giving you the flexibility to meet your functional requirements while balancing the security posture.

AWS, Azure, and Google Cloud all support Node.js as a runtime engine. At the time of this writing, only AWS and Google Cloud allow you to choose other runtime engines. As we established in Chapter 2, we have chosen Node.js as our preferred programming language and runtime. We can write all the serverless functions in Node.js for uniformity. Still, it might make sense to use a different runtime in some cases.

If you have the option to choose among different runtimes for a serverless function, you should choose the runtime with the least number of vulnerabilities. You can use the Common Vulnerabilities and Exposures (CVE),[1] National Vulnerability Database (NVD),[2] or an aggregator like CVE Details[3] website to review the vulnerabilities. We will use the CVE Details website because it provides a relatively more straightforward user interface. Still, I encourage you to become familiar with the CVE and NVD.

To search the vulnerabilities per runtime

- Visit **www.cvedetails.com**.

- Click **Version Search** under the "Search" section in the left pane.

- Enter the **Vendor Name**, **Product Name**, and **Version** based on search criteria in Table 3-1; see Figure 3-2.

- Click **Search**.

Note: This website accepts the "%" symbol as a wildcard.

Table 3-1. *CVE Details Version Search Criteria*

Runtime and Version	Vendor Name	Product Name	Version
.NET Core 2.x	Microsoft	.NET Core	2%
Go 1.x	Golang	GO	1%
Java 8.x	Oracle	JRE	1.8%
Node.js 10.x	Nodejs	Node.js	10%
Node.js 8.x	Nodejs	Node.js	8%
Python 2.x	Python%	Python	2%
Python 3.x	Python%	Python	3%
Ruby 2.x	Ruby-lang	Ruby	2%

---

[1]"Common Vulnerabilities and Exposures." The MITRE Corporation. https://cve.mitre.org
[2]"National Vulnerability Database." National Institute of Standards and Technology. https://nvd.nist.gov
[3]"CVE Details." Serkan Özkan. www.cvedetails.com

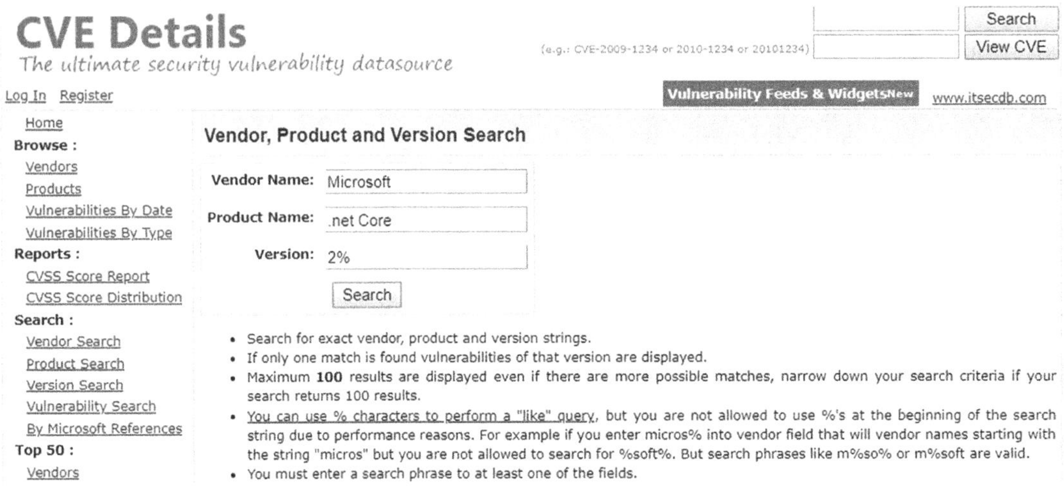

CVE Details

The ultimate security vulnerability datasource

(e.g.: CVE-2009-1234 or 2010-1234 or 20101234)

Search
View CVE

Log In Register

Vulnerability Feeds & WidgetsNew www.itsecdb.com

Home
Browse :
Vendors
Products
Vulnerabilities By Date
Vulnerabilities By Type
Reports :
CVSS Score Report
CVSS Score Distribution
Search :
Vendor Search
Product Search
Version Search
Vulnerability Search
By Microsoft References
Top 50 :
Vendors

Vendor, Product and Version Search

Vendor Name: Microsoft

Product Name: .net Core

Version: 2%

Search

- Search for exact vendor, product and version strings.
- If only one match is found vulnerabilities of that version are displayed.
- Maximum **100** results are displayed even if there are more possible matches, narrow down your search criteria if your search returns 100 results.
- You can use % characters to perform a "like" query, but you are not allowed to use %'s at the beginning of the search string due to performance reasons. For example if you enter micros% into vendor field that will vendor names starting with the string "micros" but you are not allowed to search for %soft%. But search phrases like m%so% or m%soft are valid.
- You must enter a search phrase to at least one of the fields.

Figure 3-2. *CVE Details Version Search Criteria Example*

Figure 3-3 shows the search results using Microsoft .NET as an example. Take note of the number of vulnerabilities for the specific runtime minor version (e.g., Python 2.7) or the latest version of a major version (e.g., Java 8 or Node.js 10.x).[4] Optionally, use the raw data to manually create a bar chart of the number of vulnerabilities by version for a major version to see the trend of vulnerabilities by version; see Figure 3-4. The website also provides you with statistics for the product overall when you click the version product in the search results; see Figure 3-5. You should consider reviewing the vulnerability details.

---

[4]Major version and minor versions are terms defined in semantic versioning. "Semantic Versioning 2.0.0." Tom Preston-Werner. https://semver.org

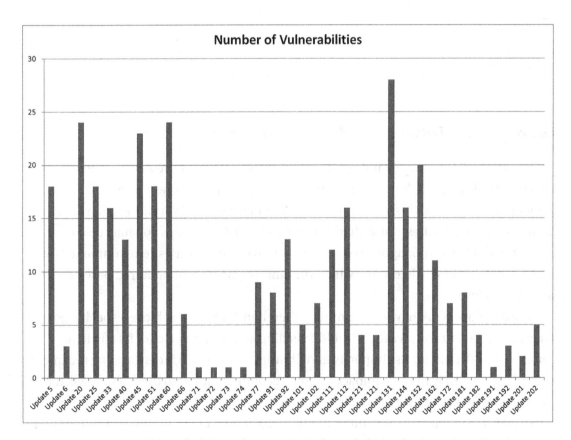

Figure 3-3. *CVE Details Version Search Results Example*

Figure 3-4. *Example Bar Chart of Java 8.x Vulnerabilities by Runtime Version Update*

CVE Details
The ultimate security vulnerability datasource

	Search
(e.g.: CVE-2009-1234 or 2010-1234 or 20101234)	View CVE

Log In Register

Vulnerability Feeds & Widgets New   www.itsecdb.com

Home
Browse :
Vendors
Products
Vulnerabilities By Date
Vulnerabilities By Type
Reports :
CVSS Score Report
CVSS Score Distribution
Search :
Vendor Search
Product Search
Version Search
Vulnerability Search
By Microsoft References
Top 50 :
Vendors
Vendor Cvss Scores
Products
Product Cvss Scores
Versions
Other :
Microsoft Bulletins
Bugtraq Entries
CWE Definitions
About & Contact
Feedback
CVE Help
FAQ
Articles

Oracle » JRE : Vulnerability Statistics

Vulnerabilities (607)   CVSS Scores Report   Browse all versions   Possible matches for this product   Related Metasploit Modules

Related OVAL Definitions : Vulnerabilities (839)   Patches (604)   Inventory Definitions (3)   Compliance Definitions (0)

Vulnerability Feeds & Widgets

Vulnerability Trends Over Time

Year	# of Vulnerabilities	DoS	Code Execution	Overflow	Memory Corruption	Sql Injection	XSS	Directory Traversal	Http Response Splitting	Bypass something	Gain Information	Gain Privileges	CSRF	File Inclusion	# of exploits
2010	1		1												
2011	3														
2012	59	3	1							2					
2013	180	1	10	4	4		1			32					2
2014	115	1	1												
2015	80														
2016	37		1	1							1	1			
2017	69	14								1	2				
2018	55	17	2								4				
2019	8	1													
Total	607	37	16	5	4		1			35	7	1			2
% Of All		6.1	2.6	0.8	0.7	0.0	0.2	0.0	0.0	5.8	1.2	0.2	0.0	0.0	

Warning : Vulnerabilities with publish dates before 1999 are not included in this table and chart. (Because there are not many of them and they make the page look bad; and they may not be actually published in those years.)

Figure 3-5. *CVE Details Vulnerability Statistics Example*

You will build an understanding of a runtime's security posture as you review the vulnerability details. You may find multiple versions have a low number of vulnerabilities, but with high severity scores. You may also find various versions have numerous vulnerabilities, but with low severity scores. Or perhaps you may discover the vulnerabilities do not apply to your application or the serverless environment. Use all these data inputs to determine which runtime engine is most preferred based on the security risk level.

The developers might want a runtime other than Node.js to achieve a specific goal. They might want to use Java for its multithreading and libraries, Go for its efficient concurrency, Python for its simplicity and libraries, and so on. Understanding the intent of the developer may have an impact on your recommendation to them if they ask for your input from a security perspective.

In addition to checking for vulnerabilities, you should check for the end-of-life (EOL) date for the runtime versions. At the time of this writing, AWS Lambda supports Python 2.7 as a runtime. The Python Software Foundation announced a January 1, 2020, EOL date[5] for Python 2.7, meaning it will no longer provide bug fixes or patches after this date. Any developers choosing to use Python 2.7 before this date will want to consider upgrading before the EOL date.

We will practice using CVE Details and researching the EOL date in Exercise 3-1.

EXERCISE 3-1: CHOOSING A RUNTIME

Objective:

In this exercise, you will practice using CVE Details to check for known vulnerabilities in runtime versions.

Relevant Information:

The development team has asked for guidance on which runtime to use for their serverless functions. They are trying to decide between Python and JavaScript since they both have the desired dependencies.

Instructions:

1. Visit www.cvedetails.com.

2. Click **Version Search** under the "Search" section in the left pane.

3. Enter "Nodejs" as the Vendor Name, "Node.js" as the Product Name, and "8%" as the Version; see Table 3-1.

4. Click the **Search** button.

5. Convert the results search table to a spreadsheet by copying and pasting the data into a spreadsheet application.

6. Optionally, create a bar chart from the spreadsheet data similar to Figure 3-4.

7. Update the search parameters by entering "Nodejs" as the Vendor Name, "Node.js" as the Product Name, and "10%" as the Version; see Table 3-1.

8. Repeat steps 4 and 5 for Node.js 10.

---

[5]"PEP 373 -- Python 2.7 Release Schedule." Python Software Foundation. 3 November 2018. www.python.org/dev/peps/pep-0373/

9. Update the search parameters by entering "Python%" as the Vendor Name, "Python" as the Product Name, and "2%" as the Version; see Table 3-1.

10. Repeat steps 4 and 5 for Python 2.

11. Update the search parameters by entering "Python%" as the Vendor Name, "Python" as the Product Name, and "3%" as the Version; see Table 3-1.

12. Repeat steps 4 and 5 for Python 3.

13. Search online for the "end-of-life" dates for Node.js 8, Node 10, Python 2, and Python 3 and record your findings.

Assess all the results and recommend the package(s) the developers should use.

Assessing Libraries and Dependencies

The developers may use libraries in their functions. Using libraries saves the developer time by leveraging existing functionality rather than writing it. There is typically no guarantee the library is efficient and without vulnerabilities. The developer of the library may have used other libraries. The number of libraries may be several layers deep. We will explore how to evaluate the dependencies used in your serverless functions.

Assessing the Dependency Tree

When a piece of code uses a library in the logic it executes, that library is called a dependency. You add a layer of code when you introduce a dependency in your code. As dependencies use other dependencies, these layers get deeper. Each dependency forms a tree branch from the tree trunk (i.e., the original piece of code). It is possible adding a single dependency can add a large tree of dependencies several layers deep, all stemming from one branch. A vulnerability may exist at any layer or branch and may affect your serverless function depending on the severity and difficulty to exploit. Therefore, it is essential to understand the dependency tree and to keep it as short and narrow as possible.

The size of a dependency tree might not be apparent when you add a dependency to your code. npm will list the number of packages (i.e., libraries) used in your Node.js project, but it is a cumulative count. You may have multiple packages in your project, but your serverless functions may only use a small subset. You can use a dependency tree tool, such as those listed in Table 3-2, to help you visualize the tree. Figure 3-6 shows an example of specific packages used by serverless functions.

Table 3-2. *Dependency Tree Tools*

Tools	License	Supported Runtime
Anvaka[1]	Free Plan	Node.js
Apache Maven Dependency Plugin[2]	Free and Open Source	Java
Bundler[3]	Free and Open Source	Ruby
DependencyWalker for .NET[4]	Free and Open Source	.NET
Depth[5]	Free and Open Source	Go
Gradle Scans[6]	Free and Paid Plans	Java
NDepend[7]	Paid Plans	.NET
Pideptree[8]	Free and Open Source	Python

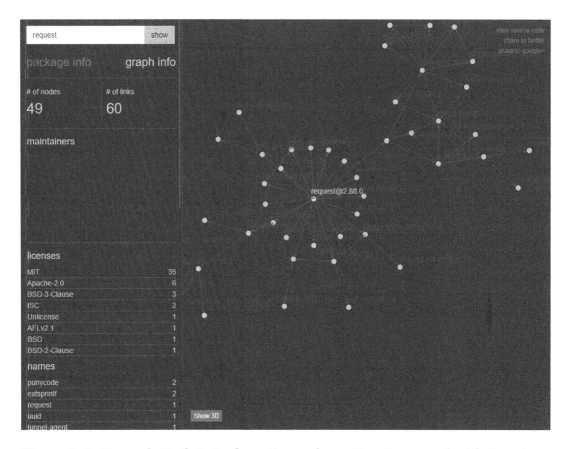

Figure 3-6. *Example Node.js Package Dependency Tree Generated with Anvaka*

A dependency tree tool will help you count the number of dependencies and see the size of the dependency tree. You can use the dependency tree to help you decide which package(s) to use when you are evaluating multiple packages that provide the same functionality. We will explore this in Exercise 3-2.

Checking for Vulnerabilities

Your dependencies should be free from known vulnerabilities whenever possible. Although you wrote your code with no vulnerabilities, you may introduce them by using libraries. Periodically checking your dependencies for vulnerabilities is a good practice to maintain the security posture of your application. Use vulnerability checkers, such as those listed in Table 3-3, to determine whether your dependencies have vulnerabilities. The tools identify which versions have known vulnerabilities and which fixed them.

In the event a package has no fixes, you should determine the security risk and provide a recommendation to accept the risk or to mitigate it by using a different package or other security control. Running these checks will help you deploy code with no known vulnerabilities, mitigated vulnerabilities, or with vulnerabilities with the risk accepted by the stakeholders.

***Table 3-3.** Library Vulnerability Checker Tools*

Vulnerability Checker	License	Supported Runtimes
Bundler Audit[9]	Free and Open Source	Ruby
Dependency-Check[10]	Free and Open Source	Python
npm audit[11]	Free and Open Source	Node.js
OSSIndex Audit.NET[12]	Free and Open Source	.NET
OSSIndex Gradle Plugin[13]	Free and Open Source	Java
OSSIndex Maven Plugin[14]	Free and Open Source	Java
OWASP Dependency Check[15]	Free and Open Source	Java, .NET *(Experimental: Ruby, Node.js, Python)*
Safety[16]	Free and Open Source	Python
Snyk[17]	Free and Paid Plans	Java, .NET, Ruby, Python, Go, Node.js
SourceClear[18]	Paid Plans	Java, Ruby, Python, Go, Node.js

Vulnerability checkers support integration into your development environment. Many organizations adopt Continuous Integration (CI) and Continuous Development (CD). CI/CD allows developers to write code, capture it in a configuration management tool or software repository, and see the code deployed in the application. You can suggest integrating vulnerability checkers into the CI/CD to automatically check for vulnerabilities and notify the developer before the code is approved.

Other Considerations

Aside from the dependency tree size and the known vulnerabilities, there are other factors you might want to consider in choosing or maintaining your packages, including

- **Last published date** informs whether the package is actively maintained. An old package may no longer have support. The maintainer may no longer check the code for vulnerabilities nor update the package to fix them.

- **Unused packages** might still exist in an existing project. Having unused code in your project will make it larger than needed, skew any security audits, and increase the attack surface of your project.

- **Older versions** are more likely to be vulnerable than newer package versions. Periodically upgrading to the latest version of packages decreases the likelihood of a vulnerability being present.

Ultimately, understanding how the developers chose and used packages and used them and whether they are maintained will sustain the security posture of your application.

EXERCISE 3-2: ASSESSING PACKAGES

Objective:

In this exercise, you will practice using Anvaka to view a dependency tree and npm audit to check for known vulnerabilities.

Relevant Information:

The development team has asked for guidance on which library to use in their Serverless Node.js functions. The functions will perform HTTP requests. They are trying to decide among the "request," "request-promise," "http-request," and "got" packages and want your suggestion based on a security perspective.

Instructions:

1. Open the source code in the **chapter03/exercise02** folder using the CLI.

2. Run **npm install** in the CLI to install the packages.

3. Open the **package.json** file and note the dependencies.

4. Visit **https://npm.anvaka.com** and generate the dependency for each of the dependencies in the "package.json" file. Capture the number of nodes and links in a table.

5. Run **npm outdated** in the CLI to determine whether the installed packages are up to date and capture which packages are outdated.

6. Visit **www.npmjs.com** and search for each package. Determine the age (in years or months) of the installed version and the age of the last published version.

7. Run **npm audit** in the CLI to determine whether the installed packages have known vulnerabilities. Determine which packages have vulnerabilities and any recommended remediations.

8. Visit **https://snyk.io**, go to the **Vulnerability DB** section, select the **npm** repository, and search for each package. Determine which packages have a history of vulnerabilities.

Assess all the results and recommend the package(s) the developers should use.

Using Static Code Analysis Tools

Static code analysis inspects the source code against a set of rules that check for common coding and security errors. Performing static code analysis is a standard security practice, but it becomes essential in a serverless environment. Traditional environments have the benefit of securing the infrastructure, operating system, platform, and so on to protect the application software and any known limitations it might have. In some respects, the serverless function code is the first line of defense because you can invoke it directly. Having well-written code that avoids common mistakes and known security vulnerabilities is imperative and can be achieved using static code analysis tools.

Static code analysis tools, such as those in Table 3-4, assess your code for common issues. They ensure the code conforms to the syntax, but also have rules to prevent against known security pitfalls. For example, Node.js provides the "eval" function that executes JavaScript code. This function is exceptionally prone to running malicious code since it evaluates any code given, and it runs with the same privileges as the main code. A static code analysis tool has rules to check for these common issues and reports any findings.

Table 3-4. *Static Code Analysis Tools*

Analysis Tool	License	Supported Runtimes
Bandit[19]	Free and Open Source	Python
Pylint[20]	Free and Open Source	Python
ESLint[21]	Free and Open Source	Node.js
SonarLint[22]	Free and Open Source	Java, .NET, Node.js, Python, Ruby
SonarQube[23]	Free Plan	Java, .NET, Node.js, Python, Ruby, Go

Wikipedia has a more thorough list of static code analysis tools.[6]

Unit Tests and Regression Tests

Performing unit tests and regression tests improves code quality and helps catch code regression. Unit tests evaluate the inputs and outputs of sections of the code to determine they perform as designed. Regression tests consist of test cases that determine whether the overall application functions as expected, and it is not regressing (i.e., getting worse). The purpose of these tests is not to explicitly check for security concerns, but you can use them to that end.

A developer can add invalid inputs into unit tests to ensure the code provides expected and secure output. For example, there might be a function that accepts a filename as an input. The unit tests can run a check for an injection attack on the input (e.g., a "myfile.jpg; cd /tmp; ls" filename) and determine whether a proper response is returned (e.g., an error code) or an undesired response is returned (e.g., the contents of the temporary directory). The unit tests allow the developer and security team to be creative in developing potential exploits to find vulnerabilities.

The team may use the regression tests to define test cases that demonstrate a certain level of security in the application. For example, there might be a test case for successfully registering for an account, but there could be test cases for a user exiting the registration process midway, a user registering again, a nonregistered user attempting

---

[6]"List of tools for static code analysis." Wikipedia. https://en.wikipedia.org/wiki/
List_of_tools_for_static_code_analysis

to access registered user functionality, and so on. The regression test allows the team to be creative in using the application in a nonstandard way and determine whether it responds acceptably and securely.

Input Validation

Input validation is the practice of writing software that checks the input it receives matches the expected format. Input validation is arguably the most effective runtime defense mechanism in a serverless environment. The Open Web Application Security Project (OWASP) Foundation[7] and the Cloud Security Alliance (CSA)[8] both published documents that define the top serverless security risks. Both define injection attacks as the highest risk, which is mitigated by input validation. Carnegie Mellon University sets the Software Engineering Institute (SEI) Computer Emergency Response Team (CERT) Secure Coding Standards,[9] which lists input validation as the top secure coding practice. With such emphasis on input validation in both serverless and non-serverless environments, it behooves us not to take it lightly.

Event Sources

Event triggers invoke (i.e., execute) serverless functions. The event generates input data and sends it to the function, which uses it in the execution logic. Table 3-5 lists the AWS,[10] Azure,[11] and Google Cloud[12] event triggers available at the time of this writing.

---

[7]"OWASP Top 10: Interpretation for Serverless." OWASP Foundation. 2017. `www.owasp.org/index.php/OWASP_Serverless_Top_10_Project`

[8]"The 12 Most Critical Risks for Serverless Applications 2019." Cloud Security Alliance. 2019. `https://blog.cloudsecurityalliance.org/2019/02/11/critical-risks-serverless-applications/`

[9]"Top 10 Secure Coding Practices." Carnegie Melon University. 2 May 2018. `https://wiki.sei.cmu.edu/confluence/display/seccode/Top+10+Secure+Coding+Practices`

[10]"Using AWS Lambda with Other Services." AWS Lambda Developer Guide. Amazon Web Services. `https://docs.aws.amazon.com/lambda/latest/dg/lambda-services.html`

[11]"Azure Functions triggers and bindings concepts." Microsoft Azure. `https://docs.microsoft.com/en-us/azure/azure-functions/functions-triggers-bindings`

[12]"Events and Triggers." Google Cloud Functions documentation. Google. `https://cloud.google.com/functions/docs/concepts/events-triggers`

Table 3-5. *Event Triggers*

Provider	Event Trigger(s)
AWS	Amazon Alexa,[24] Amazon API Gateway (i.e., HTTP),[25] Amazon CloudFront (Lambda@Edge),[26] Amazon CloudWatch Events,[27] Amazon CloudWatch Logs,[28] Amazon Cognito,[29] Amazon DynamoDB,[30] Amazon Kinesis,[31] Amazon Kinesis Data Firehose,[32] Amazon Lex,[33] Amazon Simple Email Service,[34] Amazon Simple Notification Service,[35] Amazon Simple Queue Service,[36] Amazon Simple Storage Service,[37] AWS CloudFormation,[38] AWS CodeCommit,[39] AWS Config,[40] Elastic Load Balancing (Application Load Balancer)[41]
Azure	Blob storage,[42] Cosmos DB,[43] Event Grid,[44] Event Hubs,[45] HTTP & Webhooks,[46] Microsoft Graph Events,[47] Queue Storage,[48] Service Bus,[49] Timer[50]
Google Cloud	Cloud Storage,[51] Cloud Pub/Sub,[52] Cloud Firestore,[53] Firebase Realtime Database,[54] Firebase Analytics,[55] Firebase Auth,[56] HTTP,[57] Operations and Cloud Logging[58][13]

Sanitizing per Event Type

Each event has a different input structure. We will explore two event types to illustrate how to sanitize per event type. Given there are numerous event types, I encourage you to become familiar with the specific events used in your application and implement appropriate input validations.

Amazon API Gateway Event Sanitization Example

In the "chapter03/examples-input-validation" folder, you will find a "serverless. yml" configuration file[14] that defines an AWS Lambda function. The function has an HTTP event (i.e., an API Gateway event trigger) configured for the "example/{myPathParameter}" path. When you deploy, Serverless creates the Lambda with an HTTP endpoint similar to `"https://7mzctr1gua.execute-api.us-east-1.amazonaws.com/dev/example/testParameter?testKey=testValue1&testKey=testValue2"` that

---

[13]Stackdriver was renamed to Operations, which provides Cloud Logging. "Operations (formerly Stackdriver)." Google. `https://cloud.google.com/products/operations`

[14]The "serverless.yml" configuration file uses the YAML Ain't Markup Language (YAML) format that is tab dependent and uses the "#" for comments. Learn more at "YAML: YAML Ain't Markup Language." %YAML 1.2. `https://yaml.org`

you can visit. Note: I updated "{myPathParameter}" to "testParameter" and added a query string of "testKey=testValue" to help with understanding the event data. We will explore the event input data next.

Example Input Data

In the "chapter03/examples-input-validation/src/apigateway" folder, you will find an "eventGet.json" file that captures an actual event data object generated by calling the HTTP endpoint above. You will see the event object has 91 lines of data when formatted to a human-readable format. The event data has several notable properties:

- **The "resource" property** contains the API Gateway resource from the Serverless deployment. It matches the "path" property defined in the "serverless.yml" file but prefixed with a forward slash (/).

- **The "path" property** contains the path element in the address used to call the API Gateway endpoint that triggers the Lambda function. It conforms with the "path" property defined in the "serverless.yml" file, but with the text in the curly brackets replaced with an actual value.

  - "https://" is the prefix.

  - "7mzctr1gua.execute-api.us-east-1.amazonaws.com" is the domain.

  - "/dev" is the API Gateway stage defined in the "serverless.yml" configuration.

  - "/example/testParameter" is the path.

  - "testKey=testValue1&testKey=testValue2" is the query string.

- **The "httpMethod" property** contains the HTTP method (e.g., GET, POST, PUT, DELETE, etc.) used in the HTTP request made to the specified address.

- **The "headers" property** contains the HTTP headers provided in the HTTP request.

- **The "multiValueHeaders" property** contains the information from the "headers" property but converts the subproperties into an array for repeated HTTP request header fields.

55

- **The "queryStringParameters" property** contains the keys and their last value specified in the query string. In our example, you will notice it only returned the "testValue2" key value.

- **The "multiValueQueryStringParameters" property** contains the keys and all the values specified in the query string.

- **The "pathParameters" property** contains all the path parameters and the values used in the address. In our example, you will notice the "myPathParameter" path parameter has a value of "testParameters" because we used that value in the address where "{myPathParameter}" was defined in the "path" within the "serverless.yml" configuration.

- **The "stageVariables" property** contains the stage variables defined for the API Gateway. The value is "null" unless you enabled a Serverless plugin to define stage variables.

- **The "requestContext" property** contains additional information (e.g., the API Gateway stage, the AWS account identifier, and the requestor's IP address).

- **The "body" property** contains the payload data sent in an HTTP POST as a serialized JSON string. The value is null for an HTTP GET. Review the "chapter03/examples-input-validation/src/apigateway/eventPost.json" file to see the body data for an HTTP POST.

- **The "isBase64Encoded" property** is a Boolean stating whether the payload is in base64 binary format. The value is "false" unless you enabled a Serverless plugin to convert the payload to base64.

We will explore using these properties to perform input validation.

Example Input Validation

In the "chapter03/examples-input-validation/src/apigateway" folder, you will find an "example.js" file that defines a Lambda function configured to accept both GET and POST HTTP requests. The example code illustrates different validation approaches for your consideration.

eYou will find the input validations are specific to the design of the Lambda function. They do the following

- **Accept** GET and POST HTTP requests

- **Require** a path parameter

- **Require** one query string parameter with a specific data structure for a GET

- **Reject** query string parameters for a POST

- **Require** two body properties with specific data structures for a POST

- **Execute** only for the IP address of a particular server

You will see in the code how the following event properties are used to achieve the specified input validations:

- **The "body" property** conforms to the HTTP method and has the required data elements. It should contain all the required JSON properties and test that all the required and optional JSON properties match an expected input (e.g., data type, length, and format).

  - The input validation can check that an HTTP GET has an empty body. See the "Example input validation 1" code section.

  - The input validation can check that an HTTP POST has the two required "bodyKey1" and "bodyKey2" properties and their values both strings, with lengths between 1 and 20 characters, and only uses alphanumeric characters. See the "Example input validation 2" code section.

- **The "queryStringParameters" and "multiValueQueryStringParameters" properties** conform to the HTTP method and have the required data.

  - The input validation can check that an HTTP POST has no query string parameters. See the "Example input validation 3" code section.

57

- The input validation can check that an HTTP GET has the required "testKey" property, and its value is a string, with a length between 1 and 20 characters, and only uses alphanumeric characters. It can additionally check that there is only one value for the "testKey" property in the "multiValueQueryStringParameters" property. See the "Example input validation 4" code section.

- **The "sourceIp" property**, nested under the "requestContext" property, matches a whitelisted IP.

  - The input validation can check the requestor's IP address matches the IP address specified in the "environment" property in the "serverless.yml" configuration. See the "Example input validation 5" code section.

These input validations will vary on the intent of your Lambda function. The goal is to determine how the event data might change and how your application will check its validity. You can use an API test tool like Postman[15] (see Figure 3-7) to test different variations in the address, HTTP method, query string parameters, and the body.

---

[15]Postman is a registered trademark of Postman, Inc.

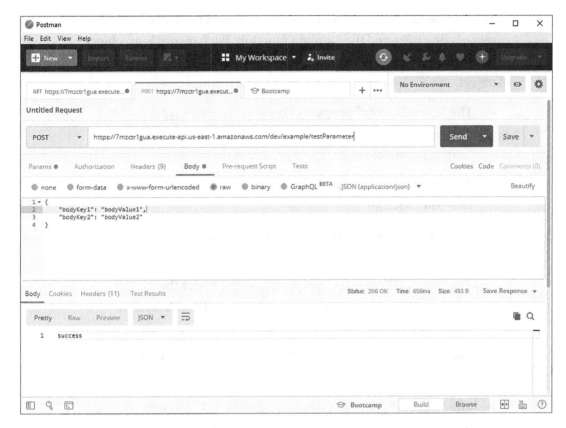

Figure 3-7. *Sending an HTTP Request Using Postman*

Amazon Simple Storage Service (S3) Event Sanitization Example

In the "chapter03/examples-input-validation" folder, you will find a "serverless.yml" configuration file which defines an AWS Lambda function. The function has an S3 event configured. When you deploy, Serverless creates the Lambda and an S3 bucket as defined in the "resources" property within the "serverless.yml" file. A file uploaded to the S3 bucket will trigger the Lambda function. We will now explore the event input data.

Example Input Data

In the "chapter03/examples-input-validation/src/s3" folder, you will find an "event.json" file that captures an actual event data object generated after uploading a file to the S3 bucket. You will see the event object has 38 lines of data when formatted to a human-readable format. The event data has several notable subproperties.

- **The "Records" property** contains an array of all the file upload records that triggered the Lambda function. Each record is an object with its properties. These are the notable properties in the record object.

  - **The "eventSource" property** contains the event type. In this case, it is "aws:s3" but will differ for a different event (e.g., "aws:dynamodb").

  - **The "eventTime" property** contains the event generation time in ISO-8601 notation.

  - **The "requestParameters" property** contains information about the request.

  - **The "sourceIPAddress" property**, nested under the "requestParameters" property, contains the IP address that performed the file upload.

  - **The "s3" property** contains information about the S3 bucket and object.

  - **The "bucket" property**, nested under the "s3" property, contains information about the S3 bucket to which the file was uploaded.

  - **The "object" property**, nested under the "s3" property, contains information about the uploaded file.

We will explore using these properties to perform input validation.

Example Input Validation

In the "chapter03/examples-input-validation/src/s3" folder, you will find an "example.js" file which defines a Lambda function configured to accept an S3 event. The example code illustrates different validation approaches for your consideration.

You will find the input validations are specific to the design of the Lambda function. They do the following

- **Reject** empty records

- **Accept** S3 event sources

- **Reject** files smaller than 10 kilobytes

- **Reject** filenames longer than 50 characters

- **Require** files with valid file extensions

- **Execute** only for the IP address of a particular server

You will see in the code how the following event properties are used to achieve the specified input validations:

- **The "Records" property** is an array with at least one object. See the "Example input validation 1" code section.

- **The "eventSource" property**, in the record object, equals "aws:s3". See the "Example input validation 2" code section.

- **The "name" property**, nested under the "s3" and "bucket" properties in the record object, equals the bucket name defined in the "serverless.yml" configuration. See the "Example input validation 3" code section.

- **The "size" property**, nested under the "s3" and "object" properties in the record object, is greater than a minimum size to filter unrealistic files. See the "Example input validation 4" code section.

- **The "key" property**, nested under the "s3" and "object" properties in the record object, has two input validations.

  - The value is smaller than a maximum size to filter files with an injection attack. See the "Example input validation 5" code section.

  - The value ends with a valid file extension. See the "Example input validation 6" code section.

  - Additionally, you can add code to read the file and inspect the MIME type equals "image/jpeg" to validate it is an actual JPEG file rather than a different file type with the JPEG file extension. Note: Be cautious in implementing this check to avoid executing any remote code embedded within the file.

- **The "sourceIpAddress" property**, nested under the "requestParameters" property in the record object, matches the IP address specified in the "environment" property in the "serverless.yml" configuration. See the "Example input validation 7" code section.

- **The "eventName" property**, in the record object, equals "ObjectCreated:Put" to filter other ways the file was created or deleted. See the "Example input validation 8" code section. Note: The "serverless.yml" file also performs the filter using the "rules" property, but it is good to validate in the code in the event an erroneous S3 event triggers the function.

- **The "eventTime" property**, in the record object, is no older than five minutes to avoid processing old records. See the "Example input validation 8" code section. Note: You could check the event time is not in the future to filter out erroneous event triggers.

These input validations will vary on the intent of your Lambda function. The goal is to determine how the event data might change and how your application should check its validity. You can use the AWS S3 Management Console (see Figure 3-8) to test different file uploads.

Figure 3-8. *AWS S3 Management Console*

Key Takeaways

In this chapter, we reviewed several topics regarding the importance of securing the application code.

We explored how to choose a runtime engine and version based on security. We used the CVE Details website to research the known vulnerabilities against runtimes and their different versions.

We learned how libraries and dependencies could introduce vulnerabilities into our serverless functions. The likelihood a dependency introduces a vulnerability increases with the size of the dependency tree. We used dependency tree tools and vulnerability checker tools to assess our libraries and dependencies.

We discussed how static code analysis tools and unit and regression tests could improve the security of the serverless application. We used static code analysis tools to catch typical programming and security mistakes. We can adapt unit and regression tests to test invalid inputs and deviate from the workflows to help identify security weaknesses.

We discussed the importance of input validation in serverless functions. We learned several events that trigger serverless functions and how they each have different data structures. We reviewed two input source and input validation techniques.

In the next chapter, we will explore how to secure the interfaces to your serverless application.

Notes

1. "Visualization of npm dependencies." Anvaka. `https://npm.anvaka.com`

2. "Apache Maven Dependency Plugin – Introduction." Apache Maven Project. `https://maven.apache.org/plugins/maven-dependency-plugin/index.html`

3. "Bundler." Bundler. `https://bundler.io`

4. "DependencyWalker.Net." GitHub. `https://github.com/isindicic/DependencyWalker.Net`

5. "depth." GitHub. `https://github.com/KyleBanks/depth`

6. "Get started with build scans." Gradle Enterprise. `https://scans.gradle.com`

7. "Why NDepend." NDepend. `www.ndepend.com`

8. "piptree." PyPI. `https://pypi.org/project/pipdeptree`

9. "bundler-audit." GitHub. `https://github.com/rubysec/bundler-audit`

10. "dependency-check." PyPI. `https://pypi.org/project/dependency-check`

11. "npm-audit." npm Documentation. `https://docs.npmjs.com/cli/audit`

12. "Audit.NET." GitHub. `https://github.com/OSSIndex/audit.net`

13. "ossindex-gradle-plugin." GitHub. `https://github.com/OSSIndex/ossindex-gradle-plugin`

14. "Welcome." Sonatype OSS Index: Maven. `https://sonatype.github.io/ossindex-maven`

15. "OWASP Dependency Check." OWASP. `www.owasp.org/index.php/OWASP_Dependency_Check`

16. "safety." GitHub. `https://github.com/pyupio/safety`

17. "Open Source Security Platform." Snyk. `https://snyk.io`

18. "Software Composition Analysis for DevSecOps." SourceClear. `www.sourceclear.com`

19. "Bandit." GitHub. `https://github.com/PyCQA/bandit`

20. "Pylint." GitHub. `https://github.com/PyCQA/pylint`

21. "ESLint." GitHub. `https://github.com/eslint/eslint`

22. "Fix issues before they exist." sonarlint. `www.sonarlint.org`

23. "Code Quality and Security." sonarqube. `www.sonarqube.org`

24. "Using AWS Lambda with Alexa." AWS Lambda Developer Guide. Amazon Web Services. `https://docs.aws.amazon.com/lambda/latest/dg/services-alexa.html`

25. "Using AWS Lambda with Amazon API Gateway." AWS Lambda Developer Guide. Amazon Web Services. `https://docs.aws.amazon.com/lambda/latest/dg/with-on-demand-https.html`

26. "Using AWS Lambda with CloudFront Lambda@Edge." AWS Lambda Developer Guide. Amazon Web Services. `https://docs.aws.amazon.com/lambda/latest/dg/lambda-edge.html`

27. "Using AWS Lambda with Amazon CloudWatch Events." AWS Lambda Developer Guide. Amazon Web Services. `https://docs.aws.amazon.com/lambda/latest/dg/with-scheduled-events.html`

28. "Using AWS Lambda with Amazon CloudWatch Logs." AWS Lambda Developer Guide. Amazon Web Services. `https://docs.aws.amazon.com/lambda/latest/dg/services-cloudwatchlogs.html`

29. "Using AWS Lambda with Amazon Cognito." AWS Lambda Developer Guide. Amazon Web Services. `https://docs.aws.amazon.com/lambda/latest/dg/services-cognito.html`

30. "Using AWS Lambda with Amazon DynamoDB." AWS Lambda Developer Guide. Amazon Web Services. `https://docs.aws.amazon.com/lambda/latest/dg/with-ddb.html`

31. "Using AWS Lambda with Amazon Kinesis." AWS Lambda Developer Guide. Amazon Web Services. `https://docs.aws.amazon.com/lambda/latest/dg/with-kinesis.html`

32. "Using AWS Lambda with Amazon Kinesis Data Firehose." AWS Lambda Developer Guide. Amazon Web Services. `https://docs.aws.amazon.com/lambda/latest/dg/services-kinesisfirehose.html`

33. "Using AWS Lambda with Amazon Lex." AWS Lambda Developer Guide. Amazon Web Services. `https://docs.aws.amazon.com/lambda/latest/dg/services-lex.html`

34. "Using AWS Lambda with Amazon SES." AWS Lambda Developer Guide. Amazon Web Services. `https://docs.aws.amazon.com/lambda/latest/dg/services-ses.html`

35. "Using AWS Lambda with Amazon SNS." AWS Lambda Developer Guide. Amazon Web Services. `https://docs.aws.amazon.com/lambda/latest/dg/with-sns.html`

36. "Using AWS Lambda with Amazon SQS." AWS Lambda Developer Guide. Amazon Web Services. `https://docs.aws.amazon.com/lambda/latest/dg/with-sqs.html`

37. "Using AWS Lambda with Amazon S3." AWS Lambda Developer Guide. Amazon Web Services. `https://docs.aws.amazon.com/lambda/latest/dg/with-s3.html`

38. "Using AWS Lambda with AWS CloudFormation." AWS Lambda Developer Guide. Amazon Web Services. `https://docs.aws.amazon.com/lambda/latest/dg/services-cloudformation.html`

39. "Using AWS Lambda with AWS CodeCommit." AWS Lambda Developer Guide. Amazon Web Services. `https://docs.aws.amazon.com/lambda/latest/dg/services-codecommit.html`

40. "Using AWS Lambda with AWS Config." AWS Lambda Developer Guide. Amazon Web Services. `https://docs.aws.amazon.com/lambda/latest/dg/services-config.html`

41. "Using AWS Lambda with an Application Load Balancer." AWS Lambda Developer Guide. Amazon Web Services. `https://docs.aws.amazon.com/lambda/latest/dg/services-alb.html`

42. "Azure Blob storage bindings for Azure Functions." Azure Functions documentation. Microsoft. `https://docs.microsoft.com/en-us/azure/azure-functions/functions-bindings-storage-blob`

43. "Azure Cosmos DB bindings for Azure Functions 1.x." Azure Functions documentation. Microsoft. `https://docs.microsoft.com/en-us/azure/azure-functions/functions-bindings-documentdb`

44. "Event Grid trigger for Azure Functions." Azure Functions documentation. Microsoft. `https://docs.microsoft.com/en-us/azure/azure-functions/functions-bindings-event-grid`

45. "Azure Event Hubs bindings for Azure Functions." Azure Functions documentation. Microsoft. `https://docs.microsoft.com/en-us/azure/azure-functions/functions-bindings-event-hubs`

46. "Azure Functions HTTP triggers and bindings." Azure Functions documentation. Microsoft. `https://docs.microsoft.com/en-us/azure/azure-functions/functions-bindings-http-webhook`

47. "Microsoft Graph bindings for Azure Functions." Azure Functions documentation. Microsoft. `https://docs.microsoft.com/en-us/azure/azure-functions/functions-bindings-microsoft-graph`

48. "Azure Queue storage bindings for Azure Functions." Azure Functions documentation. Microsoft. `https://docs.microsoft.com/en-us/azure/azure-functions/functions-bindings-storage-queue`

49. "Azure Service Bus bindings for Azure Functions." Azure Functions documentation. Microsoft. `https://docs.microsoft.com/en-us/azure/azure-functions/functions-bindings-service-bus`

50. "Timer trigger for Azure Functions." Azure Functions documentation. Microsoft. `https://docs.microsoft.com/en-us/azure/azure-functions/functions-bindings-timer`

51. "Google Cloud Storage Triggers." Google Cloud Functions Documentation. Google. `https://cloud.google.com/functions/docs/calling/storage`

52. "Google Cloud Pub/Sub Triggers." Google Cloud Functions Documentation. Google. `https://cloud.google.com/functions/docs/calling/pubsub`

53. "Google Cloud Firestore Triggers." Google Cloud Functions Documentation. Google. `https://cloud.google.com/functions/docs/calling/cloud-firestore`

54. "Firebase Realtime Database Triggers." Google Cloud Functions Documentation. Google. `https://cloud.google.com/functions/docs/calling/realtime-database`

55. "Google Analytics for Firebase Triggers." Google Cloud Functions Documentation. Google. `https://cloud.google.com/functions/docs/calling/google-analytics-firebase`

56. "Firebase Authentication Triggers." Google Cloud Functions Documentation. Google. `https://cloud.google.com/functions/docs/calling/firebase-auth`

57. "HTTP Triggers." Google Cloud Functions Documentation. Google. `https://cloud.google.com/functions/docs/calling/http`

58. "Second-Party Triggers with Stackdriver." Google Cloud Functions Documentation. Google. `https://cloud.google.com/functions/docs/calling/logging`

CHAPTER 4

Securing Interfaces

In this chapter, we will review the function triggers and provide a use case for each. We will discuss how to identify the different interfaces defined in the Serverless configuration file and function code.

Importance of Securing Interfaces

Every interface exposes the application to receiving and sending data. The data might be sensitive or not. Another party might intercept the data when moving the data from at rest to in transit. An interface is a connection where information is exchanged between two parties, services or systems, and thus makes the data vulnerable to potential interception. Therefore, we need to identify the interfaces and potential vulnerabilities to determine how to secure the interfaces.

There are two major categories of interfaces: internal and external. When the application communicates with itself, this interface is internal. When the application communicates with another application or system, this interface is external. Typically, an internal interface is less vulnerable because there is a certain level of trust. Some systems implement no security for internal interfaces because all internal components are assumed to be secure and not a threat. Cybersecurity incidents like the Stuxnet computer worm that targeted the Iranian nuclear facilities[1] highlighted the importance of implementing security for all interfaces, even internal ones. Coincidentally around the same time as the Stuxnet incident, the zero-trust[2] security concept was birthed and primarily emphasizes trusting nothing in the systems, whether internal or external. Therefore, we will explore how to identify interfaces to the application and how to secure them.

---

[1]"What is Stuxnet?" McAfee. McAfee, LLC. www.mcafee.com/enterprise/en-us/security-awareness/ransomware/what-is-stuxnet.html

[2]"What is Zero Trust? A model for more effective security." Mary K. Pratt. CSO Online. 16 January 2018. www.csoonline.com/article/3247848/what-is-zero-trust-a-model-for-more-effective-security.html

© Miguel A. Calles 2020
M. Calles, *Serverless Security*, https://doi.org/10.1007/978-1-4842-6100-2_4

Understanding Interfaces and Use Cases

Before we review how to identify the interfaces, we should examine why the interfaces exist. Every application is built with a different use case, as we established in Chapter 2. Internal and external interfaces will exist depending on the application. Therefore, we should understand why those interfaces exist before we can assess the security implications of those interfaces.

We will review the interfaces AWS, Azure, and Google Cloud provide and use cases for why they might exist. We consider interfaces as internal when both sides are within the same provider and same account. We consider them external if one side is on a different account or a different provider. These providers have a Software Development Kit (SDK) or software library that a function can use to interface with its services. These libraries use a request-response pattern, where a call using the library sends an HTTP(S) (i.e., HTTP or HTTPS) request to the service. The service acts per the request and sends a response to the library. The library captures any success and error data and invokes any asynchronous callback function specified in the request code. We review how a function interfaces with internal services via event triggers and internal requests using a library. We will also discuss why interfaces outside of AWS, Azure, and Google Cloud might exist and possible use cases. This review will guide you in starting a critical analysis of the internal and external interfaces in your application and their use cases.

Amazon Web Services (AWS)

An AWS Lambda function interfaces with other AWS services via event triggers or the AWS SDK. The AWS SDK provides an interface to almost 200 AWS services.[3] We will review each of the event triggers in more detail and give an example of how to identify interfaces via the AWS SDK.

---

[3]"AWS SDK for JavaScript." Amazon Web Services. `https://docs.aws.amazon.com/AWSJavaScriptSDK/latest/index.html`

AWS Lambda Event Triggers

We will review each of the event triggers and provide a use case.

- **Amazon Alexa Skills Kit** and **Alexa Smart Home** allow a user to issue a verbal command to Alexa-enabled devices and interact with it. You might use a skill to trigger a Lambda function to provide a contextual response rather than a static response.

- **Amazon API Gateway (i.e., HTTP)** provides an HTTP interface to Lambda functions. You might use API Gateway to allow a web application, a mobile app, or another system to make an HTTP request to trigger a Lambda function and get the desired response.

- **Amazon CloudFront (Lambda@Edge)** is a Content Delivery Network (CDN) that speeds up the content delivery time. You might use CloudFront's Lambda@Edge to trigger a Lambda function to transform CDN content before it is delivered. For example, it can update a token with a value when retrieving a static web page or insert security headers.

- **Amazon CloudWatch** captures logs in log groups and monitors AWS events.

  - Amazon CloudWatch captures **events** emitted by other AWS services[4] and triggers a Lambda function with the event information. You might use a CloudWatch event to trigger a Lambda function to create a database record or send a notification to stakeholders when a virtual machine running on AWS is shut down.

  - Amazon CloudWatch uses **streams** to trigger Lambda functions when those Lambda functions subscribe to a CloudWatch log group it has a new log entry. You might use a CloudWatch log stream to trigger a Lambda function to store CloudWatch log data in a different service or format.

---

[4]"CloudWatch Events Event Examples From Supported Services." Amazon CloudWatch Events User Guide. Amazon Web Services. https://docs.aws.amazon.com/AmazonCloudWatch/latest/events/EventTypes.html

- **Amazon Cognito** provides user authentication and access control and integrates with other identity and access management systems. A Cognito User Pool is a user credential data store that securely stores user login information and defines the access privileges to AWS services. Cognito User Pools trigger[5] Lambda functions when a user signs up and authenticates. You might use a Cognito User Pool to trigger a Lambda function to validate user metadata is complete and valid before finishing the registration process.

- **Amazon DynamoDB** is a database designed for large data sets of unstructured or semistructured schemas (i.e., Not Only Structured Query Language [NoSQL] data). DynamoDB uses streams to send events to Lambda functions when its data tables are updated. You might use DynamoDB to trigger a Lambda function to create a change record when a user updates their profile, and that action updates the associated table.

- **Amazon Kinesis** supports ingesting large amounts of data into a stream and sending it to its subscribers in real time. It supports text, images, and videos. You might use Kinesis to trigger a Lambda function to analyze text and apply metadata whenever the stream receives data.

- **Amazon Lex** allows you to build voice and text chatbots. You might use a Lex to trigger a Lambda function to validate or fulfill a command a user has sent to a bot before the bot responds.

- **Amazon Simple Email Service** (SES) allows you to send and receive emails. You might use SES to trigger a Lambda function to update an order from pending to approved when a user sends an email accepting an order.

---

[5]"Customizing User Pool Workflows with Lambda Triggers." Amazon Cognito Developer Guide. Amazon Web Services. `https://docs.aws.amazon.com/cognito/latest/developerguide/cognito-user-identity-pools-working-with-aws-lambda-triggers.html`

- **Amazon Simple Notification Service** (SNS) is a messaging service where you publish event data, and other functions and services subscribe to receive it. You organize and group SNS data into topics, similar to how you might structure a web discussion forum. You might use an SNS topic to trigger a Lambda function to update a database record. It would set an entry to an archived status when moving its associated file into long-term storage.

- **Amazon Simple Queue Service** (SQS) collects messages from input sources (e.g., SNS topic messages) and organizes them into queues. SQS sends messages from the queue and guarantees a message is delivered at least one time. You might use an SQS queue to trigger a Lambda function to process SNS events in batches.

- **Amazon Simple Storage Service** (S3) provides remote file storage and security features (e.g., file encryption, versioning, and access control). You use an S3 bucket to store the remote files. You might use S3 to trigger a Lambda function to catalog a file uploaded to an S3 bucket.

- **AWS CloudFormation** uses templates to create several resources (e.g., networking, functions, storage, and more). You might use CloudFormation to trigger a Lambda function to get the information required by the CloudFormation template while it is creating resources.

- **AWS CodeCommit** provides source control for capturing your source code and files and change history into repositories. You might use CodeCommit to trigger a Lambda function to start an internal process when code is committed to the source code repository.

- **AWS Config** enables you to audit your existing AWS resource configuration against the target configuration by using rules. It provides change history and notifications when a change is detected. You might use Config to trigger a Lambda function to resize a virtual machine. Config might send an event notifying a newly created virtual machine is larger than the maximum size.

- **AWS EventBridge** allows you to connect your application to other applications using events using event buses. AWS services send events to the default bus. AWS SaaS partners send an event to the SaaS event bus. Any custom applications send events to a custom event bus. You might want to use EventBridge to get event data from third-party SaaS applications in your application architecture (e.g., monitoring software and a custom SaaS application created by another team within the organization).

- **AWS IoT** enables you to connect several Internet of Things (IoT) devices (thermostats, cars, sensors, machinery, you name it) to AWS for management, monitoring, analysis, and more. You can define rules to trigger a Lambda function when a query returns valid data. You might create a rule to monitor errors reported from IoT devices. Your Lambda function will send a push notification to the on-site representative notifying the IoT device owner about the issue.

- **Elastic Load Balancing** distributes application or network layer[6] traffic among different servers and Lambda functions. A Network Load Balancer (NLB) redirects traffic based on the network protocol and port information. An Application Load Balancer (ALB) redirects based on the HTTP(S) request information. ALBs can trigger Lambda functions, but not NLBs. You might use an ALB to trigger a Lambda function to update a firewall to block the requestor's IP address whenever it makes an HTTP request to a honeypot web address.

- **Scheduled events** allow you to automatically trigger a Lambda function by specifying a Command Run On (CRON) expression or a trigger rate. You might want to trigger a Lambda function at midnight every day to create a sales report or every 10 minutes to status orders.

---

[6]"Information technology – Open Systems Interconnection – Basic Reference Model: The Basic Model." ISO/IEC 7498-1:1994(E). Second edition. © 1994 ISO/IEC.

AWS Interfaces via the AWS Software Development Kit (SDK)

Lambda functions can use the AWS Software Development Kit (SDK)[7] to interface with the different AWS services and resources. You might use the AWS SDK to query a DynamoDB table to get account data or trigger another Lambda function. As you review the AWS SDK documentation, you will find the use cases are numerous.

Azure

An Azure Function interfaces with other Azure services via bindings or the Azure SDK. Azure Functions use the concept of bindings to define how they are triggered and what built-in interfaces they can use. The Azure SDK provides an interface to over 100 Azure services.[8] We will review each of the bindings in more detail and provide an example of how to identify interfaces via the Azure SDK.

Azure Function Bindings

A trigger is a binding that triggers the Azure Function. An Azure Function also has input and output bindings from the Azure services with which it interfaces. An input binding specifies that the service sends data to the function. For example, a file upload to the Azure Blob storage service can trigger an Azure Function, and it has input data containing the information about the file upload. An output binding specifies that the function sends data to the service. For example, an HTTP request can trigger an Azure Function to send output data (i.e., an HTTP response). Table 4-1 lists the bindings Azure Functions support.

---

[7]"Tools & SDKs." Amazon Web Services. https://aws.amazon.com/developer/tools

[8]"Azure SDK for Node." Microsoft. GitHub. https://github.com/Azure/azure-sdk-for-node/tree/master/lib/services

Table 4-1. *Microsoft Azure Input and Output Bindings*

Binding Type	Function Trigger	Input	Output
Azure Blob storage	Yes	Yes	Yes
Azure Cosmos DB	Yes	Yes	Yes
Azure Event Grid	Yes	No	No
Azure Event Hubs	Yes	No	Yes
Azure IoT Hub	Yes	No	Yes
Azure Mobile Apps	No	Yes	Yes
Azure Notification Hubs	No	No	Yes
Azure Queue storage	Yes	No	Yes
Azure Service Bus	Yes	No	Yes
Azure SignalR Service	No	Yes	Yes
Azure Table storage	No	Yes	Yes
HTTP and Webhooks	Yes	No	Yes
Microsoft Graph	Yes[†]	Yes[†]	Yes[†]
Timer	Yes	No	No
Twilio	No	No	Yes
Twilio SendGrid[9]	No	No	Yes

[†]*Only Microsoft Graph Events support trigger, input, and output bindings. The other Microsoft Graph interfaces support input, output, or both bindings.*

Note: This table was derived from the Microsoft documentation.[10]

---

[9]"Twilio" and "SendGrid" are registered trademarks of Twilio and/or its affiliates.

[10]"Azure Functions triggers and bindings concepts." Azure Functions Documentation. Microsoft. `https://docs.microsoft.com/en-us/azure/azure-functions/ functions-triggers-bindings#supported-bindings`

We will briefly review the functionality each service provides and gives an example of a use case.

- **Azure Blob storage** allows you to store a Binary Large Object (blob), which is a binary object like an image or a video. You use containers to store blobs and have it configured to trigger whenever creating or updating blobs. You might use Blob storage to trigger an Azure Function to catalog a file when updating a blob to the container.

- **Azure Cosmos DB** is a fully managed database that supports different database APIs (e.g., Structured Query Language [SQL], Gremlin graph traversal language, MongoDB[11] document database, Azure Table storage, and Apache Cassandra[12]). You might use Cosmos DB to trigger an Azure Function to query a database table for a specific record.

- **Azure Event Grid** manages your application events. It allows your application to accept events from various publishers (i.e., sources) and route them to multiple destinations for processing. You might use Event Grid to trigger an Azure Function to process an image when uploading it to a Blob storage container.

- **Azure Event Hubs** collects data from input sources and streams them to Azure Functions for processing. It supports multiple back-end systems of various programming languages, whether hosted on-premise or in the cloud. You might use Event Hubs to trigger an Azure Function to prepare data for real-time analytics.

- **Azure IoT Hub** allows you to connect several Internet of Things (IoT) devices and establish a two-way communication. You might use IoT Hub to trigger an Azure Function to establish a keep-alive connection to the IoT device.

---

[11]"MongoDB" is a registered trademark of MongoDB, Inc.

[12]"Apache" and "Cassandra" are either a registered trademark or trademark of The Apache Software Foundation.

- **Azure Mobile Apps** enables you to build Windows, iOS, and Android apps using the native platform or cross-platform solutions. It provides several integrations for cloud-based data storage, user authentication, push notifications, and enterprise systems. You might use an Azure Function to process data from an updated Mobile Apps data table when triggered by a queue message.

- **Azure Notification Hubs** allows you to send push notifications to various devices (e.g., iOS, Android, and Windows). It uses Event Hubs to trigger the Azure Function. You might use an Azure Function to send a push notification to a mobile user when triggered by a queue message.

- **Azure Queue storage** collects messages from input sources and sends them asynchronously to Azure Functions for processing. An input source adds messages to the queue by sending a request to the queue web address with the proper credential. You can store large numbers of messages in a queue. You might use Queue storage to trigger an Azure Function to process webhook data from a continuous integration pipeline.

- **Azure Service Bus** is a message broker that supports queues and topics for publish/subscribe configurations. It provides additional messaging features (e.g., auto-forwarding, scheduled delivery, client-side batching, filtering) and security features (e.g., Role-Based Access Control [RBAC], Representational State Transfer [REST], and Advanced Message Queueing Protocol [AMQP]). You might use Service Bus to trigger an Azure Function to perform facial recognition from multiple image sources.

- **Azure SignalR** abstracts the protocols used in real-time data updates within web applications by utilizing technologies (e.g., WebSockets) to transmit data to a web application without it needing to poll for updates. You might use an Azure Function to authenticate the SignalR connection from a web-based chat room. The Azure Function might send the appropriate data response to the chat room when triggered by an HTTP request.

- **Azure Table storage** is a database designed for large data sets with unstructured or semistructured schemas (i.e., NoSQL data). You can easily scale your application due to the flexible schema. You might use an Azure Function to query an entry from an Azure Table storage data table when triggered by an HTTP request.

- **HTTP and Webhooks** provides an HTTP interface to Azure Functions. You might use an HTTP interface to allow a web application, a mobile app, or another system to make an HTTP request and to trigger an Azure Function to get the desired response.

- **Microsoft Graph** provides an API for integrating with the following Microsoft services: Azure AD (Active Directory), Excel, Intune, Outlook, OneDrive, OneNote, SharePoint, and Planner. You might use Microsoft Graph to trigger an Azure Function to keep an audit record when an Outlook calendar entry was modified.

- **Timers** allow you to specify a CRON expression to trigger an Azure Function automatically. You might want to trigger an Azure Function at midnight every day to prepare the morning shipments.

- **Twilio** is a non-Microsoft (or external) service for sending Simple Messaging Service (SMS) text messages to a mobile phone number. You might use an Azure Function to send an SMS to a user when an order has shipped when triggered by a queue message.

- **Twilio SendGrid** is a non-Microsoft (or external) service for sending email messages. You might use an Azure Function to send an email message to a user when that user's password was recently changed when triggered by a queue message.

Azure Interfaces via the Azure SDK

Azure Functions can use the Azure Software Developer Kit (SDK)[13] to interface with the different Azure services and resources. You might use the Azure SDK to create an Azure Blob storage container. As you review the Azure SDK documentation, you will find numerous use cases are possible.

---

[13]"Azure Developer Tools." Microsoft Azure. Microsoft. `https://azure.microsoft.com/en-us/tools/`

Google Cloud

A Google Cloud Function interfaces with other Google Cloud services via event triggers or the Google Cloud Client Libraries. The Google Cloud Client Libraries provide interfaces to over 100 Google Cloud services.[14] We will review each of the event triggers in more detail and provide an example of how to identify interfaces via the Google Cloud Client Libraries.

Google Cloud Function Event Triggers

We will review each of the event triggers and provide a use case.

- **Firebase Authentication** uses an SDK that provides user authentication to many types of clients (e.g., Android and iOS mobile clients and web clients). It enables users to create an account and log in using an email address and password or to sign in using a federated identity provider. You might use Firebase Authentication to trigger a Cloud Function to record the details of a newly created account.

- **Firebase Crashlytics** provides crash reports and real-time crash alerts when your mobile app experiences a crash. You can get insights into the crash and whether multiple users are affected. You might use Firebase Crashlytics to trigger a Cloud Function to send an email to the development team when a new mobile app crash is detected.

- **Firebase Realtime Database** is a fully managed NoSQL database. It provides data storage and data synchronization to Android, iOS, and JavaScript clients using its Software Development Kit (SDK). It stores all data in JavaScript Object Notation (JSON) format. Also, it provides offline support for mobile and web clients for when they experience network latency or Internet connectivity issues. You mainly use this database for real-time data synchronization across all clients. You might use Firebase Realtime Database to trigger a Cloud Function to synchronize the application database when the realtime database is updated.

---

[14]"Google API Node.js Client." Google. `https://googleapis.dev/nodejs/googleapis/latest/index.html`

- **Firebase Remote Config** allows you to update your Android and iOS mobile apps without publishing an app update. You define default values that you can override at any time. Your users will get the overridden values because the app can frequently check for the updated values. You might use Firebase Remote Config to trigger a Cloud Function to create an audit record when there is a configuration update.

- **Firebase Test Lab** allows you to test your Android and iOS mobile apps on actual devices stored in Google's data centers. You write your tests using any of the supported test frameworks, schedule the test, and Firebase Test Lab will configure physical phones to run it. You might use Firebase Test Lab to send an email to the development team when a test fails.

- **Google Analytics for Firebase** analyzes user events in Android and iOS apps using Firebase. The analysis provides insight into user behaviors, activity, and demographics. It can also provide insights into software crashes and log events when integrated with other Google services. You might use Google Analytics for Firebase to trigger a Cloud Function to update the sales report when a user makes an in-app purchase.

- **Google Cloud Endpoints** provides API Management for your application. You define your API and use that definition to create the API endpoints. Having an API endpoint allows you to monitor usage and authorize access with user authentication and API keys. You might use Google Cloud Endpoints to trigger a Cloud Function from an HTTP request authenticated and verified by an API gateway.

- **Google Cloud Firestore** is a fully managed, flexible NoSQL database. It provides data storage and data synchronization to mobile and web clients and servers. Its data model is flexible and not limited to the JSON format. It also provides offline support and the ability to query the data. You might use Google Cloud Firestore to trigger a Cloud Function to fix typos and convert all text to uppercase when a user updates their user profile.

- **Google Cloud Scheduler** allows you to automatically trigger a Google Cloud Function by scheduling an operation managed by a CRON job scheduler. You might want to trigger a Cloud Function every morning to send daily promotion emails.

- **Google Cloud Storage** allows you to store files in a storage bucket. The client application will upload the user files into the bucket, which makes them accessible to the servers for processing. The client SDK can pause and continue uploads and downloads depending on the network connectivity. You might use Google Cloud Storage to trigger a Cloud Function to update all database references to a file when deleted.

- **Google Cloud Tasks** allow you to schedule tasks to execute asynchronously, immediately, or at a scheduled time. The tasks can trigger any HTTP target and have retry logic when a task fails to complete. You might use Google Cloud Tasks to trigger a Cloud Function that is time-consuming (i.e., longer than 30 seconds) and send the result back to the application which created the Cloud Task.

- **Google Cloud Pub/Sub** allows you to ingest events from data sources and distribute them to data targets, possibly with security features (e.g., end-to-end encryption and access control). You might use Google Cloud Pub/Sub to trigger a Cloud Function to process data from various types of IoT devices.

- **Cloud Logging** allows you to store your logs from Google Cloud and AWS events. You can search and analyze the stored logs and configure it to alert you when a log event matches specified criteria. It needs Google Cloud Pub/Sub and a Cloud Logging sink to trigger a Cloud Function. You might use Cloud Logging to trigger a Cloud Function to create metric data based on security log events.

- **HTTP** provides an HTTP interface to Cloud Functions. You might use an HTTP interface to trigger a Cloud Function to allow a web application, a mobile app, or another system to make an HTTP request to that function and get the desired response.

Google Cloud Interfaces via Google Cloud Client Libraries

Google Cloud Functions can use the Google Cloud Client Libraries[15] to interface with different Google Cloud services and resources. You might use the Google Cloud Client Libraries to create a Google Cloud Storage bucket. As you review the Google Cloud Client Libraries documentation, you will find there are a lot of use cases.

External Interfaces and Use Cases

The functions might interface with services outside of the cloud provider. That interface might be based on a direct HTTP request or may use an npm package or third-party SDK. You might want to use an external interface to accept and receive payments via a payment processor. As you inspect the code, you can identify which functions interface with external systems. Each external system will have some documentation for you to review.

Identifying the Interfaces

We will review how to identify the existence of internal and external interfaces within the application. In Chapter 2, we discussed how to identify interfaces by reviewing documentation and how to identify event triggers based on the Serverless configuration file. We will now review more concrete examples of how to identify the interfaces.

Serverless Configuration File

We will review examples of how an interface is defined in the Serverless configuration file.

For example, we can identify from the "serverless.yml" configuration file shown in Listing 4-1 that four Lambda functions have HTTP event triggers from the API Gateway.

---

[15]"Google Cloud Client Libraries." Google Cloud APIs. Google. `https://cloud.google.com/apis/docs/cloud-client-libraries`

Listing 4-1. Sample Serverless Configuration with HTTP Event Triggers[16]

```
functions:
  functionAuthorizer:
    handler: src/authorizer.handler
  function1:
    handler: src/function1.handler
    events:
      - http: GET hello/world
  function2:
    handler: src/function2.handler
    events:
      - http:
          path: hello/country
          method: post
  function3:
    handler: src/function3.handler
    events:
      - http:
          path: hello/state
          method: put
          cors:
            origins:
              - http://*.website1.com
              - https://website2.com
            headers:
              - Content-Type
              - X-Amz-Date
              - Authorization
              - X-Api-Key
              - X-Amz-Security-Token
              - X-Amz-User-Agent
```

---

[16]The Serverless configuration was derived from the Serverless Framework documentation. "API Gateway." Serverless Documentation. https://www.serverless.com/framework/docs/providers/aws/events/apigateway/. "Serverless.yml Reference." Serverless Documentation. https://www.serverless.com/framework/docs/providers/aws/guide/serverless.yml/.

```
          allowCredentials: false
          maxAge: 86400
          cacheControl: 'max-age=600, s-maxage=600'
        private: true
        authorizer:
          name: functionAuthorizer
          resultTtlInSeconds: 0
          identitySource: method.request.header.Auth
          identityValidationExpression: ^Bearer .*
          type: token
function4:
  handler: src/function4.handler
  events:
    - http:
        path: hello/city
        method: post
        integration: lambda
        request:
          template:
            # A query string of ?key=value in the URL
            # is accessible in the Lambda as
            # event.queryStringParameter
            application/json: '{
              "httpMethod" : "$context.httpMethod",
              "queryStringParameter" : "$input.params(''key'')"
              }'
        response:
          headers:
            Content-Type: "'text/plain'"
            Cache-Control: "'max-age=120'"
          template: $input.path('$')
          statusCodes:
            201:
              pattern: ''
            404:
              pattern: '.*"statusCode":409,.*'
```

```
template:
  application/json: $input.path("$.errorMessage")
headers:
  Content-Type: "'application/json+hal'"
```

As we review the Serverless documentation,[17] we learn the Serverless configuration file supports two integration types (i.e., Lambda Proxy and Lambda) when triggering a Lambda function over an HTTP request. You will normally see the Lambda Proxy integration because Serverless preconfigures the request and response structures. The Lambda integration is useful when you want to customize the request and response structures, though this requires more configuration settings.

You can define a Lambda Proxy integration by adding one line to the event settings. The "function1" function configuration shows how to define an HTTP GET request to "https://<API Gateway ID>.execute-api.<AWS region>.amazonaws.com/<stage>/hello/world" that triggers the function; see Listing 4-2.

Listing 4-2. Sample Lambda Proxy Integration in the Serverless Configuration

```
function1:
  handler: src/function1.handler
  events:
    - http: GET hello/world
```

The "function2" function configuration becomes more explicit. It defines an HTTP POST request to "https://<API Gateway ID>.execute-api.<AWS region>.amazonaws.com/<stage>/hello/country" that triggers the function; see Listing 4-3.

Listing 4-3. Sample Lambda Proxy Integration in the Serverless Configuration

```
function2:
  handler: src/function2.handler
  events:
    - http:
        path: hello/country
        method: post
```

---

[17]"API Gateway." Serverless Docs. https://serverless.com/framework/docs/providers/aws/events/apigateway/

The "function3" function configuration shows the different options available to configure the trigger; see Listing 4-4. The configuration

- Enables Continuously Operating Reference Station (CORS) and

  - Allows HTTP requests originating from any subdomain of website.com

  - Allows HTTPS requests originating from the website.com domain

  - Has required headers

  - Does not allow cookies, authorization headers, or TLS client certificates

  - Has a max-age of 86,400 seconds

  - Caches the content on the browser and proxy server for 600 seconds

- Requires an API key

- Uses an authorizer that

  - Uses the "functionAuthorizer" function as its authorizer

  - Gives the authorization a time to live of zero seconds

  - Requires the "Auth" header name that matches the "^Bearer .*" regular expression

  - Is an authorization token

Listing 4-4. Sample Lambda Proxy Integration in the Serverless Configuration

```
function3:
  handler: src/function3.handler
  events:
    - http:
        path: hello/state
        method: put
        cors:
          origins:
            - http://*.website1.com
            - https://website2.com
```

```
      headers:
        - Content-Type
        - X-Amz-Date
        - Authorization
        - X-Api-Key
        - X-Amz-Security-Token
        - X-Amz-User-Agent
      allowCredentials: false
      maxAge: 86400
      cacheControl: 'max-age=600, s-maxage=600'
    private: true
    authorizer:
      name: functionAuthorizer
      resultTtlInSeconds: 0
      identitySource: method.request.header.Auth
      identityValidationExpression: ^Bearer .*
      type: token
```

You can define the Lambda integration by specifying it in the function configuration. We will not review this integration in full detail because of its more complex manual configuration. Serverless, Inc. recommends to use the Lambda Proxy integration, but I suggest you explore the documentation especially if your development team has chosen this integration. The "function4" function configuration shows the Lambda integration.

In another example, we can identify from the configuration file shown in Listing 4-5 that two Lambda functions have S3 event triggers from two S3 buckets.

Listing 4-5. Sample Serverless Configuration with S3 Event Triggers[18]

```
functions:
  function5:
    handler: src/function1.handler
    events:
      # create a new S3 bucket
```

---

[18]The Serverless configuration was derived from the Serverless Framework documentation. "S3." Serverless Documentation. https://www.serverless.com/framework/docs/providers/aws/events/s3/

```
    - s3:
        bucket: ${self:service}-${self:provider.stage}-products
        event: s3:ObjectCreated:*
        rules:
          - prefix: new/
          - suffix: .jpg
function6:
  handler: src/function2.handler
  events:
    # use an existing S3 bucket
    - s3:
        bucket: ${self:service}-${self:provider.stage}-legacy
        event: s3:ObjectRemoved:*
        existing: true
```

As we review the Serverless documentation,[19] we learn the Serverless configuration file allows you to create an S3 bucket from the Serverless deployment or using an existing S3 bucket. You can configure the Lambda functions to trigger from specific S3 events.

The "function5" function configuration will create a new bucket and will trigger the Lambda function when creating a new S3 object (i.e., file) in that bucket. The object key (i.e., path and filename) begins with "new/" and ends with ".jpg." For example, when the application uploads a file to the S3 bucket with a "new/profile-picture/b210c69f-c436-4afe-bf02-14eff40bc7fa.jpg" object key, S3 emits an event and the Lambda function triggers with the event information.

The "function6" function configuration uses an existing bucket and triggers the Lambda function when removing any S3 objects.

You can find additional examples in the "chapter04" folder.

Function Code

Now let's review examples of how the function code defines an interface. The function code can use an SDK or a direct HTTP request to interact with internal and external interfaces, as discussed earlier.

For example, the AWS Lambda function code can interface with DynamoDB using the AWS SDK. You may see code similar to Listing 4-6, which makes a query to DynamoDB.

---

[19]"S3." Serverless Docs. https://serverless.com/framework/docs/providers/aws/events/s3/

Listing 4-6. Sample Node.js Code Interfacing with DynamoDB

```javascript
const AWS = require('aws-sdk');
const dynamodb = new AWS.DynamoDB();

module.exports.handler = (event, context, callback) => {
    const params = {
        TableName: process.env.TABLE_NAME,
        ExpressionAttributeValues: {
            ':id': {
                S: process.env.ACCOUNT_ID,
            }
        },
        KeyConditionExpression: 'AccountId = :id',
    };
    return dynamodb.query(params).promise()
        .then((data) => {
            console.log(
                'Query results:',
                JSON.stringify(data),
            );
            callback();
        })
        .catch((error) => {
            console.log(`Error: ${JSON.stringify(error)}`);
            callback();
        });
};
```

As we review the AWS SDK documentation, we learn that we create a DynamoDB object, which has functions to interface with the AWS DynamoDB service. Each function requires specific inputs, which we called "params" earlier, and responds with specific outputs, which we called "data" earlier. The "params" provides the DynamoDB table name with which this function interfaces and the query it is performing.

In another example, the Azure Function code can interface with Azure Blob storage using the Azure SDK. You may see code resembling Listing 4-7, which creates a Blob storage container.

Listing 4-7. Sample Node.js Code Interfacing with Azure Blob Storage

```
const azure = require('azure-storage');
const blobService = azure.createBlobService(
    process.env. AZURE_STORAGE_CONNECTION_STRING
);

const containerName = process.env.NEW_CONTAINER_NAME;

module.exports.hello = function (context, req) {
    blobService.createContainerIfNotExists(
        containerName,
        (error, result, response) => {
            console.log(`Response: ${JSON.stringify(response)}`);
            if (error) {
                return console.log(error);
            }
            if (result) {
                return console.log(`Created container ${containerName}.`);
            }
            console.log(`Did not create container ${containerName}.`);
            context.done();
        }
    );
}
```

As we review the Azure SDK documentation, we learn the Azure Storage client library has functions to interface with the Azure Blob storage service. This Azure Function creates a container if it does not already exist.

In another example, the Cloud Function code can interface with Google Cloud Storage using the Google Cloud Storage Client Library. You may see code like in Listing 4-8, which deletes a bucket.

Listing 4-8. Sample Node.js Code Interfacing with Google Cloud Storage

```
const {Storage} = require('@google-cloud/storage');
const storage = new Storage();
const bucket = storage.bucket('albums');
```

```
exports.deleteBucket = (req, res) => {
    const bucketName = req.query.name;
    bucket.delete()
        .then((data) => {
            const apiResponse = data[0];
            console.log(JSON.stringify(apiResponse));
            res.send(`Delete bucket: ${bucketName}`);
        })
        .catch((error) => {
            console.log(`Error: ${JSON.stringify(error)}`);
        });
};
```

As we review the Google Cloud Libraries documentation, we learn the Google Cloud Storage Client Library has functions to interface with the Google Cloud Storage service. This Cloud Function attempts to delete a bucket.

In another example, the Lambda function code interfaces with a third-party payment service using a direct HTTP request. You may see code as in Listing 4-9, which asks the payment merchant service to list all payment charges against that account.

Listing 4-9. Sample Node.js Code Interfacing with an External Payment System

```
const rp = require('request-promise');
module.exports.handler = (event, context, callback) => {
    const options = {
        uri: 'https://api.stripe.com/v1/charges',
        method: 'GET',
        headers: {
            Authorization: `Bearer ${process.env.API_KEY}`
        },
    };
    return rp(options)
        .then((response) => {
            console.log(response.data.length, 'transactions');
        })
```

```
    .catch((error) => {
        console.log('Error:', JSON.stringify(error));
    });
};
```

As we review the payment processor documentation,[20] we learn the merchant provides a Representational State Transfer (REST), which uses HTTP, to interface with its service. This AWS Lambda Function uses the "request-promise" npm package[21] to form the HTTP request and process the HTTP response.

Assessing and Reducing the Attack Surface

In Chapter 2, we reviewed two tables: Table 2-2 "Sample Function Listing" and Table 2-4 "Sample Threat Model Matrix." In this section, we will use those tables as we review interfaces.

Table 2-2 helped us organize the findings from our source code review. We identified the functions, runtime, entry points, and event triggers. We noted we could add columns identifying the external and internal interfaces. We can now add those columns or review the information we captured based on the information we discussed in this chapter.

Table 2-4 helped us identify the assets, the threats against those assets, and the defense we used to protect against those threats. As we review each interface, we can reference the threat model to identify specific risks for each interface. You could update the function listing (based on Table 2-2) to include threats. You could update the threat model matrix (based on Table 2-4) to include the specific functions and interfaces. Or, you can create a new table that relates functions, interfaces, and threats as you see appropriate for your assessment. However, we will use the format previously defined in Table 2-2 with the appropriate columns in our example; see the updates in Table 4-2.

---

[20]"API Reference." Stripe. `https://stripe.com/docs/api`
[21]"request-promise." npm. `www.npmjs.com/package/request-promise`

Table 4-2. *Sample Function Listing with Interfaces and Threats Added*

Function Name	Event Trigger(s)	Internal Interface(s)	External Interface(s)	Threat(s)
login	HTTP	DynamoDB accounts table	N/A	Customer data exposed
verifyMfa	HTTP	DynamoDB accounts table	Third-party SMS service	Account hijacking

You will find the sample function listing now shows the new columns. It shows the same two sample functions with only the relevant columns displayed. It contains the sample interfaces based on the function's purpose and the relevant sample threats from Table 2-4. We could have added proposed defenses or mitigations as well.

Now that we have a format to capture our findings, we need a systematic approach for capturing the interfaces and assessing the attack surface. You can use any method that works best for you, your project, and your project schedule. We will review the Serverless configuration file and proceed with reviewing the function code as our approach.

We defined several functions in Listings 4-1 and 4-5 in the Serverless configuration. We will review each example function.

- The "functionAuthorizer" function has no event triggers, which implies it is an internal function. We see "function3" references it as its authorizer. The API Gateway will trigger the authorizer first. If it responds with a success authorization, it will forward the HTTP request to "function3." Otherwise, the API Gateway denies the HTTP request. When we review the function code, we will need to understand how it validates the authorization. Depending on the answers to the following questions, we will propose appropriate mitigations:

  - Does it check a static key against a database entry? This creates an internal interface which might be vulnerable to an injection attack.

  - Does it use a regular expression to check the key? It might be susceptible to a Regular Expression Denial of Service (ReDoS).

- Does it use a third-party service to verify a JavaScript Object Notation Web Token (JWT) claim? This creates an external interface that might need to be tuned to expire tokens based on the application requirements.

- The "function1" function uses an HTTP trigger using the Lambda Proxy integration. We find it has no authorizer or API key defined, which means any agent can access it without restrictions. Although we see the Uniform Resource Locator (URL) path "hello/world" look benign, it might still disclose customer data or return environment variables containing sensitive information. An HTTP GET method might return data from a database query that defines an interface. If this function accepts query string parameters, it might allow a request to return numerous records, which extends the function execution time, thus increasing cost and the likelihood of a DoS attack. It may also result in long database execution time, potentially increasing costs and increasing response times for other functions accessing this database. We might propose the following risk mitigations: adding an authorizer, limiting data returned, limiting or preventing query strings, and restricting the function execution time.

- The "function2" function uses an HTTP trigger using the Lambda Proxy integration. We find it has no authorizer or API key defined, which means any agent can post data without restrictions. Any agent can potentially add erroneous data to the system, increase database usage (thus defining an interface), perform injection attacks, or attempt a DoS attack with a large payload. We might propose the following risk mitigations: adding an authorizer, limiting the size of the payload, and restricting the function execution time.

- The "function3" function uses an HTTP trigger using the Lambda Proxy integration. We find it requires both an API key and an authorizer for the function to trigger. The authorizer declaration specifies a JWT claim is needed. It implements Cross-Origin Resource Sharing (CORS) to mitigate against Cross-Site Scripting (XSS) attacks. It uses an HTTP PUT method, which is similar to an HTTP POST. We might propose the same mitigations as we would for "function3" less the need for an authorizer.

- The "function4" function uses an HTTP trigger using the Lambda integration. It would behoove us to discuss with the development team why they chose this integration because it is more complex and avoids the use of authorizers. Instead, it uses request templates to validate the HTTP request at the API Gateway and deny passing the request to the function. We might propose moving to the Lambda Proxy integration in addition to any relevant recommendations from the "function 2" function.

- The "function5" function uses the S3 object created events[22] to trigger the function. This defines an internal interface to S3 that is active whenever a product image file is created, updated, or copied. When we review the function code, we will need to understand how to process the event.

  - Does it add the filename to the database record for that account? This defines a second interface.

  - Does it need to process update or copied events, or only first creation events? The function may unintentionally overwrite customer data if it processes an undesired event.

  - We might propose limiting the event to "s3:ObjectCreated:Post" to only process newly created objects and performing input sanitization on the filename to avoid a database injection attack that generates more data than expected.

- The "function6" function uses S3 object removed events to trigger the function. This defines an external or internal interface depending on whether the existing bucket is from another application or created in another service from the same application. When we review the function code, we will need to understand how to process the event.

  - Does it delete database records when the event is triggered? This defines a second interface and may result in the accidental deletion of data.

---

[22]"Configuring Amazon S3 Event Notifications." Amazon Simple Storage Service Developer Guide. Amazon Web Services. https://docs.aws.amazon.com/AmazonS3/latest/dev/NotificationHowTo.html

- Does it need to process the most recently deleted object or the removal of an older version of the object? Removing an older version may invalidate the current data set even though it did not delete the current version.

- We might propose limiting the event to "s3:ObjectRemoved:Delete" to only process the deletion of the object's current version to avoid inadvertent data deletion and performing input sanitization on the filename to prevent a database injection attack that deletes more data than expected.

As you review the Serverless configuration files, you can use the preceding assessment as an example for identifying the different interfaces and risks and proposing risk mitigations to reduce the attack surface.

We showed example interfaces defined in the function code in Listing 4-6 through Listing 4-10. We will review each example.

- Listing 4-6 defines an interface to DynamoDB and performs a query to a DynamoDB database table. The example shows a query against the same table and account, which prevents any injection attacks. Typically, this type of function will accept inputs from the HTTP URL, which has the account identifier or an HTTP query string. This function might be vulnerable to disclosing customer data if input data and the database query result in returning records for more than one user or user data from another user. That said, this code has a low likelihood of accidental disclosure because it requires the "AccountId" value to be an exact match (provided each account has a unique identifier). We might propose performing input validation on the account identifier and cross-checking the "AccountId" against the user session to confirm that the user is not accessing another user's data.

- Listing 4-7 defines an interface to Azure Blob storage and attempts to create a storage container. The example uses the same container name every time. This might be intentional if it runs on a timer to ensure the container is recreated if accidentally deleted. It behooves us to understand why a function is creating infrastructure rather than creating the infrastructure as part of the Serverless configuration deployment or the Continuous Integration (CI) and Continuous Delivery (CD) pipeline. We might propose to move this capability to the CI/CD pipeline and not to accept any inputs to avoid creating unnecessary storage containers.

- Listing 4-8 defines an interface to Google Cloud Storage and attempts to delete a storage bucket. The example uses a query string parameter to determine the container name. This function can remove any bucket name. It behooves us to understand why a function is modifying infrastructure. We might propose to perform input validation to restrict deleting critical buckets or moving the deletion to an automated process that is not triggered by an HTTP event.

As you review the code for the different functions, you can use the preceding assessment as an example for identifying the various interfaces and risks and proposing risk mitigations to reduce the attack surface.

Key Takeaways

In this chapter, we reviewed the different function event triggers for the AWS, Azure, and Google Cloud providers and discussed a use case for each event trigger. We examined how the function code can create interfaces to the AWS, Azure, Google Cloud, and external services using their respective SDKs and HTTP requests. We explored examples on how to identify the interfaces in the Serverless configuration file and function code, document any threats and risks, and propose any mitigations.

## CHAPTER 5

Configuring the Application Stack

In this chapter, we will review the organization of the Serverless configuration file. We will explore good practices for us to consider using in each configuration section.

Importance of Configuring the Application Stack

The Serverless Framework uses the Serverless configuration file to define the application stack. The "application stack" is a term referring to the different layers of applications and services used to make the application functional. For example, recall from Figure 2-2, the example ecommerce mobile app needs a mobile application, API gateway, databases, and functions. The Serverless configuration file can manage these application components, except the mobile application code. Given this configuration file can define most of your application, the components, and infrastructure, it behooves us to configure it optimally.

Understanding the Serverless Configuration

Up until now, we have been using Serverless configuration files to perform a risk assessment and identifying functions and interfaces. We will review the configuration file and its different elements in more depth.

The Serverless configuration file has three required common sections for AWS, Azure, and Google Cloud:

- **The "service" section** defines the application stack.

© Miguel A. Calles 2020
M. Calles, *Serverless Security*, https://doi.org/10.1007/978-1-4842-6100-2_5

- **The "provider" section** defines the serverless provider and provider-specific settings.

- **The "functions" section** defines the serverless functions, event triggers, and other settings.

You will see these sections defined similarly to Listing 5-1.

Listing 5-1. Required Serverless Configuration Sections

```
service: myService
provider:
  name: google
functions:
  myFunction:
    handler: myFunctionHandler
    events:
      http: path
```

These sections are used similarly across all three providers, but there are some differences. There are three additional common sections you can define:

- **The "frameworkVersion" section** defines the Serverless Framework version(s) needed to deploy the service.

- **The "plugins" section** defines the Serverless plugins to use during the deployment process or as a command-line instruction.

- **The "custom" section** defines custom variables for use in the configuration file. You can reference these custom variables by using a Serverless variable (e.g., `"${self:custom.myVariable}"`) within the configuration. Some plugins may use this section to obtain custom settings.

- **The "package" section** defines how the function code is packaged and deployed.

You will see these sections defined similarly to Listing 5-2.

Listing 5-2. Optional Serverless Configuration Sections

```
frameworkVersion: =1.0.42
plugins:
  - serverless-google-cloudfunctions
custom:
  myVariable: myValue
package:
  include:
    - src/**
    - handler.js
  exclude:
    - .git/**
  excludeDevDependencies: true
  individually: true
```

The AWS service has additional optional sections:

- **The "layers" section** defines any AWS Lambda Layers[1] to upload and deploy. You can upload up to 250 MB of data in each layer. A Lambda function can use up to five layers.

- **The "resources" section** defines any CloudFormation resources (e.g., an S3 bucket or DynamoDB database) to deploy. You can specify any resource that CloudFormation can deploy in this section.

You will see these sections defined similarly to Listing 5-3.

Listing 5-3. AWS-Specific Serverless Configuration Sections

```
layers:
  myLayer:
    path: layers/myLayer
    name: ${self:service}-${self:provider.stage}-myLayer
```

---

[1]"AWS Lambda Layers." AWS Lambda Developer Guide. Amazon Web Services.
https://docs.aws.amazon.com/lambda/latest/dg/configuration-layers.html

```
resources:
  S3BucketUploads:
      Type: AWS::S3::Bucket
      Properties:
        BucketName: ${self:custom.bucketName}
custom:
  bucketName: ${self:service}-${self:provider.stage}-uploads
```

Next, let's review some good practices for each of the sections mentioned earlier.

Good Practices for the Serverless Configuration

The Serverless configuration file will vary among the different application stacks and providers. We will review good practices for you to consider in each of the configuration files.

Defining Multiple Services

In Chapter 2, we discussed how a service is a group of functions and how the example ecommerce mobile app had three groups of functions in the application layer (see Figure 2-1). Each group of functions has one Serverless configuration file and thus deploys three services. The three services organize the functions and resources and create internal service boundaries. Each Serverless configuration file will deploy one service, which is managed independently from the other services. You might decide to create one code repository per service or have one repository (or "monorepo") with subfolders for each service depending on your project requirements and team preferences. In either case, you should have a logical grouping for each service.

You should name each service representative of its purpose. For example, you might call one service "eCommerceAccounts" because it contains functions related to user accounts. This name suggests that you will manage the account-related functions, event triggers, and any resources as a group and independent of other services. You can then add a new function without disrupting another service. Having this type of separation creates a service boundary.

Having service boundaries allows you to define service-level APIs, meaning a service must use another service's API to establish a communication. For example, a payment service might need to verify an account is active. The payment service would send an

HTTPS request to the accounts service API that executes the account lookup function. This interaction will succeed as long as the payment service conforms to the accounts service API. You should use this interservice interaction rather than having the payment service execute the accounts service function directly. Doing so creates a dependency, requires the accounts service to expand its security permissions, and adds complexity. You will also manage resources per service. For example, you can manage the accounts database independent of the payments database. Therefore, you might want to work with the application developers to confirm the services are optimally defined, especially if there is much interservice interaction.

Configuring the Provider

Other than the provider name, the provider section defines settings specific to the AWS, Azure, and Google Cloud providers. The AWS provider section has the most settings compared to those of Azure and Google Cloud. We will start with Azure and Google Cloud and conclude with AWS.

Azure

The Azure provider section allows you to define the region location to deploy the service. You can also specify the API gateway settings.

- **Region**: You should specify the region location closest to where your users will interact with the service to reduce network latency; see Listing 5-4. You can view the regions Azure supports for Azure Functions in the Azure documentation.[2]

Listing 5-4. Azure Provider Section

```
provider:
  name: azure
  location: West US
```

---

[2]"Products available by region." Microsoft Azure. Microsoft. https://azure.microsoft.com/en-us/global-infrastructure/services/?products=functions

- **API Management**: You can define an API gateway to manage your API endpoints. You should specify tags to help with organization, the appropriate authorization depending on the intent of the function, and proper Cross-Origin Resource Sharing (CORS) settings.

Listing 5-5. Azure API Management Configuration[3]

```
provider:
  apim:
   apis:
     - name: v1
       subscriptionRequired: false
       displayName: v1
       description: V1 APIs
       protocols:
          - https
       path: v1
       tags:
          - eCommerce 1.0
       authorization: none
    cors:
      allowCredentials: false
      allowedOrigins:
        - "*"
      allowedMethods:
        - GET
        - POST
        - PUT
        - DELETE
        - PATCH
      allowedHeaders:
        - "*"
      exposeHeaders:
        - "*"
```

---

[3]This configuration is based on the sample configuration provided by Serverless, Inc. "Serverless. yml Reference." Serverless Documentation. https://www.serverless.com/framework/docs/providers/azure/guide/serverless.yml/

- **Environment Variables**: This subsection defines the environment variables all functions will have. You should never include sensitive data in plaintext; instead always use encrypted versions of that data. Limit using this section to defining environment variables that every function will or might use; see Listing 5-6. You should define all other environment variables in the function configuration.

Listing 5-6. Azure Provider Section – Environment Variables

```
provider:
  name: azure
  environment:
    GLOBAL_VAR1: value1
    GLOBAL_VAR2: value2
```

Google Cloud

The Google Cloud provider section allows you to define the runtime, project, and credentials. These are the required settings. Refer to the Serverless documentation[4] for instructions on how to populate them. The provider section also allows you to define the memory size and timeout that applies to all functions:

- **Region**: Similar to the Azure region, this sets the region closest to where the users will interact with the app; see Listing 5-7. You can view the regions Google Cloud supports for Google Cloud Functions in the documentation.[5]

Listing 5-7. Google Cloud Provider Section – Region

```
provider:
  name: google
  region: us-central1
```

---

[4]"Google – Credentials." Serverless Documentation. https://serverless.com/framework/docs/providers/google/guide/credentials/

[5]"Cloud locations." Google Cloud. Google. https://cloud.google.com/about/locations/

- **Memory Size**: Cloud Functions are assigned a default memory of 256 MB. You should keep this global value small and increase it on a per-function basis; see Listing 5-8. Google Cloud charges higher prices[6] for more memory usage. More memory-intensive functions should have more memory because it reduces execution time. Be cautious with any functions that use a regular expression to validate inputs. If it is vulnerable to a Regular Expression Denial of Service (ReDoS) attack and the function has a lot of memory allocated, Google Cloud will charge a higher per-execution cost. It can become very costly if that function executes numerous times. You can use a regular expression static analysis tool to check your regular expressions.

Listing 5-8. Google Cloud Provider Section – Memory Size

```
provider:
  name: google
  memorySize: 128
```

- **Timeout**: Cloud Functions are assigned a default execution timeout of 60 seconds. You should keep this global value small and increase it on a per-function basis; see Listing 5-9. Google Cloud charges execution time in increments of 100 milliseconds.[5] The longer a function executes, the more that execution will cost. If a function is blocked during execution or is vulnerable to a ReDOS attack, it will continue executing until reaching the timeout. Google Cloud will charge you for that entire execution time, and it can become very costly if that function executes numerous times.

Listing 5-9. Google Cloud Provider Section – Timeout

```
provider:
  name: google
  timeout: 3s # only accepts seconds
```

---

[6]"Pricing." Google Cloud. Google. https://cloud.google.com/functions/pricing

- **Labels**: You should consider defining labels to help you locate and organize the functions in the Serverless deployment; see Listing 5-10.

Listing 5-10. Google Cloud Provider Section – Labels

```
provider:
  name: google
  labels:
    projectName: eCommerce
```

Amazon Web Services (AWS)

The AWS provider section allows you to define several settings. Reference the Serverless documentation[7] to see the extent of all the provider settings. We will focus on specific settings:

- **Region**: Similarly, as with the others, set the region closest to where the users will interact with the app; see Listing 5-11. You can view the regions that AWS supports for Lambda functions in the AWS documentation.[8]

Listing 5-11. AWS Provider Section – Region

```
provider:
  name: aws
  region: us-east-1
```

- **Memory Size**: Lambda functions are assigned a default memory of 1024 MB. You should keep this global value small and increase it on a per-function basis (see Listing 5-12) for the same reasons discussed in the Google Cloud section.

---

[7]"Serverless.yml Reference." Serverless Documentation. https://serverless.com/framework/docs/providers/aws/guide/serverless.yml/

[8]"AWS General Reference." AWS General Reference. Amazon Web Services. https://docs.aws.amazon.com/general/latest/gr/rande.html

Listing 5-12. AWS Provider Section – Memory Size

```
provider:
  name: aws
  memorySize: 128
```

- **Timeout**: Lambda functions are assigned a default execution timeout of 6 seconds. You should keep this global value small and increase it on a per-function basis (see Listing 5-13) for the same reasons discussed in the Google Cloud section.

Listing 5-13. AWS Provider Section – Timeout

```
provider:
  name: aws
  timeout: 3 # only accepts seconds, no "s" suffix needed
```

- **Deployment Bucket**: The Serverless Framework uploads the artifacts it used in the deployment to an S3 bucket. By default, the S3 bucket stores the files as encrypted, but they might be Internet accessible. At a minimum, you should prevent global access to these Serverless artifacts; see Listing 5-14.

Listing 5-14. AWS Provider Section – Deployment Bucket

```
provider:
  name: aws
  deploymentBucket:
    blockPublicAccess: true
```

- **Environment Variables**: This subsection defines the environment variables all functions will have. You should never include sensitive data in plaintext; instead, always use encrypted versions of that data. Limit using this section to defining environment variables that every function will or might use; see Listing 5-15. You should define all other environment variables in the function configuration.

Listing 5-15. AWS Provider Section – Environment Variables

```
provider:
  name: aws
  environment:
    GLOBAL_VAR1: value1
    GLOBAL_VAR2: value2
```

- **CloudFormation Identity and Access Management (IAM) Role**:
  When you deploy the Serverless configuration, the deployment uses
  the defined AWS credential, which typically is that of the user. This
  credential may have privileges to create resources not used in the
  Serverless configuration. You should define a specific IAM role for
  the deployment, which only has the privileges to create, update, and
  delete the resources used by the Serverless configuration; see Listing
  5-16. We will discuss IAM in Chapter 6.

Listing 5-16. AWS Provider Section – CloudFormation Role

```
provider:
  name: aws
  cfnRole: arn:aws:iam::XXXXXXXXXXXX:role/CloudFormationRole
```

- **Tags and Stack Tags**: You should consider defining custom tags
  to help you locate and organize the resources (e.g., API Gateway,
  CloudFormation stacks, Lambda functions, etc.) in the Serverless
  deployment; see Listing 5-17.

Listing 5-17. AWS Provider Section – Tags and Stack Tags

```
provider:
  name: aws
  stackTags:
    PROJECT_NAME: eCommerce
    PROJECT_VERSION: 1.0
  tags:
    PROJECT_NAME: eCommerce
    PROJECT_VERSION: 1.0
```

- **IAM Role Statements**: This subsection defines the IAM privileges all the functions will share. You should avoid setting privileges here unless it is a privilege every function needs (e.g., decrypting secrets encrypted with the KMS service); see Listing 5-18. Instead, you should define the IAM privileges within each function configuration. We will discuss this further in the next section.

Listing 5-18. AWS Provider Section – IAM Role Statements

```
provider:
  name: aws
  iamRoleStatements:
    - Effect: Allow
      Action: kms:Decrypt
      Resource: arn:aws:kms:${self:provider.region}:*:key/*
```

- **Virtual Private Cloud (VPC)**: You might use a VPC to prevent a Lambda function from being accessible from the Internet or to access resources that only exist with the VPC. You should have two VPC subnets at a minimum to ensure the Lambda function has access to the VPC in the event one of the subnets becomes available; see Listing 5-19. You only need to define the VPC in the provider section if every Lambda function needs access to the VPC.

Listing 5-19. AWS Provider Section – Virtual Private Cloud

```
provider:
  name: aws
  vpc:
    subnetIds:
      - subnet-XXXXXXXXXXXXXXXXX
      - subnet-XXXXXXXXXXXXXXXXX
    securityGroupIds:
      - sg-XXXXXXXXXXXXXXXX
```

- **Tracing**: You should consider enabling tracing for the API Gateway using AWS X-Ray; see Listing 5-20. X-Ray is an AWS service for collecting metrics and data on the API Gateway usage. It is useful in detecting potential Denial of Service attacks because it shows metrics of HTTP status codes and the web URL used to access the API Gateway. For example, if you notice numerous 403 errors for an undefined URL coming from a specific IP address, you can take measures to block that IP address.

Listing 5-20. AWS Provider Section – API Gateway X-Ray Tracing

```
provider:
  name: aws
  tracing:
    apiGateway: true
```

There are many AWS provider settings we did not discuss. You might find it beneficial to become familiar with all the settings and determine how to set them for your project. Refer to the Serverless documentation to learn more.[9]

Organizing and Defining Functions

We reviewed functions in Chapter 2 in the context of performing a risk assessment, Chapter 3 in the context of securing the code, and Chapter 4 in the context of securing interfaces. Now we will review how to organize the functions and define any function-specific settings we described earlier.

For all three providers, you can further organize the functions within a service. A service should have all the functions that relate to that service, but you might be able to organize them into subgroups. For example, say the accounts service has functions for registration, credentials, and data retrieval. You can then create three function files that contain those subgroups: "serverless-functions-registration.yml," "serverless-functions-credentials.yml," and "serverless-functions-data.yml" files; see Listings 5-21, 5-22, and 5-23, respectively.

---

[9]"AWS Provider Documentation." Serverless Framework Documentation. Serverless, Inc. www.serverless.com/framework/docs/providers/aws

Listing 5-21. Functions Section – Accounts Registration Functions

```
# serverless-functions-registration.yml
functions:
  registration1:
    handler: http
    events:
      - http: path
```

Listing 5-22. Functions Section – Accounts Login Functions

```
# serverless-functions-login.yml
functions:
  login1:
    handler: http
    events:
      - http: path
```

Listing 5-23. Functions Section – Accounts Data Functions

```
# serverless-functions-data.yml
functions:
  data1:
    handler: http
    events:
      - http: path
```

The Serverless file will reference the subgroup files; see Listing 5-24.

Listing 5-24. Functions Section – Referencing Subgroups

```
# serverless.yml
functions:
  - ${file(serverless-functions-registration.yml):functions}
  - ${file(serverless-functions-login.yml):functions}
  - ${file(serverless-functions-data.yml):functions}
```

The functions section for all providers allows you to define the events that trigger the functions. Instead of focusing on how to define events, we will focus on the recommended settings for each provider.

Azure

The Azure functions section has no Azure-specific settings to define.

Google Cloud

The Google Cloud Functions section allows you to define the memory and timeout for each function and thus override the provider settings; see Listing 5-25.

Listing 5-25. Google Cloud Functions Section – Memory Size and Timeout

```
functions:
  registration1:
    memorySize: 512
    timeout: 6s
```

AWS

The AWS functions section allows you to define several settings. Reference the Serverless documentation to see the extent of all the provider settings. We will focus on specific settings:

- **Memory Size**: You can override the memory and timeout settings defined in the provider section; see Listing 5-26.

Listing 5-26. AWS Functions Section – Memory Size and Timeout

```
functions:
  registration1:
    memorySize: 512
    timeout: 6
```

- **Environment Variables**: You can append to the provider environment variables by defining function-specific environment variables; see Listing 5-27. Remember not to use plaintext values for sensitive data; use encrypted values instead.

Listing 5-27. AWS Functions Section – Environment Variables

```
functions:
  registration1:
    environment:
      FUNCTION_VAR1: value1
```

- **Virtual Private Cloud**: You can override the provider VPC settings or define the VPC setting for specific functions; see Listing 5-28.

Listing 5-28. AWS Functions Section – VPC

```
functions:
  registration1:
    vpc:
      subnetIds:
        - subnet-XXXXXXXXXXXXXXXXX
        - subnet-XXXXXXXXXXXXXXXXX
      securityGroupIds:
        - sg-XXXXXXXXXXXXXXXXX
```

- **Layers**: You can define which layers to use; see Listing 5-29.

Listing 5-29. AWS Functions Section – Layers

```
functions:
  registration1:
    layers:
      - arn:aws:lambda:region:XXXXXXXXXXXX:layer:LayerName:Y
```

- **IAM Role Statements**: You should define IAM privileges for each function; see Listing 5-30. You will need a plugin to enable this setting because it does not exist natively in the Serverless Framework. Remember to use the least amount of privileges for the function to execute properly. We will discuss IAM in Chapter 6.

Listing 5-30. AWS Functions Section – IAM Role Statements

```
functions:
  registration1:
    iamRoleStatements:
      - Effect: Allow
        Action: s3:DeleteObject
        Resource: arn:aws:s3:::${self:custom.bucketName}/*
```

Pinning the Framework Version

For all three providers, you can define which version(s) of the Serverless Framework to use when deploying the service. You can specify a specific version (see Listing 5-31), which is a recommended setting for production deployments. Having varying versions is typically not a problem. Still, for reproducibility and testability, it is a good idea to use an exact version because a future version might introduce a bug or a breaking change into the Serverless Framework.

Listing 5-31. Framework Version Section – Specific Version

```
frameworkVersion: '=1.42.0'
```

You can also specify a minimum and maximum version range; see Listing 5-32. You might want to use this option while developing the application to give flexibility in upgrading to the latest version of Serverless. Make sure to limit the maximum version to be less than the next major version to avoid any backward-compatibility issues. When the application is close to being final or is ready for final production deployment, you should consider using a specific version.

Listing 5-32. Framework Version Section – Version Range

```
frameworkVersion: '>=1.42.0 <2.0.0'
```

Using Plugins

While AWS allows you to use optional plugins to deploy their functions, Azure and Google require their respective plugins. There are some recommended plugins to consider for each cloud provider. There are more plugins to explore in the Serverless Plugins GitHub page.[10] Before you install any plugin, you should review the GitHub page and its source code.[11]

Azure

You will need the "serverless-azure-functions" plugin to deploy Azure Functions; see Listing 5-33. You might want to consider adding the "serverless-webpack" plugin[12] that optimizes the function upload size.

Listing 5-33. Azure Plugins Section

```
plugins:
  - serverless-azure-functions
  - serverless-webpack
```

Google Cloud

You will need the "serverless-google-cloudfunctions" plugin to deploy Google Cloud Functions; see Listing 5-34. You might want to consider adding the "serverless-webpack" plugin[13] too.

Listing 5-34. Google Cloud Plugins Section

```
plugins:
  - serverless-google-cloudfunctions
  - serverless-webpack
```

---

[10]"Serverless Plugins." GitHub. https://github.com/serverless/plugins

[11]Serverless plugins might introduce vulnerabilities to your development environment and application environment. Inspecting the source code might help you find potential security concerns. "Insecure Serverless Plugins: Why You Should Inspect the Source Code." Miguel A. Calles. Secjuice. March 29, 2020. www.secjuice.com/ insecure-serverless-plugins-why-you-should-inspect-the-source-code

[12]"serverless-webpack." GitHub. https://github.com/serverless-heaven/serverless-webpack

[13]"serverless-webpack." GitHub. https://github.com/serverless-heaven/serverless-webpack

AWS

You should consider using the following plugins:

- The **"serverless-iam-roles-per-function" plugin**[14] allows you to define IAM roles per function; see Listing 5-35.

- The **"serverless-stack-termination-protection" plugin**[15] prevents accidental deletion of the CloudFormation stack used to deploy the Serverless service; see Listing 5-35.

- The **"serverless-webpack" plugin**[16] optimizes the function artifact package size; see Listing 5-35. You will need a webpack configuration file for this to work; see Listing 5-36. Reference the GitHub page for more information.

Listing 5-35. AWS Plugins Section

```
plugins:
  - serverless-iam-roles-per-function
  - serverless-stack-termination-protection
  - serverless-webpack
```

Listing 5-36. An Example of a Serverless Webpack Plugin "webpack.config.js" Configuration File[17]

```
const slsw = require('serverless-webpack');
const nodeExternals = require('webpack-node-externals');
const { isLocal } = slsw.lib.webpack;
module.exports = {
    entry: slsw.lib.entries,
    target: 'node',
```

[14]"serverless-iam-roles-per-function." GitHub. https://github.com/functionalone/serverless-iam-roles-per-function

[15]"serverless-stack-termination-protection." GitHub https://github.com/miguel-a-calles-mba/serverless-stack-termination-protection

[16]"serverless-webpack." GitHub. https://github.com/serverless-heaven/serverless-webpack

[17]This configuration was derived from the Serverless Webpack examples. "webpack.config.js." Serverless Webpack. GitHub. https://github.com/serverless-heaven/serverless-webpack/blob/master/examples/include-external-npmpackages/webpack.config.js

```
  externals: [nodeExternals()],
  mode:isLocal ? 'development' : 'production',
};
```

Using the Custom Section

You can use the custom section for all three providers. It is a good place to store variables for use in other sections. For example, you might want a standard naming convention for the per-function IAM role statements; see Listing 5-37.

Listing 5-37. Custom Section – IAM Roles Name Variable

```
custom:
  stack: ${self:service}-${self:provider.name}
  iamRolesPrefix: ${self:custom.stack}-${self:provider.stage}
functions:
  registration1:
    iamRoleStatementsName: ${self:custom.iamRolesPrefix}-reg1
    iamRoleStatements:
      - Effect: Allow
        Action: s3:DeleteObject
        Resource: arn:aws:s3:::${self:custom.bucketName}/*
```

You might also want to specify settings for a plugin; see Listing 5-38.

Listing 5-38. Custom Section – Plugin Settings

```
custom:
  serverless-iam-roles-per-function:
    defaultInherit: true
  serverlessTerminationProtection:
    stages:
      - prod
  webpack:
    includeModules: true
```

AWS-Specific Configuration Settings

The following sections discuss configuration settings specific to AWS.

Defining the Packaging

All three providers allow you to define how Serverless deploys its function artifacts by specifying which files to include and exclude. AWS allows you to specify having one artifact per Lambda function; see Listing 5-39. This setting, when used in conjunction with the "serverless-webpack" plugin, deploys Lambda functions with small artifact sizes and improves Lambda function performance.

Listing 5-39. AWS Package Section

```
package:
  individually: true
```

Using AWS Lambda Layers

The AWS provider allows you to define immutable AWS Lambda Layers, meaning a deployment cannot modify them. You can define up to five layers. You should limit who has access to these layers by restricting them to a specific account or accounts. You should use layers for files with large file sizes (e.g., text databases and runtime files) that you will use in your Lambda function code. You typically would not use layers for npm packages unless it's a package that is too large to import into your "package.json" file. You might choose layers over an S3 bucket when you need immutable data; a file in an S3 is modifiable. You might also consider retaining all versions of the layers. Otherwise, the deployment will delete older layers when it creates newer ones.

Listing 5-40. AWS Layers Section[18]

```
layers:
  myLayer:
    path: layers/myLayer
    name: ${self:service}-${self:provider.stage}-myLayer
    allowAccounts:
```

---

[18]The configuration was derived from the sample configurations provided by Serverless, Inc. "AWS - Layers." Serverless Documenation. https://www.serverless.com/framework/docs/providers/aws/guide/layers/

```
      # only share with the current account
      - 'Fn::Join':
          - ''
          - - Ref: 'AWS::AccountId'
    retain: true
```

Defining Resources

The AWS provider allows you to use a CloudFormation template to create custom resources. You can use the CloudFormation template reference[19] for information on creating custom resources. You should consider organizing files similar to the functions organization; see Listing 5-41.

Listing 5-41. AWS Resources Section – Referencing CloudFormation Templates

```
# serverless.yml
resources:
  - ${file(serverless-resources-s3.yml):resources}
```

In each resource definition, you should evaluate every setting and ensure there is least privilege, least access, and any encryption at-rest and in-transit settings. The S3 resource example in Listing 5-42 shows the access control and Cross-Origin Resource Sharing settings.

Listing 5-42. AWS Resources Section – S3 CloudFormation Template

```
# serverless-resources-s3.yml
resources:
  Resources:
    S3BucketUploads:
      Type: AWS::S3::Bucket
      Properties:
        BucketName: ${self:custom.uploadsBucketName}
        AccessControl: Private
        CorsConfiguration:
```

---

[19]"Template Reference." AWS CloudFormation User Guide. Amazon Web Services. https://docs.
aws.amazon.com/AWSCloudFormation/latest/UserGuide/template-reference.html

```
CorsRules:
  - AllowedMethods:
      - GET
      - HEAD
    AllowedOrigins:
      - "*"
```

Key Takeaways

In this chapter, we explored good practices to follow in the Serverless configuration file. We discussed using multiple Serverless configuration files to define services based on groups of functions. We reviewed how to further group functions and resources within a service. We reviewed the configuration sections and how they were common yet different among the AWS, Azure, and Google Cloud providers. Finally, we discussed good practices to consider for each section.

CHAPTER 6

Restricting Permissions

In this chapter, we will discuss how we might use permissions in AWS, Azure, and Google Cloud. We might consider them as a first-line defense in our serverless environment from attacks on functions and account takeovers. Therefore, we should understand how to implement them. We will learn the permission capabilities each provider has and how we might use them.

Importance of Restricting Permissions

Permissions in a serverless or public cloud environment are conceptually similar to those in a private cloud environment. Both give you settings to define "what" is available to use and "who" has access. On a Windows computer, the Information Technology (IT) department determines which services a regular user can access vs. those of an administrator. This separation of duties typically prevents a regular user from installing unwanted and malicious software and impairing the level of security the organization desires. A malicious actor can potentially access sensitive data, modify the infrastructure, or perform other malicious activities if this person has compromised a computer with little or no permissions restricting access. The situation is similar in a serverless environment; a malicious actor can potentially access other services or take over an account if the permissions have little or no restrictions.

In Chapter 4, we discussed the importance of securing interfaces. We reviewed the different interfaces your serverless application might use and how to identify their existence. Listing 4-3 provided an example code for a function querying an AWS DynamoDB database. Let's suppose the function code was not performing input validation, and it had the permissions to delete records. A malicious actor has determined how to send a "delete record" command via the function input. That actor can then potentially remove all the database records. Now let's suppose the function had

© Miguel A. Calles 2020
M. Calles, *Serverless Security*, https://doi.org/10.1007/978-1-4842-6100-2_6

permissions that allowed access to any AWS service. Let's also suppose a malicious actor has determined how to send a Linux shell command via the function input. That actor can now execute any AWS CLI command. Given it might be possible for a malicious actor to take over your entire account, we should restrict the function permissions.

Another example may be account hijacking. In general, there are two types of accounts: user accounts (used by persons) and service accounts (used by machines). Either of those accounts might be compromised. A malicious actor can take over an account by breaking into one of the two types of accounts and changing the login credentials.[1] Let's suppose we have a service account for our CI/CD pipeline. We grant the account more permissions than necessary for it to deploy all the different Serverless configurations; maybe it was too difficult or time-consuming to restrict the permissions, or we decided to restrict it later due to a tight schedule. We gave the account administrator privileges; we created access keys for authentication and gave them access to the AWS console. Suppose a malicious actor somehow obtained the secret keys. This person can now log in to the AWS console, use the administrator privileges to create new keys while revoking the existing keys, and modify other accounts to prevent anyone else from accessing the account; this person has successfully taken over the privileged account. There are multiple ways a malicious actor can take over an account; therefore, restricting permissions in accounts is essential.

We will learn how to restrict permissions by first understanding what they are. We will learn the general principles before getting into the specifics for AWS, Azure, and Google Cloud.

Understanding Permissions

AWS, Azure, and Google Cloud each implement permissions slightly differently. We will explore how each provider implements permissions after we review the general principles that apply to all three providers.

---

[1]"What Is Account Takeover Fraud?" Sydney Vaccaro. Chargeback. December 11, 2018. `https://chargeback.com/what-is-account-takeover-fraud/`

General Principles

All three providers have an Identity and Access Management (IAM) service that defines user accounts and service accounts and their privileges. The IAM service allows us to define "who" can access "what." The "who" is a type of account (or principal). Typically, there are two types of IAM accounts: a user account (or user principal) and a service account (or service principal). There is also a provider account that grants access to the provider service but is different than the IAM accounts. This chapter mainly focuses on IAM accounts. Having both user and service accounts allow us to differentiate how an account interacts with the provider. A user account typically has access to the provider's console (sometimes called a portal), which is a web-based interface; the user authenticates with a username and password. A service account typically has access to the provider's APIs; the service authenticates with a secret key. All three providers support the concept of user and service accounts, though they implemented them differently.

Although an account can successfully authenticate to access the provider's console or APIs, it cannot perform any actions without first defining permissions for the account. All providers' IAM services support the Principle of Least Privilege (PoLP)[2] and Role-Based Access Control (RBAC),[3] to some extent, and allow us to define "what" can be accessed.

PoLP suggests assigning the minimum number of permissions needed to perform an action and assumes it can take no action without assigned permissions. For example, we should only get a read privilege to a database if we only need to read from the database. We should not be able to perform a create, update, or delete action on a database. Furthermore, we should limit the read privilege to a specific database if we only need the data from that one database. We should not be able to read a database from the finance department, for example, if we are in the engineering department. At the time of this writing, AWS and Google Cloud support limiting access to specific resources. However, Google Cloud only provides limited support. RBAC suggests defining roles and the actions they can perform. For example, a data entry role enters data into a database.

---

[2]"Least Privilege." Michael Gegick & Sean Barnum. Cigital. September 14, 2005. www.us-cert. gov/bsi/articles/knowledge/principles/least-privilege

[3]"Role-Based Access Controls." David Ferraiolo & Richard Kuhn. 15th National Computer Security Conference (NCSC). October 13, 1992. https://csrc.nist.gov/publications/detail/ conference-paper/1992/10/13/role-based-access-controls

That role would have the permissions to perform a write action to that database. Auditor roles read data from the database. That role would have the permissions to perform a read action to the database. An administrator role can make any changes to a database. That role would have all the permissions to perform any actions to the database. A user can have multiple roles and should use the appropriate role to execute the desired actions.

The combination of RBAC with PoLP reduces the risk of any given role having excessive or overly permissive permissions. Each provider implements PoLP and RBAC differently, and their terminology varies too. We will review how permissions are applied in a general sense and distinguish how each provider implements them.

We define a "role" to contain the necessary permissions to perform an operation or access a resource. The role might define read permissions to a storage object or write permissions to a database resource, for example. We define the role based on the type of operations we need a group of accounts to perform. For example, we might define one role for users to perform security audits, another role for writing data to a database, or another role for deploying a Serverless configuration. The role defines the permissions but not the accounts who can use it. We must assign a role to an account or group of accounts to grant the permissions to those accounts; this is a role assignment.

We established the "user account," "service account," "role," and "role assignment" as IAM terms in a general sense. Figure 6-1 shows us how these terms relate to each other. It will help us understand how each provider uses these terms and their principles. Table 6-1 compares the general terms against the terms the providers use.

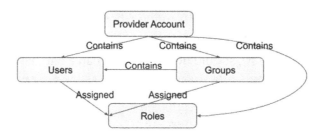

Figure 6-1. *Relationship Among General IAM Terms*

Table 6-1. Comparing Identity and Access Management (IAM) Terms

IAM Term	AWS	Azure	Google Cloud
User Account	User (with AWS management console access)	Active Directory User	Member (Google, G Suite, or Cloud Identity account)
Service Account	Service Role or User (with programmatic access)	Service Principal	Member (service account)
Role	Policy	Role Definition	Role
Role Assignment	Attach	Role Assignment	Policy (or IAM permissions)

Some terms might be confusing because they are overloaded. AWS can have IAM users, which can be a user account or a service account. In contrast, Google Cloud uses "member" but distinguishes them as either a Google, G Suite, or Cloud Identity account, or a service account. AWS uses the term "role" to assign permissions to an AWS service, whereas "policy" is the role assigned to a user account or a service role. AWS assigns roles by "attaching" policies to groups, users, or roles. In contrast, Google Cloud uses a policy (or IAM permission) to assign roles to members. Keep these differences in mind while reading how each provider implements IAM. If the terminology starts to become confusing, it might help to think about this general principle: IAM allows us to define an assignment (or policy or attachment) of "who" (a type of account) can access "what" (via a permission list or a role).

Amazon Web Services (AWS)

AWS provides the Identity and Access Management (IAM) service to manage permissions. It allows you to specify access to AWS services and resources.[4] IAM uses different types of settings which work together to give and restrict access:

- **Policies** define the permissions that grant access to AWS services and resources.

- **Groups** define the policies available to their assigned users.

---

[4]"Actions, Resources, and Condition Keys for AWS Services." AWS Identity and Access Management User Guide. Amazon Web Services. https://docs.aws.amazon.com/IAM/latest/UserGuide/reference_policies_actions-resources-contextkeys.html

- **Users** define the accounts that can access the AWS provider account. You can give users access to the AWS console, programmatic access (via the AWS CLI, SDK, and APIs), or both, specify the policies available to that user, and add users into a group.

- **Roles** specify the policies used by AWS services.

- **Identity providers** define the external services with which you can integrate third-party (or federated) logins.

Figure 6-2 depicts the relationship for settings. We will explore each concept with examples where appropriate.

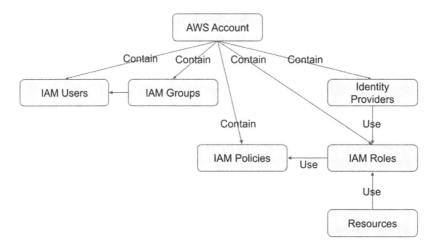

Figure 6-2. *Relationship Among AWS IAM Settings*

Policies

We use policies to define a logical grouping of permissions. We might want to define policies that allow access to a specific AWS resource. These policies might be organized by read, write, create, and delete permissions. Having a convention in defining policies allows us to assign multiple policies and thus grant their respective permissions to the AWS resources. AWS does have managed (i.e., predefined) policies[5] we can use too.

---

[5]"Managed Policies and Inline Policies." AWS Identity and Access Management User Guide. Amazon Web Services. `https://docs.aws.amazon.com/IAM/latest/UserGuide/access_policies_managed-vs-inline.html`

We will create a policy to give read access to a DynamoDB table, but no other access (e.g., edit or delete). We define policies against services, which is DynamoDB, in this case. We specify the actions taken against those services, which we will choose as "read" actions. We can choose to limit those actions against specific resources (e.g., a specific table named "ch6"). We can add a request condition for the user to enter a valid Multi-Factor Authentication (MFA) credential before the action is executed or limit the actions to specific IP addresses. Lastly, we give the policy a name (such as "DDB-Chapter6-ReadOnly-Policy"). We can use the AWS console to edit the policy visually (see Figure 6-3) or use AWS Policy JSON (see Listing 6-1) to define the policy.

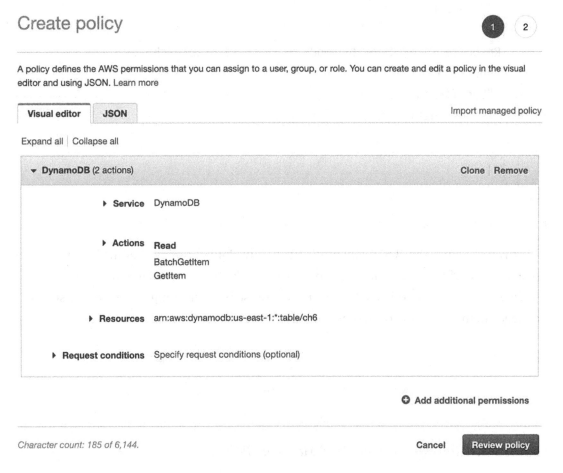

Figure 6-3. *An Example of Using the AWS Policy Visual Editor*

Listing 6-1. AWS Policy JSON

```
{
  "Version": "2012-10-17",
  "Statement": [
    {
      "Sid": "VisualEditor0",
      "Effect": "Allow",
      "Action": [
        "dynamodb:BatchGetItem",
        "dynamodb:GetItem"
      ],
      "Resource": "arn:aws:dynamodb:us-east-1:*:table/ch6",
      "Condition": {
        "BoolIfExists": {
          "aws:MultiFactorAuthPresent": "true"
        }
      }
    }
  ]
}
```

Now we can use the "DDB-Chapter6-ReadOnly-Policy" policy to grant a user the privileges to perform the "read" actions against the "ch6" DynamoDB table. You can use the AWS managed policies where it makes sense (e.g., granting a user administrator privileges to the AWS console); see Figure 6-4.

Figure 6-4. *An Example of an AWS Managed Policy*

Let's explore the sections in our new JSON policy from Listing 6-1.

Statements

A policy contains one or more statements. The visual editor shows these as different sections. The JSON policy shows each statement as an object in the "statements" array. Each statement defines a set of permissions and their effect on the actions taken on the specified resources when meeting the condition.

Effect

The effect defines whether to allow or deny actions. By default, AWS denies access to all resources. An "allow" effect enables performing actions against the specified resources, as seen in our new policy. We typically do not use a deny effect unless we need to override an allow effect. For example, you might assign two policies to a user where the first policy allows access to all databases, and you assign a second policy to deny access to specific databases.

Actions

The actions define the allowed or denied operations. You specify the service and its operations. Our new policy specified the DynamoDB service and the following read operations: BatchGetItem, GetItem, Scan, and Query. We can use wildcards when defining our actions (e.g., "dynamodb:List*" to specify all "List" operations or "dynamodb:*" to specify all operations against DynamoDB). We should avoid using an overly permissive operation (e.g., "dynamodb:*") that encompasses all operations for a service. We must be cautious when using wildcards to prevent creating an action with more operations than we desire. Having an action with "dynamodb:*" allows or denies all operations against the specified resource. Although this permissive action is easy to configure, it might grant undesired results (e.g., deleting databases used by other applications). We should use wildcards sparingly and with caution.

Resources and Amazon Resource Names (ARNs)

We first saw the Amazon Resource Names[6] (ARNs) in Chapter 5. The ARN is a naming convention that acts as an "address" to reference AWS resources. The ARNs follow the formats specified in Listing 6-2.

---

[6]"Amazon Resource Names (ARNs)." AWS General Reference. Amazon Web Services. https://docs.aws.amazon.com/general/latest/gr/aws-arns-and-namespaces.html

Listing 6-2. Amazon Resource Name (ARN) Formats

```
arn:partition:service:region:account-id:resource-id
arn:partition:service:region:account-id:resource-type/resource-id
arn:partition:service:region:account-id:resource-type:resource-id
```

The ARNs have at least six components:

1. All ARNs have a value of "arn" in the first component.

2. The second component specifies the AWS partition. For the US services, we specify the "aws" value. Other AWS regions may have a partition name identifying the physical location (e.g., the "aws-cn" identifies resources in AWS China [Beijing] region).

3. The third component specifies the service. We used "dynamodb" as the value in the preceding policy.

4. The fourth component specifies the region. We defined "us-east-1" as the value because the DynamoDB table exists in that region. Some services (e.g., S3) have resources that are global (not specific to a region), so their region value is empty.

5. The fifth component specifies the account identifier (ID). We specified "*" as the value because that is our example account ID. The asterisk is a wildcard for any account ID. Some services (e.g., S3) do not require an account ID, and thus the value is empty.

6. The sixth and subsequent components specify the type of resource and its identifier. We defined "table/ch6" specifying the resource type as a table and the table name as the identifier. The format varies among the different AWS resources (e.g., S3 buckets use the bucket name as the value). In contrast, the CloudWatch Logs use a value like "log-group:log-group-name:*" that has multiple components.

When a policy uses an ARN, we can specify a specific ARN or use wildcards in the sixth and subsequent components except where it is the resource type. We can take advantage of wildcards in our policies to apply to multiple resources of the same type. For example, if all the application databases have the same prefix, we can use an ARN with a wildcard that applies to them all. The ARN "arn:aws:dynamodb:us-east-1:*:table/ch6*" will refer to all tables with names starting with "ch6" that exist in the "us-east-1" region for any account. We could have specified an account ID (e.g., "123456789012") that would limit access to only that account. We must be cautious when using wildcards to avoid giving permissions to more resources than we desire. Having an ARN like "arn:aws:dynamodb:us-east-1:*:table/*" that uses a wildcard for the table name grants privileges to tables that might not be part of our application. Although this permissive ARN might be satisfactory when only one application exists in the AWS, it might become an issue when introducing additional apps or when a user should not access data from all the tables.

Conditions

We can use conditions when we want to add a safeguard before granting the permissions. Specifying an MFA condition requires a user to enter a valid MFA code before granting the permissions. We might want to enable an MFA condition as a confirmation before deleting any resources. We can also specify an IP address range in the conditions. We might want to use it to make the office network the only location when granting permissions. We might want to consider one or both when we need to exercise caution in granting permissions.

Groups

We want to attach policies to groups rather than attaching policies directly to users. We can categorize users into groups that need the same permissions. Most companies or projects have super administrators, administrators, developers, viewers, and deployment users per project. Super administrators typically have all privileges to all resources. Administrators usually have all or most privileges against project resources. Developers generally need the read and write privileges against project resources but may also need the create and delete privileges. Viewers usually have read privileges against project resources. Deployment users are used in a CI/CD pipeline and generally need to create, delete, read, and write privileges to deploy the Serverless configurations. Having all users categorized standardizes the privileges and minimizes having users with unique privileges, which might become complicated to manage.

We will create a group that contains multiple policies and will name it "DDB-Chapter6-ReadWrite-Group." This group will allow its users to read and write the "ch6" database. We will attach the "DDB-Chapter6-ReadOnly-Policy" and "DDB-Chapter6-WriteItems-Policy" policies; see Figure 6-5. The group will have the permissions defined in each policy.

Figure 6-5. *An Example of Attaching Policies to a Group*

This group will have the following permissions:

- From the "DDB-Chapter6-ReadOnly-Policy" policy:
  - "dynamodb:BatchGetItem"
  - "dynamodb:GetItem"
  - "dynamodb:Scan"
  - "dynamodb:Query"
- From the "DDB-Chapter6-WriteItems-Policy" policy:
  - "dynamodb:BatchWriteItem"
  - "dynamodb:UpdateTimeToLive"
  - "dynamodb:PutItem"
  - "dynamodb:UpdateItem"

Any users we add to this group will inherit these permissions.

Users

We create users to grant persons or machines (such as those from a CI/CD pipeline) access to AWS resources. We will create an administrator user. This user will have programmatic access (which enables using AWS developer tools to deploy the Serverless configuration) and console access (which allows access to the AWS management console); see Figure 6-6.

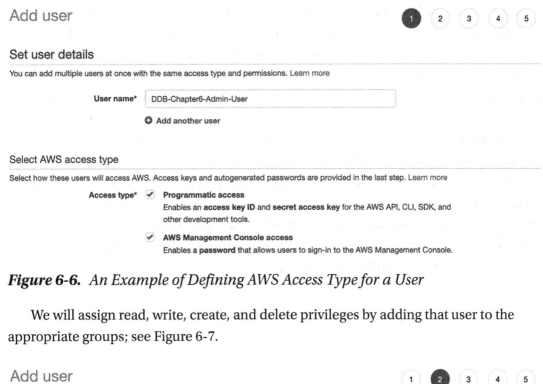

Figure 6-6. *An Example of Defining AWS Access Type for a User*

We will assign read, write, create, and delete privileges by adding that user to the appropriate groups; see Figure 6-7.

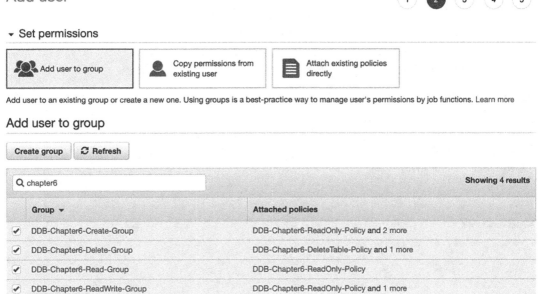

Figure 6-7. *An Example of Assigning Groups to a User*

The user can log in to the AWS console to access the database and can affect the database using the Serverless Framework and AWS Command-Line Interface (CLI).

We might use multiple groups to support the roles of each user. We might assign a developer user the"DDB-Chapter6-ReadWrite-Group" group, but maybe not the "DDB-Chapter6-Create-Group" and "DDB-Chapter6-Delete-Group" groups. If a specific user needs a privilege not defined in an existing group, we should create a new group because another user may need that privilege too. We might assign the developer users to a "Developer" group that has the appropriate policies.

We can create an access key for a user that has programmatic access. We will use it to deploy a Serverless configuration. We created another user named "ServerlessDeploy" with programmatic access and attached the AWS managed "AdministratorAccess" policy; see Figure 6-8. We would generally avoid granting full administrator privileges, but we are doing this to simplify the example.

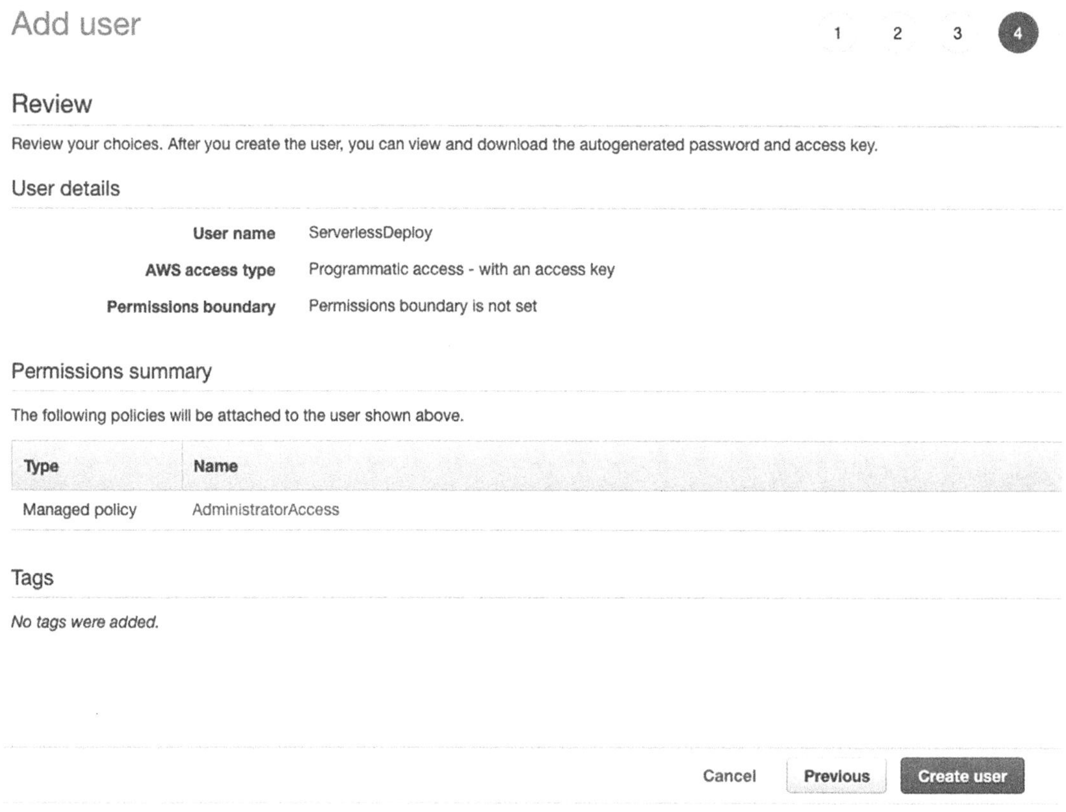

Add user

1   2   3   **4**

Review

Review your choices. After you create the user, you can view and download the autogenerated password and access key.

User details

User name	ServerlessDeploy
AWS access type	Programmatic access - with an access key
Permissions boundary	Permissions boundary is not set

Permissions summary

The following policies will be attached to the user shown above.

Type	Name
Managed policy	AdministratorAccess

Tags

No tags were added.

Cancel   Previous   **Create user**

Figure 6-8. *An Example of Creating a User for Deploying a Serverless Configuration*

The AWS console prompts us to download the access key in the last step in the user creation process; see Figure 6-9.

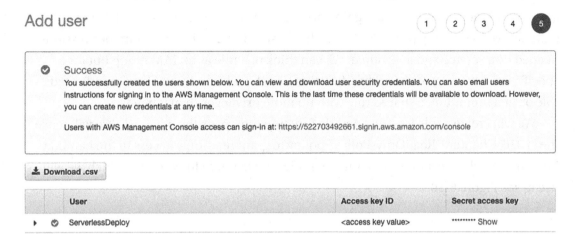

Figure 6-9. *An Example of Obtaining the Access Key*

We will add the access key to the AWS credentials file or store them as environment variables. In our example, we will store the access key as environment variables. In the example, we can use the Linux/macOS[7] "export" command (see Listing 6-3) or the Windows env command (Listing 6-4).

Listing 6-3. Defining AWS Environment Variables in Linux or macOS Terminals

```
export AWS_ACCESS_KEY_ID='<accessKeyId>'
export AWS_SECRET_ACCESS_KEY='<secretAccessKey>'
```

Listing 6-4. Defining AWS Environment Variables in Windows PowerShell

```
env:AWS_ACCESS_KEY_ID='<accessKeyId>'
env:AWS_SECRET_ACCESS_KEY='<secretAccessKey>'
```

Now we can deploy the Serverless configuration using the "sls deploy" command.

---

[7]macOS is a registered trademark of Apple, Inc.

Service Roles

We assign service roles to AWS services, other AWS accounts, and identity providers. We grant permissions to roles by assigning policies. Unlike users and groups, it is better to be granular when defining permissions. Each role should have the minimum permissions needed by a service and a resource. We can think of a role as an IAM group but for a specific resource (e.g., one Lambda function). Each Lambda should have a dedicated role or, at a minimum, a shared role with no more privileges than it needs.

We will create a role for one Lambda function that reads the database. We will reuse the "DDB-Chapter6-ReadOnly-Policy" policy to grant read-only access to the Lambda function. We choose a role name that identifies the Lambda function for which we will use it; see Figure 6-10.

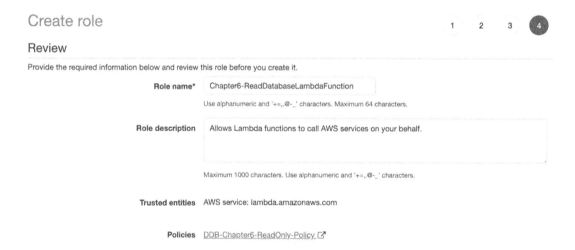

Figure 6-10. *An Example of Creating a Policy*

When we create the "ReadDatabaseLambdaFunction" Lambda function, we will assign it to the "Chapter6-ReadDatabaseLambdaFunction" role, which grants read access to the Chapter 6 DynamoDB table resource.

Identity Providers

We integrate with identity providers when we have a user management system with existing users. The users will use their existing login credentials to access AWS services, which simplifies user management. The identity provider must support either the Security Assertion Markup Language (SAML) protocol or the OpenID Connect protocol (we will discuss both in Chapter 9). Some identity providers allow you to have different login sessions that grant the appropriate permissions. We will not integrate with an identity provider because the integration varies per provider.

Azure

Azure provides the Active Directory (AD) and IAM services to manage permissions. They allow you to specify access to Azure services.[8] AD has many more features and capabilities than needed for deploying functions, and we will focus on those relevant to deploying Serverless configurations:

- **AD administrative roles** define the permissions that grant access to Azure services.

- **AD groups** define users and their access. We can create it as a security group (to grant permissions to Azure resources) or an Office 365 group (to give access to Office 365 services).[9] We can associate Azure resources to security groups, which associate those services to their users.

- **AD users** define the users that can access the Azure account. We can assign users to roles and groups.

- **Role definitions** define the permissions that grant access to users, groups, and service principals for Azure services.

- **Application registrations** represent the application and how it is accessed.

- **Scopes** define the levels for granting access. The scope can be the management group (topmost level), subscription, resource group, or resource (lowest level). Allowing access at a high level gives access to its lower levels.

---

[8]"Azure Resource Manager resource provider operations." Azure RBAC documentation. Microsoft. https://docs.microsoft.com/en-us/azure/role-based-access-control/resource-provider-operations

[9]"Create a basic group and add members using Azure Active Directory." Azure Active Directory fundamentals documentation. Microsoft. https://docs.microsoft.com/en-us/azure/active-directory/fundamentals/active-directory-groups-create-azure-portal

Figure 6-11 depicts the relationship for settings. We will explore each concept with examples where appropriate.

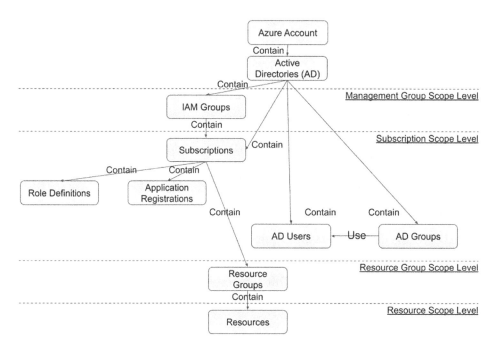

Figure 6-11. *Relationship Among Azure IAM Settings*

Active Directory (AD) Administrative Roles

We use administrative roles to define a set of permissions within the Azure AD. Azure AD comes with built-in (i.e., predefined) roles.[10] We might want to create a custom role that grants specific permissions (e.g., reading audit logs). Roles should be named based on the function a user performs (e.g., security auditor). Creating custom roles is unavailable in the free tier, and thus we will not create one. You can review Azure documentation for the procedure to create a custom role.[11]

---

[10]"Built-in roles for Azure resources." Azure RBAC documentation. Microsoft. `https://docs.microsoft.com/en-us/azure/role-based-access-control/built-in-roles`

[11]"Create and assign a custom role in Azure Active Directory." Enterprise user management documentation – Azure AD. Microsoft. `https://docs.microsoft.com/en-us/azure/active-directory/users-groups-roles/roles-create-custom`

AD Groups

We use security groups to give users access to the Azure Portal for viewing and managing our serverless applications. We will create one group named "Chapter6SecurityGroup" (see Figure 6-12). We should add the global administrator (the user that created the Azure provider account) as the owner, at a minimum, and add administrator users later.

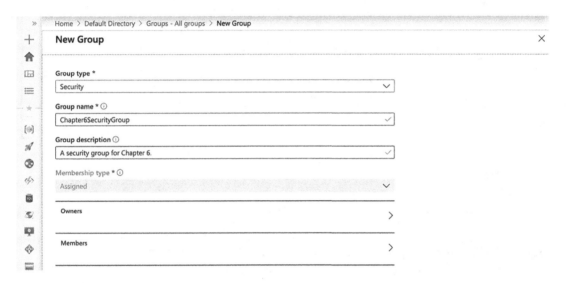

Figure 6-12. *An Example of Creating an Active Directory (AD) Group*

We can now add our users to this group.

AD Users

We create a user to grant a person access to the Azure Portal or Office 365. We will create an administrator user. We will assign this user to the "Chapter6SecurityGroup" (see Figure 6-13). This user will have access to the Azure Portal.

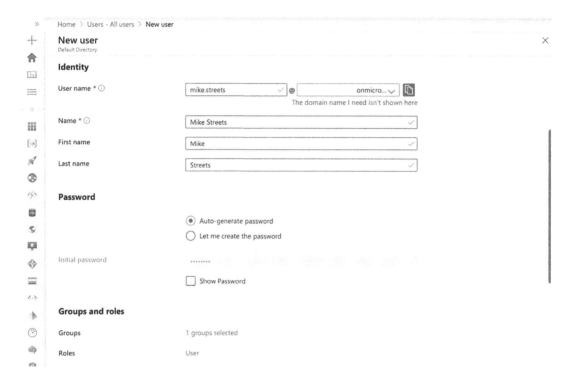

Figure 6-13. *An Example of Creating an Active Directory User*

Role Definitions

We use role definitions to define a set of permissions within an Azure subscription, which contains the billing plan and the deployed serverless applications. The subscription comes with built-in roles. We might want to create and assign one role per serverless application or assign multiple built-in roles. We should base the role definitions on RBAC,[12] where users only have the minimum permissions needed to perform their responsibilities. Microsoft recommends having owner roles (administrators), contributor roles (managers), and reader roles (viewers).

We will create a custom contributor role. The built-in contributor roles grant access to manage specific services or all the services. This new role has the permissions common to all contributor roles but cannot manage any services. This new role allows us

---

[12]"What is role-based access control (RBAC) for Azure resources?" Azure RBAC documentation. Microsoft. `https://docs.microsoft.com/en-us/azure/role-based-access-control/overview`

to create additional contributor roles that add to this "base" contributor role. We will use the Azure CLI to create the role[13] because the Azure Portal cannot create custom roles at the time of this writing.

The example screen captures and Azure CLI all assume we have logged in to the Azure Portal and Azure CLI.

We will need the subscription ID for the following examples. We can use the Azure Portal to obtain it; see Figure 6-14.

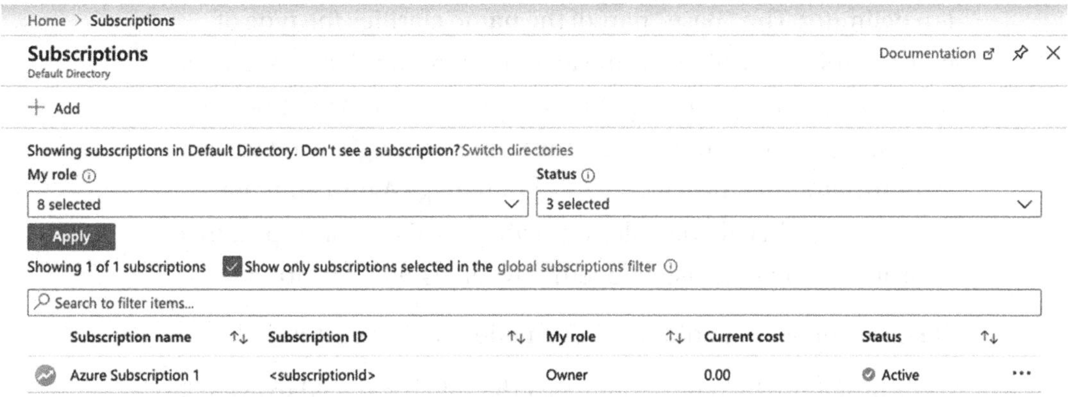

Figure 6-14. *An Example of Displaying an Azure Subscription Identifier (ID)*

We create a JSON file named "ContributorBaseRole.json," which defines the new custom role; see Listing 6-5.

Listing 6-5. An Example Azure Custom Role Definition

```
{
  "Name": "Contributor - Base",
 "Description": "Manage deployments; no resources defined.",
  "Actions": [
    "Microsoft.Authorization/*/read",
    "Microsoft.Resources/deployments/*",
    "Microsoft.Resources/subscriptions/resourceGroups/read",
    "Microsoft.Support/*"
  ],
```

---

[13]"Custom roles for Azure resources." Azure RBAC documentation. Microsoft. https://docs.microsoft.com/en-us/azure/role-based-access-control/custom-roles

```
  "NotActions": [],
  "AssignableScopes": ["/subscriptions/<subscriptionId>"]
}
```

The JSON role definition has the following properties:

- **Name** defines the role's name, which we defined as "Contributor - Base" to describe its purposes and facilitate sorting. The "Contributor" part of the name defines the type of role. The "-" is a delimiter. The "Base" part of the name clarifies the type of contributor role, which has the least amount of privileges needed to be a contributor. This naming convention allows us to define additional contributor roles. For example, we might want to have a contributor role that can create and manage Azure Function Apps. We would call this role "Contributor - FunctionApp," and all contributor roles are listed together when listed and sorted.

- **Description** gives additional information for the custom role.

- **Actions** define the permissions that the role is allowed to exercise. We defined the minimum set of permissions needed to deploy; view the list of permissions in the Microsoft Azure documentation.[14]

- **NotActions** defines the permissions to deny a role from exercising. We did not define any restrictions because IAM does a deny by default. We could attempt to restrict all other permissions. Still, we run the risk of restricting the permissions we intend to allow. It might be better to use this property to limit permissions to any resources defined in the allowed permissions. For example, we might allow the contributor role to register for support and create and update tickets, but not read them. We might want only the contributor's supervisor

---

[14]"Azure Resource Manager resource provider operations." Azure RBAC documentation. Microsoft. https://docs.microsoft.com/en-us/azure/role-based-access-control/resource-provider-operations

to read tickets. To achieve this, we add the "Microsoft.Support/ supportTickets/read" to the "NotActions" similarly how the "Actions" are defined. Read more about using deny statements in the Azure documentation.[15]

- **AssignableScopes** define at what level to assign a role. We set the subscription (with identifier "<subscriptionId>") as the scope. We will discuss scopes in further detail later.

We use the Azure CLI to create the custom role; see Listing 6-6.

Listing 6-6. Creating an Azure Custom Role Using the Azure CLI

```
az role definition create --role-definition \
ContributorBaseRole.json
```

Note   We split the command across two lines using a backslash to make it easier to read on the page. Press the Enter key after the backslash to continue the command on the next line.

The Azure CLI command returns a JSON response, which includes the "id" and "name" properties; see the example response in Listing 6-7. These properties indicate the Azure CLI command successfully created the custom role.

Listing 6-7. An Example Response After Creating an Azure Custom Role

```
{
  "assignableScopes": [
    "/subscriptions/<subscriptionId>"
  ],
  "description": "Manage deployments; no resources defined.",
  "id": "/subscriptions/<subscriptionId>/providers/Microsoft.Authorization/
roleDefinitions/<roleId>",
  "name": "<uniqueName>",
```

---

[15]"What is role-based access control (RBAC) for Azure resources?" Azure RBAC documentation. Microsoft. https://docs.microsoft.com/en-us/azure/role-based-access-control/ overview#deny-assignments

```
"permissions": [
  {
    "actions": [
      "Microsoft.Authorization/*/read",
      "Microsoft.Resources/deployments/*",
      "Microsoft.Resources/subscriptions/resourceGroups/read",
      "Microsoft.Support/*"
    ],
    "dataActions": [],
    "notActions": [],
    "notDataActions": []
  }
],
"roleName": "Contributor - Base",
"roleType": "CustomRole",
"type": "Microsoft.Authorization/roleDefinitions"
}
```

We can now see the new role in the Azure Portal; see Figure 6-15. We can assign the role to AD users, groups, or service principals.

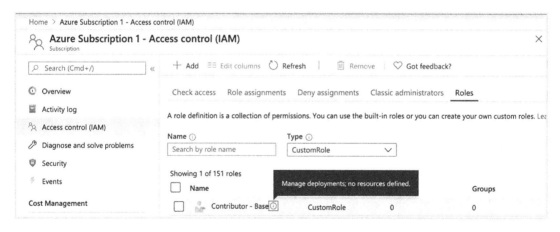

Figure 6-15. *An Example of a Custom Role Displayed in the Azure Portal*

Application Registrations

We use application registrations to define application objects and service principal objects.[16] An application object represents the application and is only registered in one Azure AD tenant[17] (i.e., instance). In contrast, a service principal object represents how an Azure AD tenant can access the application.[18] We create a service principal in the same tenant (i.e., the same Azure AD), which defines the credentials to access the application resources. We also use a service principal to create and deploy an application.

We can choose to make our application available to multiple tenants. To do this, we grant the other tenants access to the Azure AD application object. Each tenant will need to create a service principal object to access the application resources associated with the application object. We will focus on single-tenant applications in our examples.

We will first create a service principal object and use it to create the application object; see Listing 6-8.

Listing 6-8. An Example of Creating an Azure Service Principal Object Using the Azure CLI

```
az ad sp create-for-rbac -n "MyAppSP"
```

The Azure CLI command returns a JSON response, which includes the "appId" and "password" properties; see the example response in Listing 6-9. These properties indicate the Azure CLI command successfully created the custom role.

---

[16]"Application and service principal objects in Azure Active Directory." Microsoft identity platform documentation. Microsoft. https://docs.microsoft.com/en-us/azure/active-directory/develop/app-objects-and-service-principals

[17]"Microsoft identity platform developer glossary: tenant." Microsoft identity platform documentation. Microsoft. https://docs.microsoft.com/en-us/azure/active-directory/develop/developer-glossary#tenant

[18]"Application and service principal objects in Azure Active Directory." Microsoft identity platform documentation. Microsoft. https://docs.microsoft.com/en-us/azure/active-directory/develop/app-objects-and-service-principals

Listing 6-9. An Example Response After Creating an Azure Service Principal
Object

```
{
  "appId": "<appId>",
  "displayName": "MyAppSP",
  "name": "http://MyAppSP",
  "password": "<uniquePassword>",
  "tenant": "<tenantId>"
}
```

We can now see the new service principal object in the Azure Portal; see Figure 6-16.

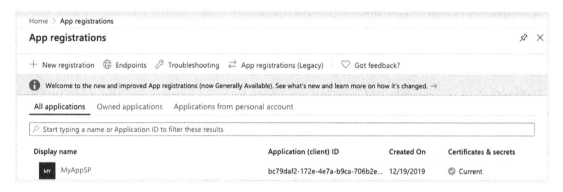

Figure 6-16. *An Example of a Service Principal Object Displayed in the Azure*
Portal

We can use the service principal to create a Function App using the Serverless
Framework. We will need the following information before deploying:

- Azure subscription ID

- Azure application ID (i.e., the service principal ID)

- Azure application password

- Azure tenant ID

We store these values as environment variables. In the example, we will use the
Linux/macOS "export" command (see Listing 6-10) or the Windows env command
(see Listing 6-11).

Listing 6-10. Defining Azure Environment Variables in Linux or macOS Terminals

```
export AZURE_SUBSCRIPTION_ID='<subscriptionId>'
export AZURE_TENANT_ID='<tenantId>'
export AZURE_CLIENT_ID='<appId>'
export AZURE_CLIENT_SECRET='<uniquePassword>'
```

Listing 6-11. Defining Azure Environment Variables in Windows PowerShell

```
env:AZURE_SUBSCRIPTION_ID='<subscriptionId>'
env:AZURE_TENANT_ID='<tenantId>'
env:AZURE_CLIENT_ID='<appId>'
env:AZURE_CLIENT_SECRET='<uniquePassword>'
```

Now we can deploy the Serverless configuration using the "sls deploy" command.

Scope

We use the scope to define where our role definitions and service principal objects apply. The lowest scope is the resource level, and the topmost scope is the management group level. The topmost scope can affect all the lower levels, while the lowest level can only affect its own. Creating a role definition or service principal object in the resource scope will limit them to that resource; other resources do not inherit the role. Creating them in the management scope makes the role applicable to the resources, resource groups, and subscriptions within a management group.

Resource Level

A resource is the instance of an Azure service. When we deploy a Function App using the Serverless Framework, we use the Function App service to create a unique Function App (i.e., a resource). Any other services defined in the Serverless configuration file will create the appropriate resources. We can choose to create a role definition that only applies to those resources.

Resource Group Level

A resource group allows us to manage a group of resources without having to modify each resource individually. The Serverless Framework automatically creates a resource group for all the resources it deploys. We can choose to create a role definition that applies to the resource group, and all its resources will inherit that role definition.

Subscription Level

A subscription defines the services available based on the billing plan. All created resources are associated with a subscription. We can choose to create a role definition that applies to a subscription, and all its resource groups and resources will inherit the role definition. Defining the role definition at the subscription allows us to reuse it without having to create it for each resource group or resource.

We might choose to put each application in a separate subscription, thus allowing us to segregate all the resources from other applications. The approach also allows us to define the appropriate billing plan for each application and to get billing statements for each application.

Management Group Level

A management group allows us to group multiple subscriptions. We can choose to create a role definition that applies to a management group, and all its subscriptions (and their resource groups and resources) will inherit the role definition. Defining the role definition at the management group allows us to reuse it without having to create it for each subscription, resource group, or resource.

We might choose to use a management group to administer multiple applications based on similarity.[19] We might organize them by business unit, application type, security requirements, and so on.

Google Cloud

Google Cloud provides the Cloud IAM service to manage permissions. It allows you to specify access to Google Cloud services and resources.[20] Cloud IAM uses different types of settings which work together to give and restrict access:

---

[19]"Organize your resources with Azure management groups." Azure management groups documentation. Microsoft. `https://docs.microsoft.com/en-us/azure/governance/management-groups/overview`

[20]"Overview." Identity and Access Management documentation. Google. `https://cloud.google.com/iam/docs/overview`

- **Roles** define the permissions that grant access to Google Cloud resources.

- **Members** define the identities allowed to access Google Cloud resources.

- **Policies** assign members to roles.

- **Scopes** define the levels for granting access. The scope can be an organization (topmost level), a folder, a project, or resource (lowest level). Allowing access at a high level gives access to its lower levels.

- **Identity and organization** use a G Suite domain or a Google Cloud Identity domain to create an organization.

Figure 6-17 depicts the relationship for settings. We will explore each concept with examples where appropriate.

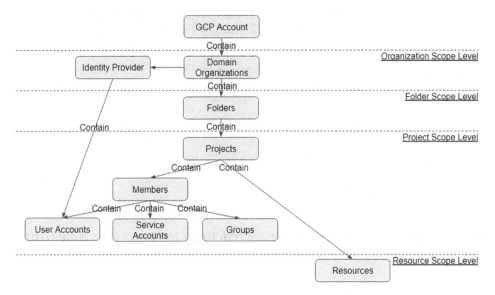

Figure 6-17. *Relationship Among Google Cloud IAM Settings*

Roles

We use roles to define a logical grouping of permissions. We might want to define roles that allow access to a specific Google Cloud resource. These policies might be organized by read, write, create, and delete permissions. Having a convention in defining policies allows us to assign multiple roles and thus grant their respective permissions to the Google Cloud resources. Additionally, Google Cloud also has predefined roles we can utilize.[21]

We will create a custom role to deploy a Serverless configuration.[22] We define policies against the Cloud Functions, Deployment Manager, Cloud Logging, and Cloud Storage services. We will leverage the Cloud Functions Developer, Deployment Manager Editor, Logging Admin, and Storage Admin predefined roles to create a new role. We will use the Google Cloud console to assign predefined roles (see Figure 6-18) and name it "Serverless Deploy" (see Figure 6-19).

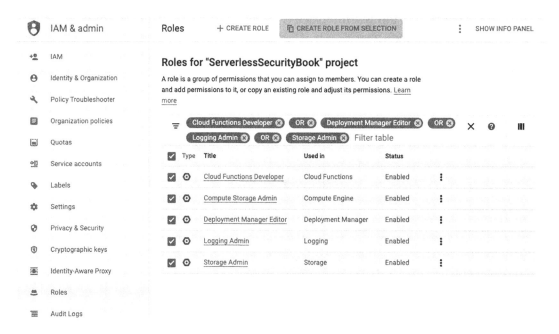

Figure 6-18. *An Example of Assigning a Predefined Role to a New Role Using the Google Cloud Console*

---

[21]"Understanding roles." Identity and Access Management documentation. Google. `https://cloud.google.com/iam/docs/understanding-roles`

[22]"Creating and managing custom roles." Identity and Access Management documentation. Google. `https://cloud.google.com/iam/docs/creating-custom-roles`

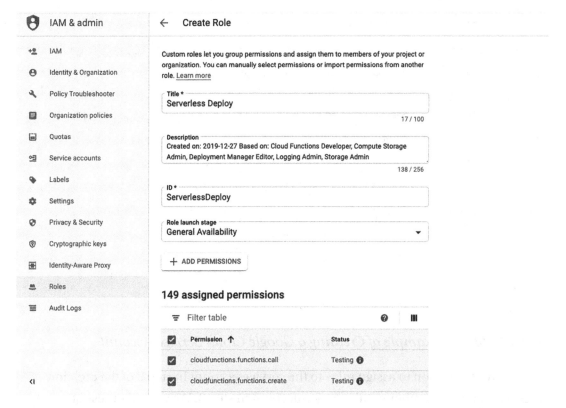

Figure 6-19. *An Example of Naming the New Role Using the Google Cloud Console*

Now we can use this role when defining a policy.

Members

We define members to grant persons or machines access to Google Cloud resources. A person who is a member will have a Google, G Suite, or Cloud Identity account. A machine that is a member will have a Cloud IAM service account. We can use a Google Group (a collection of members who need the same privileges) as a member. Furthermore, we can allow external members (i.e., those not within the organization) by specifying "authenticated users and all users." "Authenticated users" are any users with a Google, G Suite, and Cloud Identity account, and "all users" include anyone on the Internet. We will create a service account named "Serverless Framework Deploy" to deploy a Serverless configuration; see Figure 6-20.

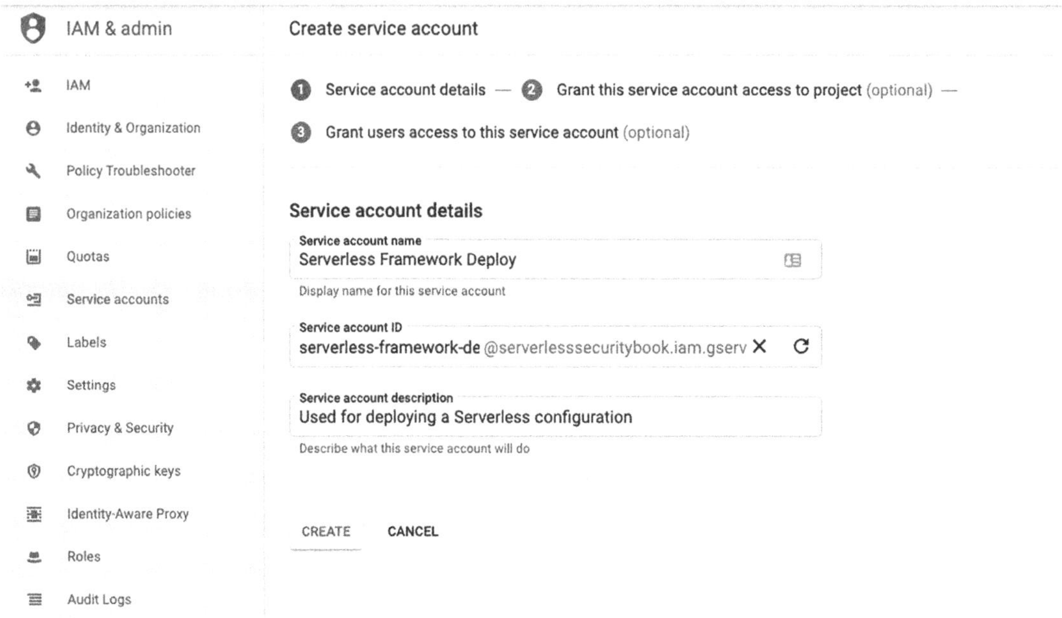

Figure 6-20. *An Example of Creating a Google Cloud Service Account*

We have the option to assign roles to the service account in step 2 of the creation process and add a member to this service account in step 3. We will skip these steps because we will cover step 2 in the policies section, and step 3 introduces some complexities.[23] When we grant members access to a service account, they inherit the service account permissions. The service account might have more permissions than a user account because it needs to create and modify resources. The user account might inherit access to resources not intended for that user. Therefore, we will focus on creating the private key for now, which we will need to deploy the Serverless configuration.

We will create a private key for the "Serverless Framework Deploy" service account; see Figure 6-21. We will use this private key in our Serverless configuration.

---

[23]"Understanding service accounts." Identity and Access Management documentation. Google. https://cloud.google.com/iam/docs/understanding-service-accounts

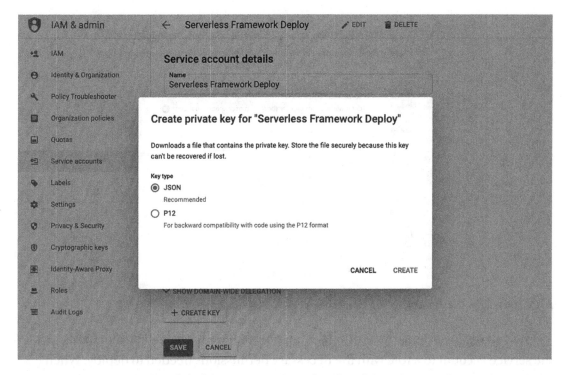

Figure 6-21. *An Example of Creating a Google Cloud Service Account Private Key*

The Google Cloud console will automatically download a private key file. We will reference its file path in the Serverless configuration file. When we deploy using the "sls deploy" command, Google Cloud will verify the key before it begins creating the resources defined in the Serverless configuration.

Policies

We use policies to associate or bind members and roles.[24] When we define a policy, we can bind one or more members to one role. We need multiple policies to bind multiple roles to one member. We can choose to apply a time-based or resource-based condition to a policy. We will create a policy to bind the "Serverless Framework Deploy" service account to the "Serverless Deploy" role; see Figure 6-22.

---

[24]"Understanding policies." Identity and Access Management documentation. Google.
`https://cloud.google.com/iam/docs/policies`

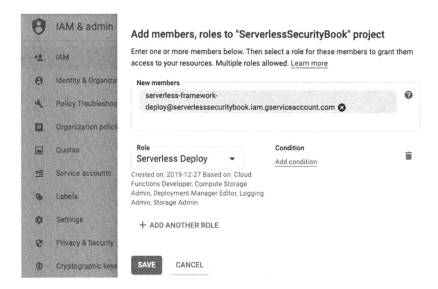

Figure 6-22. *An Example of Creating a Google Cloud Policy*

We can deploy a Serverless configuration now that we have a policy that binds the service account to a role with the necessary permissions needed to deploy. When we deploy using the "sls deploy" command, Google Cloud will verify the service account's permissions before it begins creating the resources defined in the Serverless configuration.

Scope

We use the scope to define where our policies, roles, and service accounts apply. The lowest scope is the resource level, and the topmost scope is the organization level. Creating a policy in the resource level will limit access to that resource, and the policy does not apply to other resources. Creating a policy in the organization scope will make it applicable to its resources, projects, and folders.

Resource Level

The resource level contains one resource, which is the instance of a Google Cloud service. When we deploy a Cloud Function using the Serverless Framework, we use the Cloud Function service to create a unique Cloud Function (i.e., a resource). Some Google Cloud services support applying policies to resources, and we can choose to create a policy that only applies to a resource.

Project Level

The project level contains one project which might contain multiple resources.[25] When we deploy a Cloud Function using the Serverless Framework, we deploy to a specific project. Any other services defined in the Serverless configuration file will create the appropriate resources. When we apply a policy to a project, all its resources inherit that policy.

Folder Level

The folder level contains one folder, which includes projects and other folders.[26] Having folders allows us to manage a group of projects without having to modify each resource individually. When we apply a policy to a folder, all its folders and projects inherit that policy.

Organization Level

The organization level contains one domain, which includes folders and projects.[27] The organization level may seem similar to the folder level. A folder enables us to organize other folders and projects within an organization. An organization can contain projects without needing folders. When we apply a policy to an organization, all its folders and projects inherit that policy.

Identity and Organization

We can use G Suite or Google Cloud Identity to create an organization based on the domain. Both G Suite and Cloud Identity are premium services. Still, Cloud Identity has a free version[28] at the time of this writing. Irrespective of the service, we need a

---

[25]"Creating and Managing Projects." Resource Manager documentation. Google. https://cloud.google.com/resource-manager/docs/creating-managing-projects

[26]"Creating and Managing Folders." Resource Manager documentation. Google. https://cloud.google.com/resource-manager/docs/creating-managing-folders

[27]"Creating and Managing Organizations." Resource Manager documentation. Google. https://cloud.google.com/resource-manager/docs/creating-managing-organization

[28]"Sign up for Cloud Identity from the GCP console." Setup steps for GCP administrators. Google. https://support.google.com/cloudidentity/answer/7389973?hl=en&ref_topic=7555414#

valid domain name we can verify.[29] We use that domain name to create an organization resource.[30] When the organization exists, we can assign policies to the organizational users and create projects. We will not set up an identity and organization here because the domain name verification varies between G Suite and Google Cloud.

Implementing Permissions

This section provides a suggestion on how to implement permissions. It is not a prescription since your organization and project requirements will ultimately dictate how to define the permissions. We will start with the general principles to provide context when working with providers. We will adopt approaches for implementing the general principles among AWS, Azure, and Google Cloud with consideration of their differences.

General Principles

We should use PoLP and RBAC when implementing permissions. To successfully take advantage of both concepts, we should consider using a model. The model enables us to define a high-level approach. Keeping it high level makes it easier to communicate and becomes a useful reference during implementation. The model can also translate to Azure and Google Cloud scopes. We will define a general permissions model for us to adopt when discussing each provider. The model will apply PoLP and RBAC and will use different IAM permission levels.

Organization Level

We will use an organization to be the topmost level in our model. An organization contains all the user accounts, projects, and resources of a similar kind. We can relate it to a business unit within a company that has employees, projects, and resources to operate the business. The entire company is an organization, but it might have

---

[29]"Verify your domain for Cloud Identity." Setup steps for GCP administrators. Google. `https://support.google.com/cloudidentity/topic/7390701?hl=en&ref_topic=7555414`

[30]"Creating and Managing Organizations." Resource Manager documentation. Google. `https://cloud.google.com/resource-manager/docs/creating-managing-organization`

smaller organizations within it. The organization structure might be large and have multiple levels. If possible, the model should have an organization that contains only the necessary user accounts, projects, and resources for the application(s) to function correctly.

Having a small organization can have multiple benefits:

- There are fewer user accounts to manage within an organization.

- Each organization can have only the settings and permissions it needs.

- We can segregate data and access by using multiple organizations.

- A breach in one organization has little or no impact to another organization.

There are some drawbacks:

- Managing user accounts in multiple organizations might become burdensome.

- It requires due diligence to enforce required settings and permissions across all organizations.

- Sharing data across organizations has architectural and security implications.

- More auditing is needed to detect breaches in multiple organizations.

Every approach has its benefits and drawbacks. Your company or project might choose to have one large organization to meet its requirements. We will assume a small organization in our model because it is useful for small businesses with a small number of projects, and large enterprises with numerous projects can also leverage it.

It might make sense to have an organization with other organizations under it when we have a large organization and want to manage them, similar to a small organization. This approach could help with keeping similar organizations aligned in the administration and billing. We assign a group of user accounts to the master organization and assign them to its child organization if they need access. We can apply security settings across the master and child organizations. We will assume the master organization will only have the minimum required child organizations to keep the group of organizations as small as possible.

Project Level

An organization might have multiple projects. We will consider each project as supporting one application. An organization might need numerous projects to support the different applications it needs to operate. For example, an ecommerce website might have a customer-facing website, a back-office website for processing orders, and a reporting system. We will treat each as having its own project. Having one project for each application allows us to group all its resources and separate them from the other projects' resources.

There might be projects that could potentially support other projects and organizations. For example, the accounting system and human resources system likely support every organization. These projects should be under separate organizations, whether it is one for each project or one for them all. They would need to share data with all the projects that need access. For example, the accounting system may need sales information from the ecommerce reporting system. Depending on the business requirements, each organization might have an instance (or copy) of the project that applies to them all, and each is maintained separately.

Development Stage Level

Each project usually has at least two development stages: development and production. We want two separate instances of project resources for each development stage to avoid making changes to production (live) projects. We can grant permission to developers in the development stage, whereas we might limit or deny this access in production. Developers might introduce changes that break a project, and we want a safe place for them to test our changes. We should only allow privileged users and the CI/CD pipeline access to production resources. A developer might have access to the production stage but limited to read privileges. The roles for each user should be different among the different stages as appropriate.

Role Level

Each project will have its roles, although the same role can be copied (or leveraged) into all projects. We should tailor the project's role to that project. For example, although each project might need an auditor role, the auditor may only need access to specific resources. Whenever possible, a role should define what resources it can access and with what privileges.

We will define roles based on RBAC and PoLP. We will use RBAC and PoLP to define roles for the user accounts that need to access resources and roles for service accounts. A user account might have different roles and will need to switch roles to perform their desired access. Service accounts might need to deploy different Serverless configurations. There could be one service account with a role that has permissions to deploy all the resources from all the Serverless configurations, or there can be one service account for each (or groups of) Serverless configuration(s). The service account should have the minimum number of permissions to deploy Serverless configurations. The goal is to prevent a user account or service account from having more permissions than needed when performing a task.

Resource Level

Each resource will have its own permissions and inherited permissions. Inherited permissions are those applied at higher levels (organization, project, or role) and automatically assigned to the resource. We might apply specific permissions to a resource when its higher level does not include them. We define permissions at the resource level when a resource needs permissions to access other resources or a user account needs access to resources not defined in a role.

Accounts

A user or service account might apply at any level. An account might have permissions from an organization, a project, a role, or a resource. We typically create an account in the organization and apply the permissions to the levels.

We want to ensure an account can access the correct project and development stage. We might need to create one account for each project and each stage. This approach could be burdensome. Some identity providers and some of the provider IAM capabilities allow for using temporary credentials, thus allowing an account to choose which project and stage to access. We will briefly discuss this approach in the appropriate provider sections, but not provide specific details to implement because the integration will vary by the identity provider.

Example Permissions Model

We are going to depict a model for an ecommerce organization; see Figure 6-23.

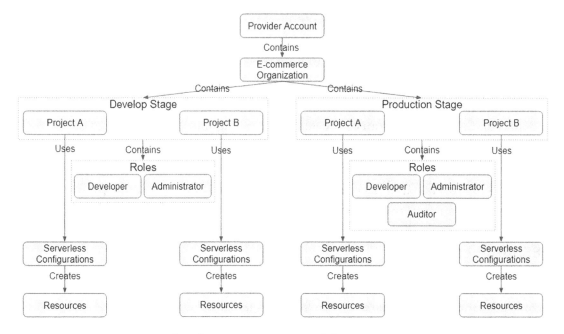

Figure 6-23. *An Example of a Permissions Model*

The organization has two projects: a website for customers to make orders (Project A) and a back-office system for processing orders (Project B). Each project has multiple Serverless configurations to create all the necessary resources. There are two development stages: one for developing and improving the projects (Develop) and another for the live system (Production). Each project will have developer and administrator roles for both development stages. The Production stages of each project will have an additional role for an auditor.

We are using one provider account to define our model and to contain the ecommerce organization. We will discuss how to organize provider accounts and organizations in the next chapter.

We grouped the project and development stage levels. Grouping each project by development stage provides the following benefits:

- Live and development resources are logically separated.

- Develop and live roles are separated and have different permissions, even if named similarly.

- The stages themselves can become an organization.

We could have instead grouped by project, but it might introduce the complications of mixing multiple stages within the same organization.

You might have noticed we did not depict users in the diagram. Users might exist on multiple levels, such as the provider account, the organizations, and projects. Users have been omitted from the diagram for simplicity.

We will explore how to implement the general permissions model and where to create users within each provider.

AWS

We will discuss how we might implement the levels in the general permissions model for AWS based on the AWS permissions principles we reviewed earlier in this chapter.

Organization Level

You might have noticed we did not define an organization level or a scope for AWS earlier in this chapter. AWS does support organizations but implements them differently than Azure, Google Cloud, and the general permissions model. An AWS organization is simply an AWS account. Our AWS account is the organization from the general permissions model. We will discuss AWS organizations further in the next chapter. AWS does not explicitly have a scope concept, though it is somewhat built-in. For example, applying permissions to a policy affects the groups, users, roles, and resources that use them. For simplicity, we will use one AWS account to be our ecommerce organization.

Project and Development Stage Levels

Within this AWS account, we will identify the projects and the development stages by a common prefix (namely, "<projectName>-<stage>"). For example, all the IAM settings and resources will begin with "projectA-develop" for the Project A Develop stage. At the time of this writing, AWS does not support segregating resources within an account. We will discuss how to achieve segregation in the next chapter. Having a naming prefix is sufficient to differentiate the IAM settings and resources. We will specify the appropriate settings in the Serverless configuration; see Listing 6-12.

Listing 6-12. Example Serverless Configuration Naming

```
service: projectA
provider:
  name: aws
  stage: develop # or production
```

The Serverless configuration automatically uses the "service" and "stage" properties to name resources prefixed with the "<projectName>-<stage>" naming convention.

Role Level

We will create multiple IAM settings for each project and development stage that define the role level from the general permissions model; see Table 6-2.

Table 6-2. *AWS IAM Settings for Each Project and Development Stage*

IAM Setting	Develop Stage		Production Stage	
	Project A	Project B	Project A	Project B
Policies	developer, admin	developer, admin	developer, admin, auditor	developer, admin, auditor
Groups	developer, admin	developer, admin	developer, admin, auditor	developer, admin, auditor
Developer Group Policies	developer	developer	developer	developer
Admin Group Policies	admin	admin	admin	admin
Auditor Group Policies	Not Applicable	Not Applicable	auditor	auditor

Note: Each item in the table will be prefixed with the appropriate project and stage at implementation. For example, the "developer" policy for Project A in the Develop stage has a "projectA-develop-developer" policy name.

There are four sets of policies and groups for each project and its development stage. The policy for each project will have the permissions needed to access the different resources within the project and its stage. The developer policy in the Develop stage will have more permissions than its counterpart policy in the Production stage. We create groups similarly named as the policies. This allows us to associate the policies to groups based on RBAC. Now that we have the groups and policies in place, we can create users.

Users

The user creation can become a bit tedious if we want to segregate permissions by stage. Without using an identity provider, we would create an IAM user for a person. A developer named Amy Smith might have an IAM user named "amy.smith" and we would assign that user to the "projectA-develop-developer," "projectB-develop-developer," "projectA-production-developer," and "projectB-production-developer" groups. Amy Smith now has access to the Develop and Production stages. She needs to be diligent and mindful about which project is being affected. Ideally, the Production stage policies will prevent any accidental changes. Still, the developer might accidentally make changes in Production if the policy is overly permissive. We should consider having the developer log in to a user account that only has access to the Develop or the Production stage, never both at the same time.

We can choose to have multiple IAM users per developer. Our developer might have a user with a name containing "production" and another containing "develop." For example, Amy Smith might have "amy.smith.develop" and "amy.smith.production" IAM users. We assign the "amy.smith.develop" user to the "projectA-develop" and "projectB-develop" groups, and similarly for the Production IAM users and groups. This approach segregates access between the Develop and Production resources. Unfortunately, this approach puts the added burden to the developer and the AWS account administrator in maintaining multiple sets of accounts.

Although I stated earlier we would avoid giving examples using an identity provider and discuss AWS organizations in the next chapter, I feel it is essential to mention how we would use both in segregating access to Develop and Production resources for a single person. If we had set up an identity provider, we could create an IAM role[31] for each RBAC role similar to how we created a group. When the user logs in to the identity provider, it would ask the user which role to assume, and the user would have a temporary credential to access the AWS resources using the selected role.[32] We could also use multiple AWS organizations, one for each development stage, that contain the appropriate resources. We would create IAM users in the master AWS organization and create IAM roles[33] to access the resources in AWS child organizations. A user will select the desired role when logging in to the IAM user account and will have access to

---

[31]"Creating a Role for a Third-Party Identity Provider (Federation)." AWS Identity and Access Management User Guide. Amazon Web Services. https://docs.aws.amazon.com/IAM/latest/UserGuide/id_roles_create_for-idp.html

[32]"Providing Access to Externally Authenticated Users (Identity Federation)." AWS Identity and Access Management User Guide. Amazon Web Services. https://docs.aws.amazon.com/IAM/latest/UserGuide/id_roles_common-scenarios_federated-users.html

[33]"Creating a Role to Delegate Permissions to an IAM User." AWS Identity and Access Management User Guide. Amazon Web Services. https://docs.aws.amazon.com/IAM/latest/UserGuide/id_roles_create_for-user.html

the resources for the respective development stage.[34] Both these options are suitable alternatives, but require more effort to set up.

If we are using a CI/CD pipeline to deploy the Serverless configurations, we will want to create a policy, possibly a group, and a user account with only programmatic access. The Serverless configuration supports specifying an AWS CloudFormation role, which deploys with that role irrespective of the user that performs the deployment. It is a good idea to create at least one AWS CloudFormation role to use in our Serverless configurations to ensure the deployment only uses the required permissions. It will help prevent creating unwanted resources and accidentally deleting resources if the role only has the permissions to create the necessary resources. We will create additional IAM settings to support a CI/CD pipeline and specify an AWS CloudFormation role; see Table 6-3.

Table 6-3. *AWS IAM Settings for CI/CD Pipelines and CloudFormation Roles*

IAM Setting	Develop Stage		Production Stage	
	Project A	Project B	Project A	Project B
Policies	developer, admin cicd, slsdeploy	developer, admin cicd, slsdeploy	developer, admin, auditor cicd, slsdeploy	developer, admin, auditor cicd, slsdeploy
Groups	developer, admin cicd	developer, admin cicd	developer, admin, auditor cicd	developer, admin, auditor cicd
Roles	slsdeploy	slsdeploy	slsdeploy	slsdeploy
Developer Group Policies	developer	developer	developer	developer
Admin Group Policies	admin	admin	admin	admin
Auditor Group Policies	Not Applicable	Not Applicable	auditor	auditor
CI/CD Group Policies	cicd	cicd	cicd	cicd
SlsDeploy Role Policies	slsdeploy	slsdeploy	slsdeploy	slsdeploy

---

[34]"Providing Access to an IAM User in Another AWS Account That You Own." AWS Identity and Access Management User Guide. Amazon Web Services. https://docs.aws. amazon.com/IAM/latest/UserGuide/id_roles_common-scenarios_aws-accounts. html#id_roles_common-scenarios_aws-accounts-example

We added a "cicd" policy and added a "cicd" group that uses that policy. We can now create a user (with programmatic access only) that our CI/CD pipeline can use to log in to AWS to deploy the Serverless configurations. This CI/CD user will have the permissions defined in the "cicd" policy and group.

We also added an "slsdeploy" policy and created an "slsdeploy" role that uses that policy. We will use this role as the CloudFormation role in the Serverless configurations by specifying the policy's ARN.

Resource Level

We use Serverless configurations to create resources. When we deploy, the Serverless Framework will create one IAM role for each Serverless configuration based on the permissions defined in the "iamRoleStatements" property. Each function that the Serverless Framework creates during the deployment will use the IAM role created for its Serverless configuration. Having the Serverless Framework create the IAM role and each function using it is a convenient feature, but it does have its downside.

Using one set of IAM role statements (permissions) that applies to each Lambda function can grant overly permissive roles to each function. Each function should only have the minimum required permissions to execute based on PoLP successfully. Having a blanket role that, for example, allows deleting database records will grant that permission to every function, even if that function only needs to read the database. Let's suppose that a Lambda function that reads the database is vulnerable to an injection attack when it executes a delete command. That exploit is successful because the function has the delete database records permission. Still, it would have failed if it only had the read permission. It is a good practice to apply PoLP and only give the required permissions to each function.

The Serverless Framework does not support specifying IAM role statements to each function. Still, we can use a plugin, such as the Serverless IAM Roles per Function Plugin,[35] to help us achieve the desired result. We specify the permissions common to every function in the "iamRoleStatements" property. Then we install the plugin and define the settings in the "custom" property that allow each function to inherit the permissions from the "iamRoleStatements" property; see Listing 6-13.

---

[35]"Serverless IAM Roles Per Function Plugin." GitHub. `https://github.com/functionalone/serverless-iam-roles-per-function`

Listing 6-13. Serverless Configuration Settings for the Serverless IAM Roles per Function Plugin

```
custom:
  serverless-iam-roles-per-function:
    defaultInherit: true
```

We can now define the IAM role statements for each function; see Listing 6-14.

Listing 6-14. Example Serverless Configuration with Role Statements per Function

```
provider:
  name: aws
  iamRoleStatements:
    - Effect: "Allow"
      Action: kms:Decrypt
      Resource: "*"
functions:
  getTransaction:
    handler: getTransaction.handler
    iamRoleStatements:
      - Effect: "Allow"
        Action: dynamodb:GetItem
        Resource: " arn:aws:dynamodb:*:*:table/Transactions"
  deleteTransaction:
    handler: deleteTransaction.handler
    iamRoleStatements:
      - Effect: "Allow"
        Action: dynamodb:DeleteItem
        Resource: "arn:aws:dynamodb:*:*:table/Transactions"
```

When the Serverless Framework deploys the updated configuration, it will create three roles: one role for the "iamRoleStatements" property, one role for the "getTransaction" function, and one role for the "deleteTransaction" function. The "getTransaction" function gets the "dynamodb:GetItem" permission, whereas the "deleteTransaction" gets the "dynamodb:DeleteItem" permission. Both functions also get the "kms:Decrypt" permission. Any functions that do not have their own "iamRoleStatements" property will use the role from the common "iamRoleStatements" property.

Azure

We will discuss how we might implement the levels in the general permissions model for Azure based on the Azure permissions principles we reviewed earlier in this chapter.

Organization Level

You might have noticed we did not define an organization level for Azure earlier in this chapter. Azure does support organizations but only within the Azure DevOps service. We can treat the Azure account as the organization, similar to our AWS approach, since we might or might not use the Azure DevOps service. We can also choose to use a management group to define an organization. Any subscriptions added to the management group are part of the organization, and we can use the scope to apply permissions to all items under it. We will create an "ecommerce" management group[36] to define our organization.

Development Stage Level

We will create one subscription[37] for each stage: one subscription for the Develop stage and another for the Production stage, thus allowing us to segregate the resources.

Project Level

We will use the Serverless configuration "service" property to identify the project in the resource names. We will specify the appropriate settings in the Serverless configuration; see Listing 6-15.

---

[36]"Create management groups for resource organization and management." Azure management groups documentation. Microsoft. `https://docs.microsoft.com/en-us/azure/governance/management-groups/create`

[37]"Create an additional Azure subscription." Azure Cost Management + Billing documentation. Microsoft. `https://docs.microsoft.com/en-us/azure/billing/billing-create-subscription`

Listing 6-15. Example Serverless Configuration Naming

```
service: projectA
provider:
  name: azure
  region: West US 2
  stage: develop # or production
```

The Serverless configuration automatically uses the "service," "stage," and "region" properties to name resources prefixed with the "sls-<region>-<stage>-<projectName>" naming convention.

Role Level

At the time of this writing, the Serverless Framework Azure plugin has no support for specifying custom role definitions. It will use the role definition from the service principal or the AD user used when deploying the Serverless configuration.

Users

We will create the users in an Azure Active Directory tenant. The users are primarily used to access Microsoft and Azure services (e.g., Office 365). We have the option of using the Serverless Framework Azure interactive login (which redirects to a browser login page). Still, the Serverless Framework documentation recommends using service principals.[38] We will follow the recommended approach for deploying Serverless configurations. Still, it is advisable to have AD users for administration purposes.

We will create service principals to deploy the Serverless configuration. All users that need to deploy Serverless configurations can each have their own service principal. When we create service principals, we will specify the subscription as the scope. We can now have service principals for each subscription, thus meaning we cannot use a service principal from the Develop subscription to deploy Serverless configurations to the Production stage.

---

[38]"Azure – Credentials." Serverless Docs. `https://serverless.com/framework/docs/providers/azure/guide/credentials/`

The service principal uses the built-in "Contributor" role,[39] which can manage resources without accessing their content. We can create a custom IAM role definition within each subscription to define the least amount of privileges needed to deploy a Serverless configuration. Defining custom IAM role definitions allows us to apply PoLP and restrict what types of resources we can deploy.

We mentioned each user could have its service principal. Still, it presents a similar burden as using multiple AWS access keys. We could consider using temporary service principles when deploying.

Resource Level

We use Serverless configurations to create resources. When we deploy, the Serverless Framework will create a resource group containing all resources defined in the Serverless configuration. Each function can process triggers and inputs and send outputs based on the bindings specified in the Serverless configuration. Aside from bindings, the functions have no IAM permissions.

Google Cloud

We will discuss how we might implement the levels in the general permissions model for Google Cloud based on the Google Cloud permissions principles we reviewed earlier in this chapter.

Organization and Development Stage Levels

Google Cloud explicitly supports an organization by using a domain to define the organization. Having the ability to use domain names to create organizations gives us some flexibility. We can use different domain names for the Develop and Production stages and treat the domain organization as the development stage level. We did not explore using different domain names in the AWS and Azure setups. For simplicity and uniformity, we will use one domain name to create our organization and use folders to group the Develop projects and the Production projects.

---

[39]"Built-in roles for Azure resources." Azure RBAC documentation. Microsoft. `https://docs.microsoft.com/en-us/azure/role-based-access-control/built-in-roles#contributor`

Project Level

We will create a Google Cloud project for each project and development stage (four projects in total): a Project A Develop project, a Project A Production project, a Project B Develop project, and a Project B Production project. We put the two Develop projects in the Develop folder and similarly for the Production projects. What makes Google Cloud different is the project resources are segregated by project. In contrast, AWS and Azure have the project resources in the same account and subscription, respectively.

Role Level

We have the option of creating custom roles or using predefined roles. Google Cloud documentation[40] and the Serverless Framework documentation[41] both suggest using predefined roles as custom roles have known limitations. For this reason, we will use predefined roles.

Users

We will create user accounts and groups. The Google Cloud organization also functions as an identity provider that lets us manage user accounts and groups. We will create user accounts for individual persons. We will create groups based on roles: a developer group, an administrator group, and an auditor group. We can now assign users to each group, thus allowing us to manage the user permissions as a group rather than by each user.

We will create service accounts within each project to deploy the Serverless configurations. All users that need to deploy Serverless configurations can each have a separate service account, or we can assign a service account to a group. Although it requires more administration, assigning a service account to each user account allows revoking that user account without affecting other user accounts. Each user will need a service account and its associated key to deploy a Serverless configuration to the appropriate project. We will assign the service accounts the predefined roles necessary

---

[40]"Understanding IAM custom roles." Identity and Access Management documentation. Google. `https://cloud.google.com/iam/docs/understanding-custom-roles`

[41]"Google – Credentials." Serverless Docs. `https://serverless.com/framework/docs/providers/google/guide/credentials/`

to deploy the Serverless configuration, which, at the time of this writing, include the Deployment Manager Editor, Storage Admin, Logging Admin, and Cloud Functions Developer roles.

We mentioned each user could have its own private key. Still, it presents a similar burden as using multiple AWS access keys. We could instead consider using short-lived service account credentials[42] when deploying.

Resource Level

We use Serverless configurations to create resources. When we deploy, the Serverless Framework will create a deployment configuration for all resources defined in the Serverless configuration. The resources will inherit the permissions from its higher scope levels. It will also create additional permissions needed for the resources to process an event. For example, a Cloud Function that accepts an HTTP trigger will create the permissions to allow all users (i.e., the entire Internet) to execute that function by calling its HTTP address. At the time of this writing, the Serverless Framework does not support specifying specific permissions for each function.

Key Takeaways

This chapter is the longest and rightly so. We wanted to ensure we establish a foundation before discussing how to use permissions. Similarly how we used Chapter 1 to develop a foundation for this book, this chapter had a foundation section. Having an understanding of how permissions work prepares us for creating our own, robust permissions model, and diligently applying it will improve the overall security of our serverless application. Let's recap what we discussed.

In this chapter, we first addressed the importance of permissions to limit function injection attacks and account takeovers. Restricting permissions to functions and accounts that have limited access reduces the risk of a successful attack from happening. After setting that precedence, we reviewed permissions principles before exploring how to apply those principles.

---

[42]"Creating short-lived service account credentials." Identity and Access Management documentation. Google. `https://cloud.google.com/iam/docs/creating-short-lived-service-account-credentials`

We started by discussing general permissions principles. These principles were necessary to address first because each provider approaches principles differently and uses similar terms, but with varying definitions. We established that we would use the Principle of Least Privilege (PoLP) and Role-Based Access Control (RBAC) as foundations for principles. After establishing the general principles, we reviewed how permissions work in AWS, Azure, and Google Cloud.

After understanding permissions principles in a general sense and for each provider, we discussed how to use these principles to implement permissions. We first established a general permissions model. This model helped us to develop an approach to adopt within AWS, Azure, and Google Cloud. Without this model, relating the implementation across all three providers might prove to be confusing and complicated. The model is a suggested approach and not a prescription when implementing permissions because your requirements will dictate our final setup. However, the method might be beneficial in giving us a starting point.

CHAPTER 7

Account Management

In this chapter, we will discuss how we might manage our account to reduce risk and improve security. The provider account allows us to access multiple services and create numerous resources. We will learn how we might use various accounts to organize the resources we create and how to secure our account by implementing standard practices.

The Importance of Account Management

Each provider account has a main/central/master/root account that gives us access to the provider's services. With this account, we can use services to build the applications we need for our businesses. When we use these services, we can incur costs as little as pennies and as much as several thousand dollars per month. If someone manages to take over an account, that actor can use the services in our account and create a costly bill. Therefore, we want a secure provider account to protect the main account from someone compromising it.

We can structure our provider accounts to minimize our exposure. Rather than having all our applications in one provider account, we can choose to use multiple provider accounts. Distributing our applications across multiple provider accounts reduces the impact of any damage from a compromised provider account. Still, there is a trade-off because we need to manage more provider accounts. If one provider account is taken over or compromised, we can limit the extent of the damage to one application.

© Miguel A. Calles 2020
M. Calles, *Serverless Security*, https://doi.org/10.1007/978-1-4842-6100-2_7

Understanding Provider Accounts

We briefly discussed organizations and multiple accounts in the previous chapter. The focus of the last chapter was permissions, and any mention of provider accounts was in that context. This chapter focuses on managing the accounts and using organization concepts where appropriate. We will review general and provider-specific principles.

General Principles

The providers have general consumer services in addition to cloud services. Having an account gives us access to both. A person might use cloud services with a personal account for business purposes. We should consider having separate accounts similar to how most professionals have both personal and professional email addresses. Having both personal and professional accounts provides mental compartmentalization on how we interact with the providers. It limits the scope of financial liabilities to the affected legal entity.

In addition to separating personal and professional accounts, we might want to consider using different accounts for different applications and development stages. In the previous chapter, we discussed an example model using one account containing one organization and two projects, each project having two development stages. We will expand on this model to take advantage of having multiple accounts; see Figure 7-1. Note: We omitted the roles from the diagram as we are assuming each account will have IAM permissions.

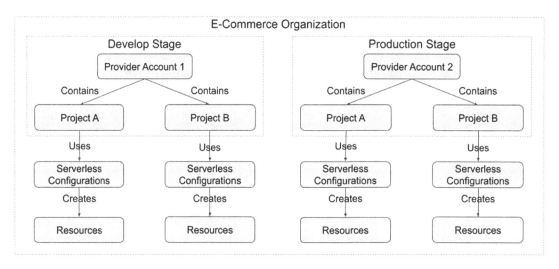

Figure 7-1. *An Example of a Permissions Model Using Multiple Provider Accounts*

178

We restructured the example model from Chapter 6 to treat all provider accounts as the organization. We used one provider account per development stage. Doing this allows us to further separate develop and production resources rather than solely relying on IAM permissions.

Furthermore, it allows us to have the same IAM user account name for both accounts. For example, both the develop and production accounts can have an "amy.smith" user account. However, we can still adopt the "amy.smith.develop" and "amy.smith.production" accounts, as previously discussed. We can also leverage the example permissions model from Chapter 6, even if we use multiple accounts.

Having multiple accounts provides nonsecurity-related benefits. Each provider might impose technical limits on each account. Having all the projects and their resources in the same provider account means they all share the same limits. Assuming the provider cannot increase the limits, we would need to ensure our development has no negative impact on the operational resources. However, with separate accounts, the provider limits apply to each account. Therefore, using resources on one account does not affect the other accounts.

We will explore how we might set up our two-development-stage account model for each provider.

Amazon Web Services (AWS)

AWS provides AWS Organizations[1] to manage multiple AWS accounts. AWS recommends having multiple accounts because it is a security best practice.[2] We can, therefore, implement the model we defined earlier; see Figure 7-2. Visit `https://console.aws.amazon.com/organizations` to set up the organization structure.

---

[1]"AWS Organizations." Amazon Web Services. `https://aws.amazon.com/organizations`

[2]"AWS Organization Features." Amazon Web Services. `https://aws.amazon.com/organizations/features`

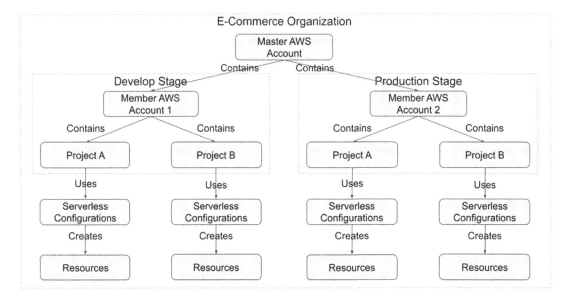

Figure 7-2. *Example of an AWS Organization*

We first start with one AWS account, which we designate as the master account. We use this account to create an organization that contains member accounts. We add a member account by creating a new AWS account or inviting an existing AWS account. Let's create a new member account; see Figure 7-3.

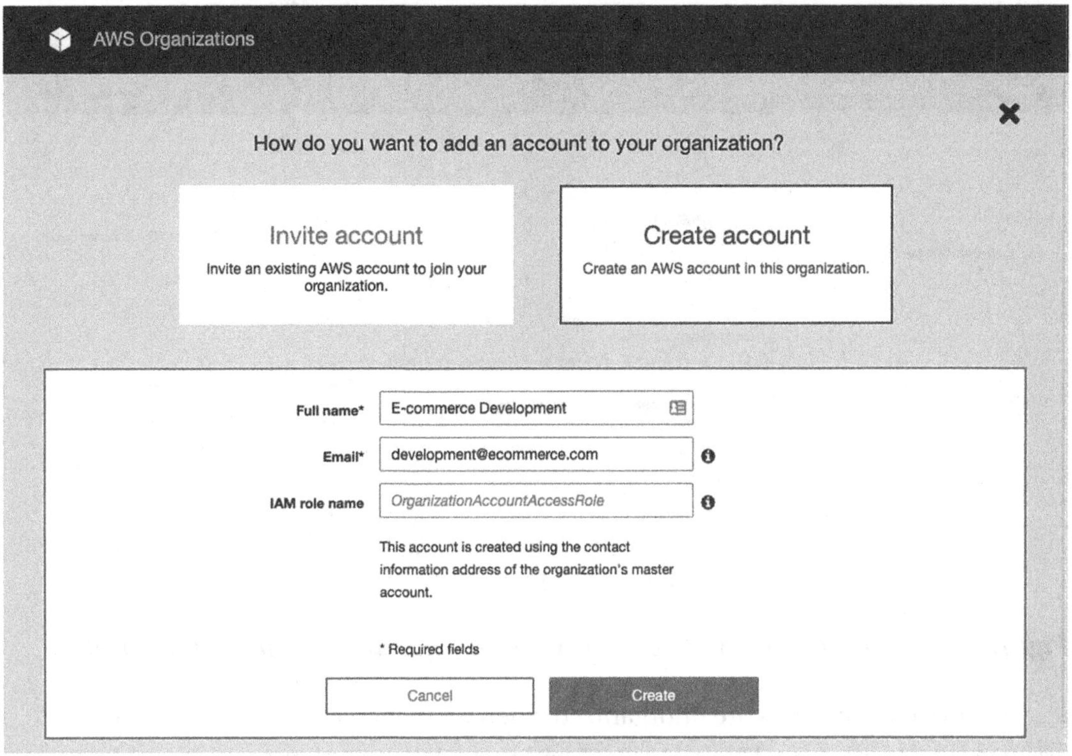

Figure 7-3. *Creating an AWS Member Account*

We specify the account name, the email address that owns the member account, and optionally an IAM role name. AWS Organizations automatically creates a service role in the member account that gives trust access to the master account.

We will create two member accounts named "Develop" and "Production." Each account will use a separate email address, preferably a group mailing list. We can organize the member accounts into an organizational unit (OU); see Figure 7-4.

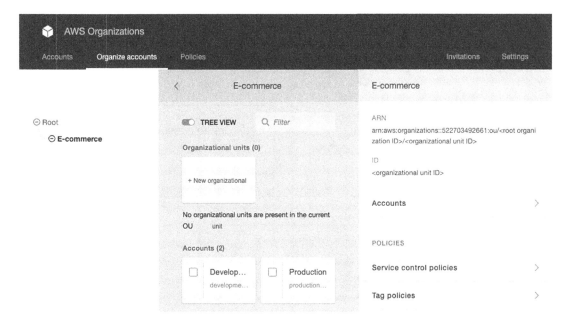

Figure 7-4. *Organizing AWS Member Accounts into an Organizational Unit*

The member accounts are unorganized when we first create them. We created an organizational unit named "Ecommerce" and moved the member accounts under it. Using organizational units allows us to organize multiple member accounts, especially when we have numerous organizations.

Other benefits of using AWS Organizations include

- Centralized billing, auditing, monitoring, and security

- Applying permissions across multiple member accounts using Service Control Policies

- Sharing resources across member accounts

Now that we have our two member accounts organized under an OU, we can set up our projects. We can now deploy the development resources in the AWS develop member account and deploy the production resources in the AWS production member account. We can set up any security, auditing, and monitoring settings across all accounts to meet the business requirements.

Azure

Azure supports having an organization by using the Azure Active Directory (AD).[3] We can implement the model we defined earlier by leveraging Microsoft Active Directory; see Figure 7-5.

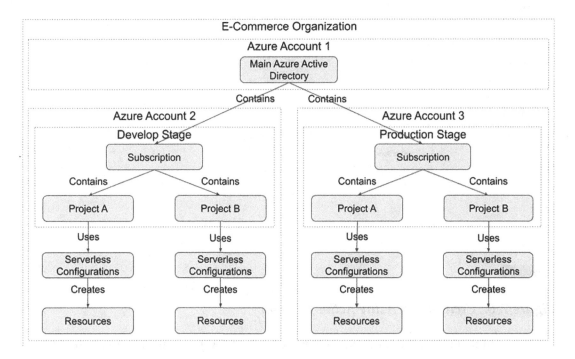

Figure 7-5. *Organizing Azure Accounts into an Organization Using Active Directory*

We will create three Azure accounts: one acting as the "master" account, one used for the develop stage, and one used for the production stage. Each account will use a separate email address, preferably a group mailing list. We will create an AD tenant in the master account for all accounts to use; see Figure 7-6.

---

[3]"Sign up your organization to use Azure Active Directory." Azure Active Directory fundamentals documentation. Microsoft. https://docs.microsoft.com/en-us/azure/active-directory/fundamentals/sign-up-organization

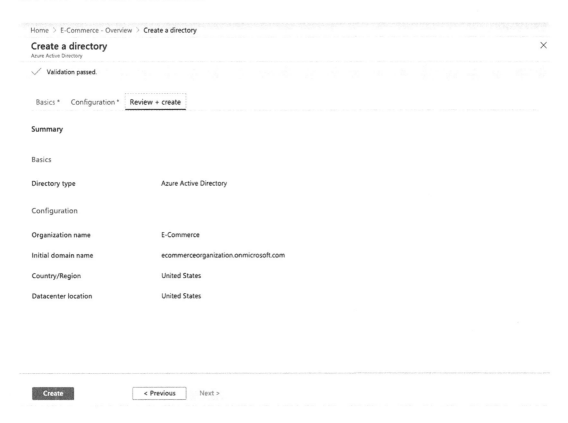

Figure 7-6. *Creating an Azure Active Directory*

We want to let the other accounts have access to the AD tenant. We can invite the different email addresses to the AD tenant; see Figure 7-7.

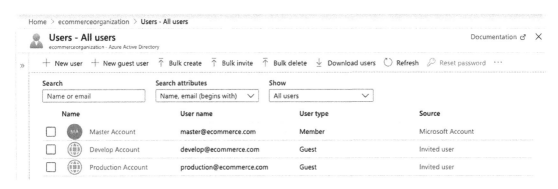

Figure 7-7. *Inviting Others to an Azure Active Directory*

We will create subscriptions in the other two accounts so we can deploy resources. We will assign the subscriptions to the AD tenant in the master account by changing the directory; see Figure 7-8.

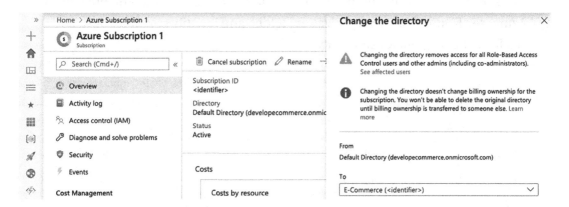

Figure 7-8. *Assigning Subscriptions to an Azure Active Directory Tenant*

The master account now centralizes the develop and master subscriptions under one AD. This approach centralizes user management.

The subscription billing remains with the develop and production Azure accounts. If the business requirements specify centralized billing, the master account could create the subscriptions and change its ownership to AD tenants within the other accounts. The other AD tenants can use direct federation to reduce the administrative overhead.[4]

Google Cloud

In Chapter 6, we discussed how Google Cloud provides identity and organizations. Google Cloud documentation recommends using organizations as a best practice.[5] We should follow this approach instead of having multiple Google Cloud accounts. AWS implements organizations via a master account and Azure via AD. However, Google Cloud implements organizations by relating it to a domain name using G Suite or

---

[4]"Direct federation with AD FS and third-party providers for guest users (preview)." External Identities documentation. Microsoft. `https://docs.microsoft.com/en-us/azure/active-directory/b2b/direct-federation`

[5]"Best practices for enterprise organizations." Get started with Google Cloud. Google. `https://cloud.google.com/docs/enterprise/best-practices-for-enterprise-organizations`

Google Cloud Identity. The organization manages the projects it owns instead of the accounts that created them. Therefore, the organization approach we used in the previous chapter is sufficient.

That said, we could use multiple accounts similar to what we implemented for AWS and Azure; see Figure 7-9. The organization, folder, and identity resources have been omitted from the diagram for simplicity.

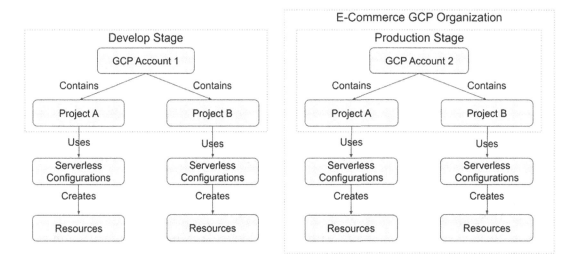

Figure 7-9. *Alternate Approach for Organizing Projects in Google Cloud*

We could choose to use Google Cloud organizations to manage all production resources. All other development stages could use a separate Google Cloud account. This allows us to separate resources while centrally administering the production resources. We lack certain benefits (e.g., centralized billing) by using this approach, but achieve any desired resource separation.

Securing Accounts

In addition to making use of multiple provider accounts, we want to secure them to prevent account hijacking, illegal changes or purchases, or unauthorized deleting of applications or data.

General Principles

The following general principles are useful in protecting a provider account and worthy of discussion:

- Using a service or group email address for the account

- Specifying contact information

- Specifying alternate contacts

- Using a secure and robust password

- Enabling Multi-Factor Authentication (MFA)

- Creating additional users to perform different functions

- Avoiding creating access keys or service principals in the primary account

- Enabling security questions

Using a service or group email address allows having a trusted group of persons to get email notifications about the account. This allows those trusted individuals to perform account recovery procedures. Whereas using an individual's email address might put the business in a tough situation. Let's suppose the contact was an individual that unexpectedly became unavailable, and no one else has access to the account. Any account recovery requests would go to that person's email inbox and would be inaccessible. Instead, using a group email address will result in having account notices sent to multiple persons, thus allowing multiple people to notice and take action on account changes, service notices, and potential issues.

We want to specify contact information to ensure we get adequately notified when the provider needs to contact us. Likewise, password recovery procedures might leverage contact information. We should consider using a physical address not listed on any public-facing website to avoid someone attempting to take over the account using social engineering or password recovery. A small business might only have one physical location, so they might want to consider getting a mailbox from a third party to use as the mailing address for the provider account. If the contact information asks for a birthday, consider using a date not tied to a person's birthdate.

We should consider using alternate contacts to ensure there are backups for getting notifications. We want to consider using group email addresses for these alternate contacts for the reasons mentioned earlier. The provider might allow you to specify alternate contacts for different domains (e.g., billing) and security contacts, and we should consider determining those to send appropriate communications to individuals that would typically support those business areas.

Having a strong password might seem apparent, but it is worth mentioning to avoid this common pitfall. Some companies might have a default password they use when setting up accounts. This password is easy to remember and makes it convenient to share among its employees. Yet it might become known by someone outside the company. Other companies might reuse a password for multiple websites, and that password might now be listed in hacker databases.[6] We should use long passwords, difficult to guess, unique, and changed periodically, to avoid someone accessing our provider account.

MFA provides another layer of protection in the event someone discovers our password or manages to reset the password. Upon successfully entering a matching username and password, the provider will request an MFA one-time password. Failing to enter this one-time password prevents access to the account, and good MFA practices should then require the user to log in again. Also, consider using a physical MFA device for increased security because a malicious party will need to obtain it physically. This does mean only the individuals who have physical access to the device can log in to the provider account and might be difficult for a business with companies in different locations. The next principle will address this situation. We do have the option of using virtual MFA devices. This is an excellent alternative for all user accounts. Still, we should avoid it for the main provider account because any digital data is subject to getting hacked. Yet, it is better to use a virtual MFA device than not enforcing MFA in your provider account at all.

Next, we should consider creating the following user accounts that allow us to perform the actions we might perform in the main provider accounts:[7]

- Read-only user account to view the account, but not make any undesired changes

---

[6]"Google warns BILLIONS of website passwords have been hacked – how to check yours now." Sean Keach. *The Sun*. January 15, 2020. `www.thesun.co.uk/tech/9734757/google-passwords-hacked-how-to-check`

[7]These user accounts should have strong passwords and have MFA enabled.

- Security administrator to make permission changes and create new user accounts

- Billing user account to generate billing reports and make payments

- Administrator user account to perform administrator actions for designated account services or projects

Creating access keys or service principals for the master account typically grants the same privileges that account has in the web-based management console. Anyone that obtains access to them has unrestricted access to the AWS provider account. Therefore, we should avoid creating access keys or service principals for the master account and create them for individual user accounts in which we can restrict access.

We should enable any security questions. These questions provide additional security when the answers are difficult to guess. Given these questions are used for account recovery, it is best to answer them in a manner that is difficult to guess.[8]

In the next section, we will review some of these general principles and provider-specific account settings.

AWS

When you log in to the AWS Management Console, click your account name at the top-right menu bar and select "My Account." This will take you to your account page.

Update your account information and contact information to use a group email address, a secure password, and an appropriate mailing address and phone number; see Figure 7-10.

---

[8]"The Hulk Was My Best Friend As A Kid: Advice on Answering Security Questions." Miguel A. Calles. Secjuice. January 5, 2020. www.secjuice.com/advice-on-answering-security-questions

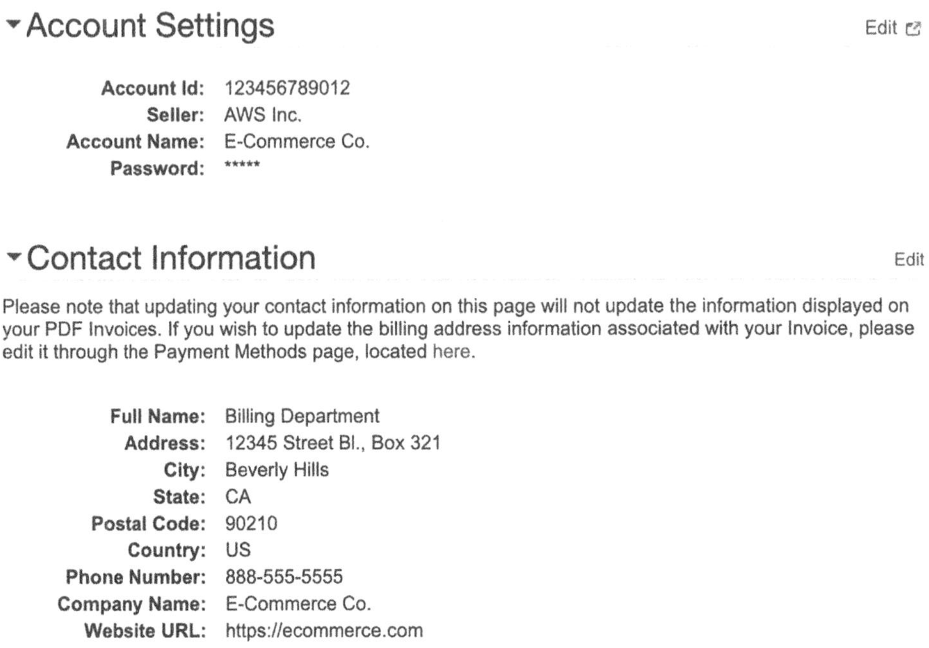

▾ Account Settings

Account Id:	123456789012
Seller:	AWS Inc.
Account Name:	E-Commerce Co.
Password:	*****

▾ Contact Information

Edit

Please note that updating your contact information on this page will not update the information displayed on your PDF Invoices. If you wish to update the billing address information associated with your Invoice, please edit it through the Payment Methods page, located here.

Full Name:	Billing Department
Address:	12345 Street Bl., Box 321
City:	Beverly Hills
State:	CA
Postal Code:	90210
Country:	US
Phone Number:	888-555-5555
Company Name:	E-Commerce Co.
Website URL:	https://ecommerce.com

Figure 7-10. *Updating AWS Account Information*

Further down, you will see the alternate contacts and security challenge questions. AWS does not require these sections by default; see Figure 7-11. Use the previously mentioned guidance when enabling these settings.

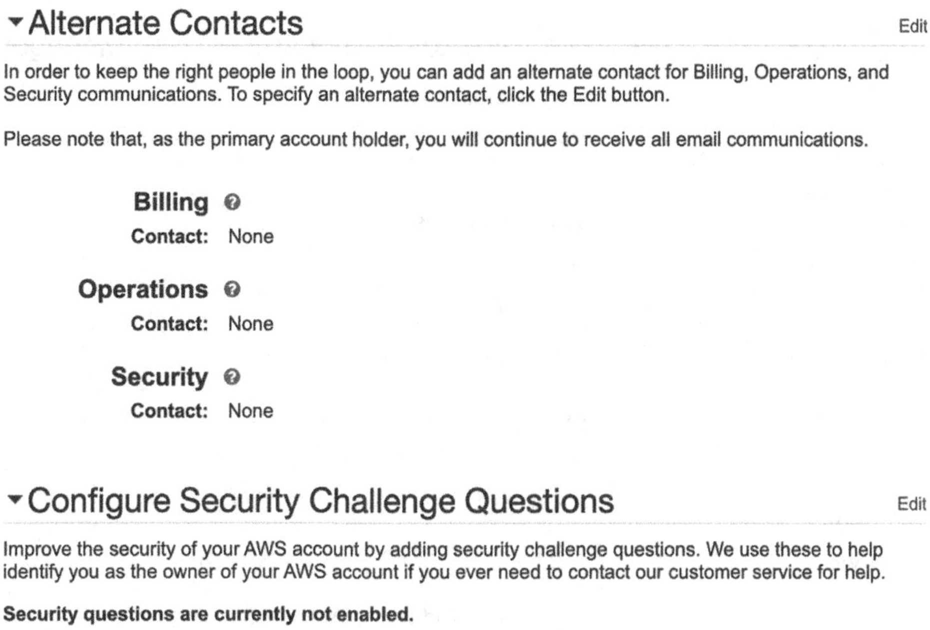

▾ Alternate Contacts

Edit

In order to keep the right people in the loop, you can add an alternate contact for Billing, Operations, and Security communications. To specify an alternate contact, click the Edit button.

Please note that, as the primary account holder, you will continue to receive all email communications.

Billing ❓
Contact: None

Operations ❓
Contact: None

Security ❓
Contact: None

▾ Configure Security Challenge Questions

Edit

Improve the security of your AWS account by adding security challenge questions. We use these to help identify you as the owner of your AWS account if you ever need to contact our customer service for help.

Security questions are currently not enabled.

Figure 7-11. *AWS Alternate Contacts and Security Challenge Questions Sections*

Go to the IAM service to see the IAM dashboard. You will see a security status section with recommended master account security settings; see Figure 7-12.

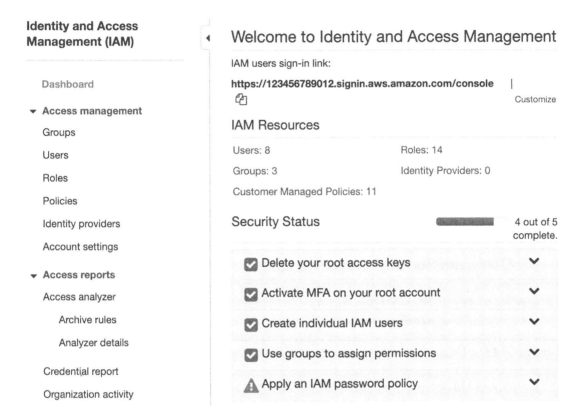

Figure 7-12. *AWS Security Status*

You should already be compliant with the "Delete your root access keys" item. If not, create an IAM user, create an access key to replace the existing master account (i.e., root) access keys, and delete the root access keys. By doing this, you become compliant with the "Create individual IAM users" item.

AWS does not enable MFA by default. Click the "Activate MFA on your root account" section, or click your account name at the top-right menu bar (not shown) and select "My Security Credentials." Add an MFA device and follow the on-screen instructions. The next time you log in, you are prompted to enter a one-time password; see Figure 7-13.

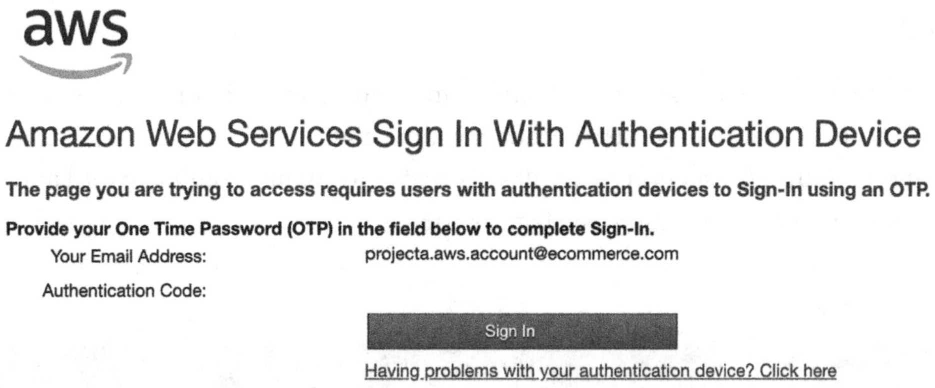

Amazon Web Services Sign In With Authentication Device

The page you are trying to access requires users with authentication devices to Sign-In using an OTP.

Provide your One Time Password (OTP) in the field below to complete Sign-In.

Your Email Address: projecta.aws.account@ecommerce.com

Authentication Code:

Sign In

Having problems with your authentication device? Click here

Figure 7-13. *AWS One-Time Password Prompt Example*

You will become compliant with the "Use groups to assign permissions" item when implementing a permissions model, as discussed in Chapter 6.

It is a good idea to comply with the "Apply an IAM password policy" item. This will require all IAM users' passwords to comply with the password policy you specify; see Figure 7-14.

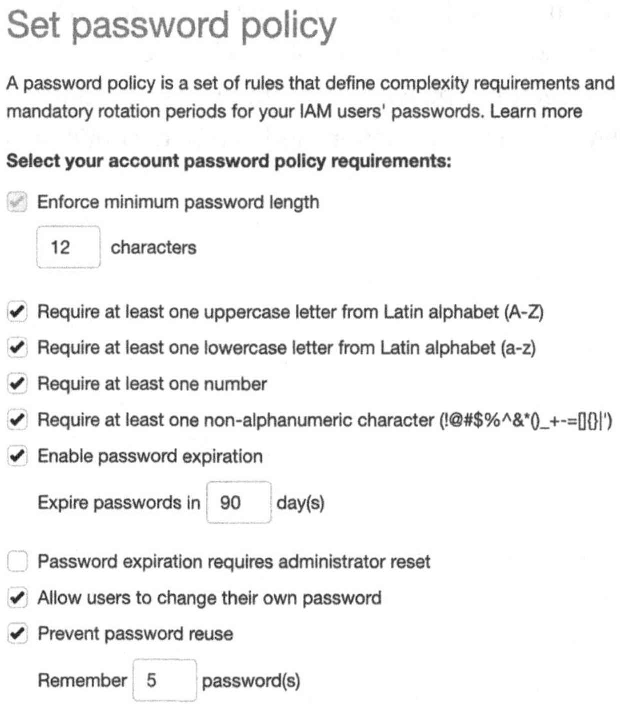

Set password policy

A password policy is a set of rules that define complexity requirements and mandatory rotation periods for your IAM users' passwords. Learn more

Select your account password policy requirements:

☑ Enforce minimum password length

[12] characters

☑ Require at least one uppercase letter from Latin alphabet (A-Z)

☑ Require at least one lowercase letter from Latin alphabet (a-z)

☑ Require at least one number

☑ Require at least one non-alphanumeric character (!@#$%^&*()_+-=[]{}|')

☑ Enable password expiration

Expire passwords in [90] day(s)

☐ Password expiration requires administrator reset

☑ Allow users to change their own password

☑ Prevent password reuse

Remember [5] password(s)

Figure 7-14. *AWS IAM Password Policy Example*

Azure

We will review some of the general principles and how to apply them to Azure. Visit `https://account.microsoft.com` to update your account settings.

Visit the "Your Info" section. You will see options to change your password and update your contact information; see Figure 7-15.

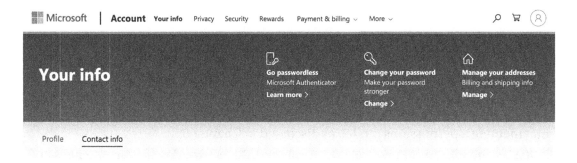

Figure 7-15. *Azure Account Information*

Change your password to be a strong password. Manage your addresses per the previously mentioned guidance. I suggest avoiding passwordless login for your master account for a similar reason as having a virtual MFA device.

Visit the "Security" section. You will see multiple security options to enable two-step verification (i.e., MFA), contact information, and additional options; see Figure 7-16.

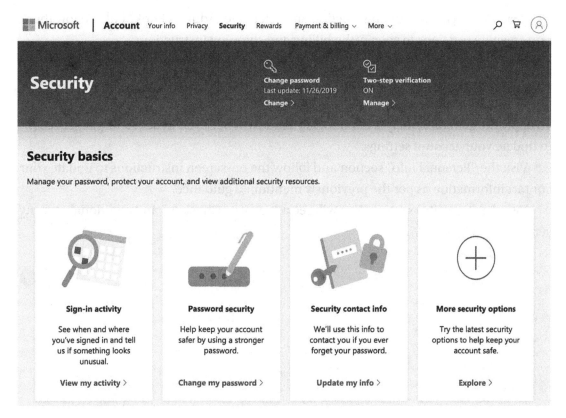

Figure 7-16. *Azure Security Section*

Click the two-step verification and follow the on-screen instructions to enable it.

Click the "More security options" section, go to the "Identity verification apps" section, and follow the on-screen instructions to enable an identity verification app (i.e., a virtual MFA device).

Optionally, go to the "Windows Hello and security keys" section and follow the on-screen instructions to set up a security key (which is like a physical MFA device, but does not require a username or password). This is a useful convenience feature and has comparable security since the security key requires a fingerprint or PIN to log in.[9]

Go to the "Recovery code" section and follow the on-screen instructions to print your recovery code as a backup method to access your account.

---

[9]"Sign in to your Microsoft account with Windows Hello or a security key." Windows Support. Microsoft. `https://support.microsoft.com/en-us/help/4463210/ windows-10-sign-in-microsoft-account-windows-hello-security-key`

Visit the "Payment & billing" section and select the "Address book" link. Follow the on-screen instructions to specify the billing and shipping instructions.

Google Cloud

To apply the general principles to Google Cloud, visit `https://myaccount.google.com` to update your account settings.

Visit the "Personal info" section and follow the on-screen instructions to update your contact information as per the previously mentioned guidance.

Visit the "Security" section. You will see a "Security Checkup" and additional security settings; see Figure 7-17.

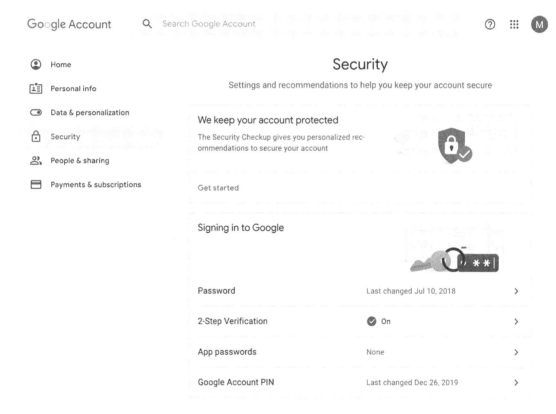

Figure 7-17. *Google Cloud Security Checkup and Security Settings*

Click the "Security Checkup" and follow the on-screen instructions to address any findings.

Return to the "Security" section and click the "2-Step Verification" button. You will see options to enable voice calls, SMSs, authenticator apps (i.e., virtual MFA device), and security keys (which is like a physical MFA device)[10] to enable MFA. Follow the on-screen instructions to enable all or some of the MFA options.

Key Takeaways

We extended the permissions model concepts from Chapter 6 by leveraging multiple provider accounts. We proposed using one account per development stage, thus separating and isolating the resources. This approach allows us to leverage the permissions model with the added protection of having different accounts to access its resources.

We concluded by reviewing the general principles to protect our account. We covered having basic security hygiene, such as using strong passwords and enabling multi-factor authentication, to minimize the risk of an unwanted party logging in to our provider account. Additionally, we explored updating contact information and using group email addresses to assist in password recovery situations.

Although this chapter is not specific to implementing and using the Serverless Framework and serverless technologies, protecting your provider account is still an essential aspect of keeping your serverless application secure. The remaining chapters will focus more on protecting the provider infrastructure to ensure the overall serverless application is more secure and has less risk.

---

[10]"Use a security key for 2-Step Verification." Google Account Help. Google. `https://support.google.com/accounts/answer/6103523`

## CHAPTER 8

Secrets Management

In this chapter, we will discuss how you might protect our secrets using provider services. We will explore the various ways AWS will enable us to encrypt secrets. Based on this exploration, we will select an approach that has a balance between encryption and convenience, and explore that approach in Azure and Google Cloud.

The provider allows us to encrypt your secrets in multiple ways. We will explore the various ways AWS will enable us to encrypt secrets. Based on this exploration, we will select an approach that has a balance between encryption and convenience, and explore that approach in Azure and Google Cloud.

The Importance of Secrets Management

Serverless functions may need to interface with external services, which may require a username and password, an API key, or a secret key to verify the account and validate the session. For example, your application may need to process credit card transactions, and the payment processor API might require an API key unique to your account to accept API requests. If someone obtains access to this API key, that individual might start processing unauthorized credit card transactions. These illegal transactions could result in financial loss, customer complaints, or other actions degrading the business brand. Therefore, we must take extra measures to protect secrets, like an API key, to reduce risk.

Protecting Secrets

We want to avoid accidentally disclosing secrets to help prevent scenarios like those previously discussed. We should take as many measures as possible, and as practical, to protect our secrets. We should have a business process for protecting secrets and a secure software process in our application.

© Miguel A. Calles 2020
M. Calles, *Serverless Security*, https://doi.org/10.1007/978-1-4842-6100-2_8

The business process might be the responsibility of the Information Technology, Information Security, or Cybersecurity departments or the application team if the organization is small. Whoever is responsible, having a process in place, is essential and need not be elaborate. It might be as simple as using a password manager to store all secrets and limiting who has access to it. Some organizations might store a physical sheet of paper containing the passwords in a safe, and the knowledge of the safe's code is limited. Both situations, in essence, have the same process in different mediums, digital vs. physical. Whatever process our business adopts, we need to use it consistently and periodically reassess it.

The secure software process is likely a shared responsibility between the software development team and the team responsible for the business process. It is a shared responsibility because the software developers need to develop software that securely uses the secrets, and the business process team might be involved in establishing the process and auditing it. We will discuss the general principles for how you might develop your secure software process for protecting secrets and how you might implement them for each provider.

General Principles

As a general rule, the source code should not contain any secrets (i.e., usernames, passwords, or keys). We can consider a few approaches for protecting secrets in the Serverless configuration file:

- Reference an environment variable.

- Reference a provider service that contains the value.

- Use an encrypted value in the Serverless configuration file.

We can use environment variables for any information we do not want to save in the source code. For example, we will obtain an API key from the environment variable to access a payment gateway; see Listing 8-1.

Listing 8-1. An Example of Referencing an Environment Variable Containing an API Key

```
const { API_KEY } = process.env;
console.log('API_KEY:', API_KEY.replace(/\w/g, '*'));
```

We can store the credit payment vendor's API key in the environment as a variable named "apiKey" which our Node function can reference. We will need to update our Serverless configuration to define the environment variable and make it accessible for the function; see Listing 8-2.

Listing 8-2. An Example of Defining an Environment Variable in the Serverless Configuration

```
functions:
  chargeCC:
    handler: src/functions/chargeCC.handler
    events:
      - http:
          method: post
          path: chargeCC
    environment:
      API_KEY: 40d5263a-0952-4fa2-94c6-882b92523e5c
```

You might notice defining the API key in the Serverless configuration has the actual API key value. The configuration might be captured in a repository[1] and no longer kept secret. We have moved the API key from the function source code to the Serverless configuration, which diminishes the security patch or software update. We should have the Serverless configuration file reference the "apiKey" value rather than storing it.

We can define the environment variable containing the API key in the CI/CD pipeline that deploys the Serverless configuration; see Listing 8-3.

Listing 8-3. An Example of Referencing an Environment Variable in the Serverless Configuration

```
functions:
  chargeCC:
    handler: src/functions/chargeCC.handler
    events:
```

---

[1]You can safely remove the API keys from the repository if you accidentally committed them to GitHub or any other git repository. "Removing Sensitive Data & Plaintext Secrets from GitHub." Miguel A. Calles. Secjuice. March 1, 2020. www.secjuice.com/ github-complete-cleaning-sensitive-secrets

```
    - http:
        method: post
        path: chargeCC
  environment:
    API_KEY: ${env:API_KEY}
```

The CI/CD pipeline should have limited access and have security measures (e.g., up-to-date software, host-based firewalls) in place to reduce the risk of accidentally disclosing the environment variables.

We can reference a provider service that contains the API key, which centralizes where the value is stored. We will see examples in the AWS, Azure, and Google Cloud sections. We want to use IAM permissions to limit who and what functions have access to the value.

We can use encryption in combination with the previous three approaches we have discussed. Using encryption further reduces the risk of disclosing the secret API key by the CI/CD server, the function, or the developer. In the event the environment variables are disclosed, only the encrypted version of the API key is made known. The recipient will need to decrypt the encrypted data to obtain the API key. Remember, using a stronger encryption method will better protect the secrets.[2,3]

The decryption algorithm should leverage well-known algorithms rather than building a custom decryption algorithm which may introduce unknown vulnerabilities. We should consider using an encryption-decryption capability included in the provider's libraries.

We will now explore how to protect secrets using provider capabilities.

---

[2]"Cracking SSL Encryption is Beyond Human Capacity." Flavio Martins. Digicert. August 21, 2014. www.digicert.com/blog/cost-crack-256-bit-ssl-encryption

[3]"Encryption 101: How to break encryption." Vasilios Hioureas. MalwareBytes Labs. March 6, 2018. https://blog.malwarebytes.com/threat-analysis/2018/03/encryption-101-how-to-break-encryption

Amazon Web Services (AWS)

In AWS, we can leverage the Systems Manager (SSM) Parameter Store,[4] Secrets Manager,[5] Key Management Service,[6] or a combination to manage our secrets. SSM Parameter Store enables us to store the values in plaintext (i.e., unencrypted) and ciphertext (i.e., encrypted) when at rest. We can reference them in our Serverless configuration or Lambda function code. Secrets Manager enables us to store values in ciphertext at rest and can reference them in our Serverless configuration or Lambda function code. KMS allows us to encrypt and decrypt data using customer master keys (CMKs), which are unique encryption keys we generate within AWS. SSM Parameter Store and Secrets Manager use KMS to encrypt and decrypt the ciphertext. These are the three services we'll consider to manage our secrets.

Scenario: Using AWS Systems Manager (SSM) Parameter Store

We will explore how to use SSM Parameter Store to store our secrets in plaintext and ciphertext. We can use the AWS Management Console to create a parameter as a "String" (i.e., plaintext) (see Figure 8-1) or a "SecureString" (i.e., ciphertext) (see Figures 8-2 and 8-3).

---

[4]"AWS Systems Manager Parameter Store." AWS Systems Manager User Guide. Amazon Web Services. https://docs.aws.amazon.com/systems-manager/latest/userguide/systems-manager-parameter-store.html

[5]"What Is AWS Secrets Manager?" AWS Secrets Manager User Guide. Amazon Web Services. https://docs.aws.amazon.com/secretsmanager/latest/userguide/intro.html

[6]"What is AWS Key Management Service?" AWS Key Management Service Developer Guide. Amazon Web Service. https://docs.aws.amazon.com/kms/latest/developerguide/overview.html

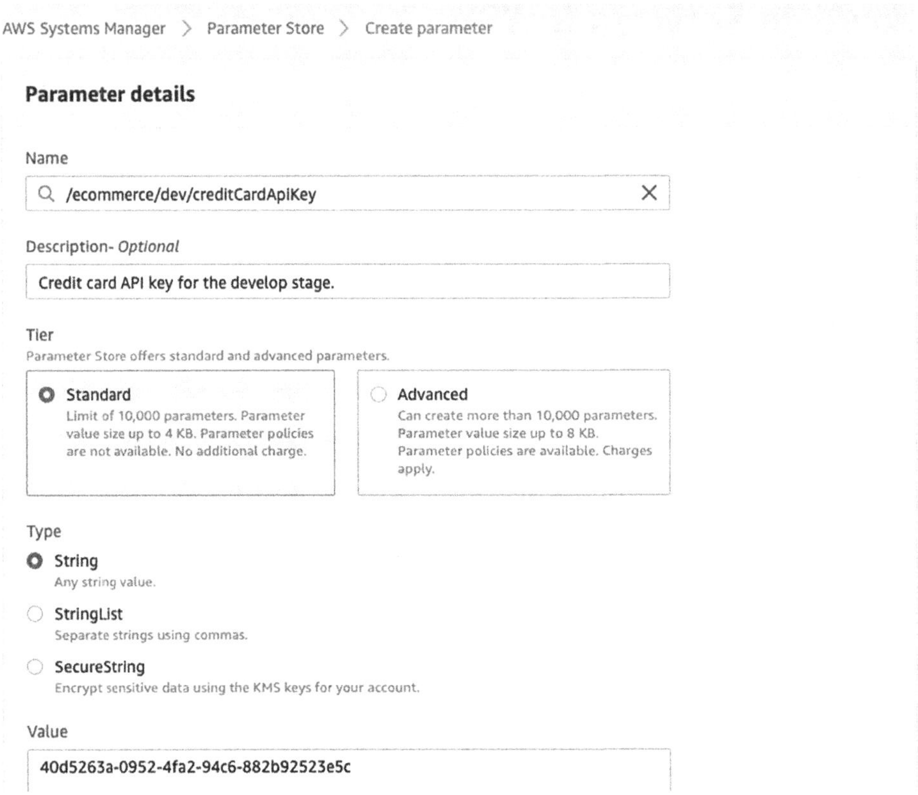

Figure 8-1. *An Example of Creating an AWS SSM String (Plaintext) Parameter*

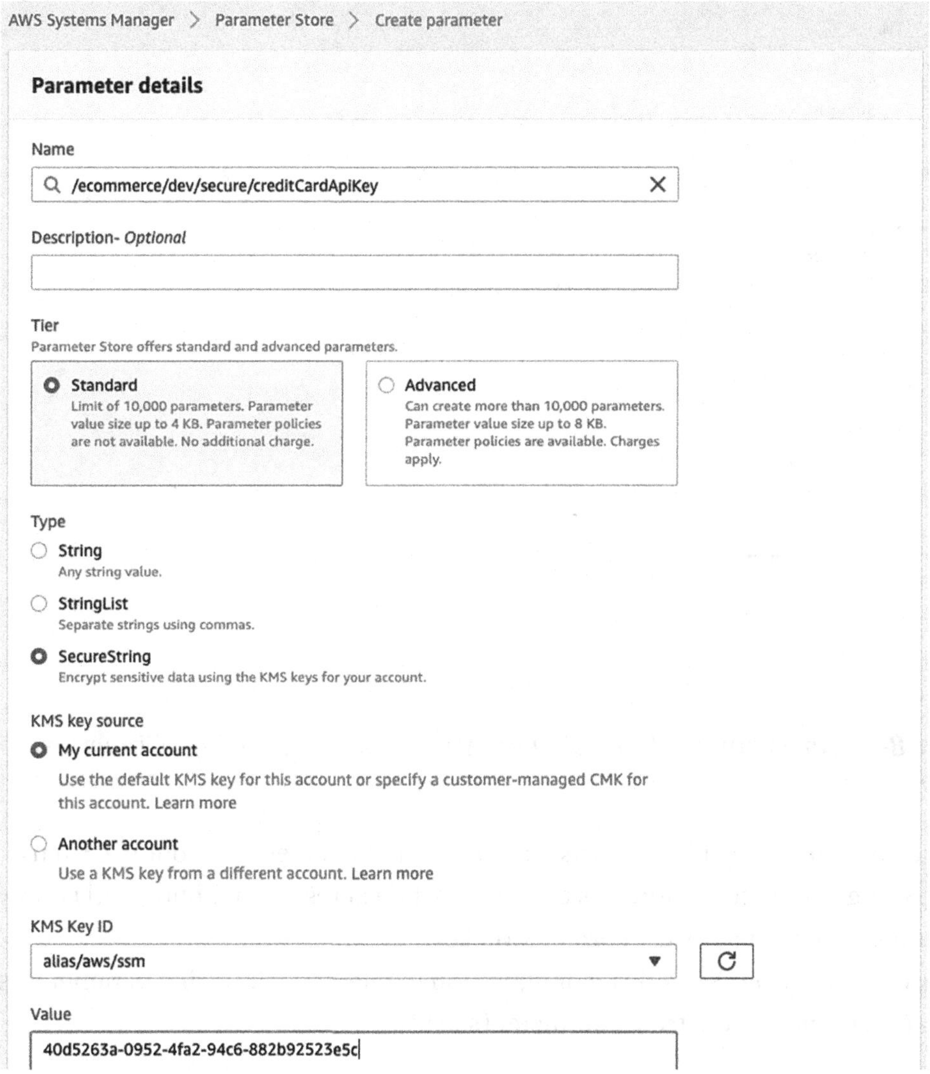

Figure 8-2. *An Example of Creating an AWS SSM SecureString (Ciphertext) Parameter, Part 1*

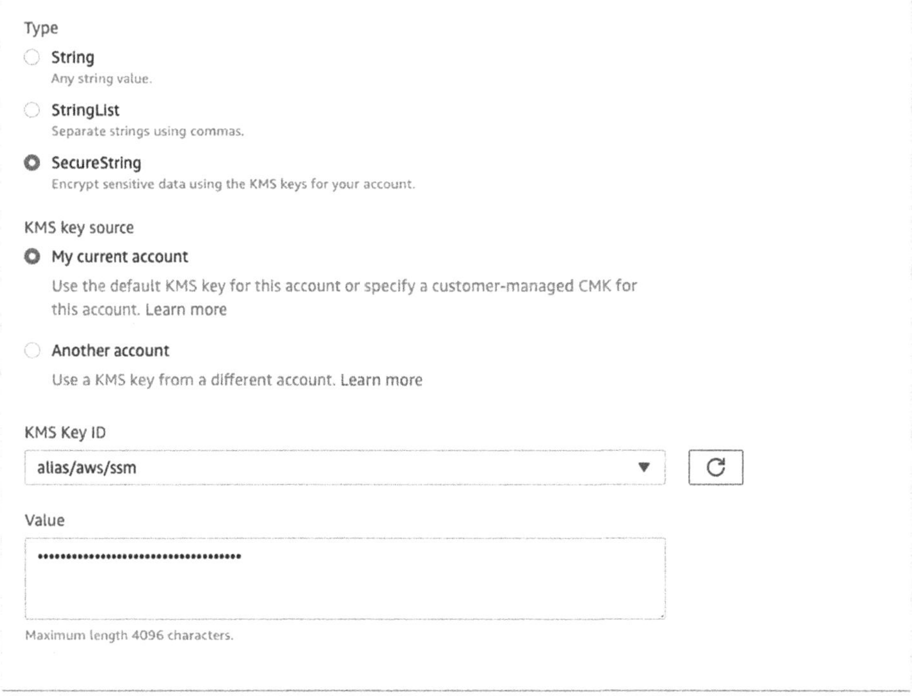

Type

○ **String**
Any string value.

○ **StringList**
Separate strings using commas.

● **SecureString**
Encrypt sensitive data using the KMS keys for your account.

KMS key source

● **My current account**
Use the default KMS key for this account or specify a customer-managed CMK for this account. Learn more

○ **Another account**
Use a KMS key from a different account. Learn more

KMS Key ID

| alias/aws/ssm ▼ | | C |

Value

| •••••••••••••••••••••••••••••••••• |

Maximum length 4096 characters.

Figure 8-3. *An Example of Creating an AWS SSM SecureString (Ciphertext) Parameter, Part 2*

The String parameter is stored as plaintext, whether at rest, in motion, or in use. The SecureString parameter is stored as ciphertext when at rest or in motion and is converted to plaintext when in use by the correct KMS key.

We can update our Serverless configuration to reference the String parameter (see Listing 8-4) or the SecureString parameter (see Listing 8-5).

Listing 8-4. An Example of Referencing an AWS SSM String Parameter in the Serverless Configuration

```
custom:
  ssmPath: /ecommerce/${self:provider.stage}/creditCardApiKey
functions:
  chargeCC:
    handler: src/functions/chargeCC.handler
```

```
events:
  - http:
      method: post
      path: chargeCC
environment:
  API_KEY: ${ssm:${self:custom.ssmPath} }
```

Listing 8-5. An Example of Referencing an AWS SSM SecureString Parameter in the Serverless Configuration

```
custom:
  ssmPath: /ecommerce/${self:provider.stage}/secure/creditCardApiKey
functions:
  chargeCC:
    handler: src/functions/chargeCC.handler
    events:
      - http:
          method: post
          path: chargeCC
    environment:
      API_KEY: ${ssm:${self:custom.ssmSecure}~true}
```

With either approach, the parameter value is passed in plaintext to the Lambda function environment variables; see Figure 8-4.

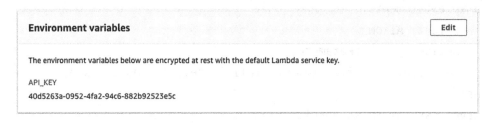

Figure 8-4. *An Example of AWS Lambda Environment Variables Containing Plaintext Secrets*

Anyone able to access the Lambda function configuration section or disclose the environment variables during the Lambda function runtime can obtain the API key. To avoid this risk, we can dynamically get the SSM parameter during the Lambda function runtime. Listing 8-6 shows an example Serverless configuration for specifying the SSM parameter name to a Lambda function. (Listing 8-6 has the appropriate IAM permissions to allow the Lambda function to access the SSM parameters and uses the Serverless IAM Roles per Function plugin we discussed in Chapter 6.) Listing 8-7 shows an example of using the SSM parameter name to obtain an SSM SecureSring parameter. Setting the "WithDecryption" value to "true" retrieves an SSM SecureString parameter, whereas setting it to "false" retrieves an SSM String parameter.

Listing 8-6. Updating the Serverless Configuration to Use the SSM Parameter Name

```
custom:
  arnPrefix: arn:aws:ssm:${self:provider.region}:*:parameter
  ssmPath: /ecommerce/${self:provider.stage}/secure/creditCardApiKey
functions:
  chargeCC:
    handler: src/functions/chargeCC.handler
    events:
      - http:
          method: post
          path: chargeCC
    environment:
      PARAMETER_NAME: /ecommerce/${self:provider.stage}/secret/
creditCardApiKey
    iamRoleStatements:
      - Effect: Allow
        Action: ssm:GetParameter
        Resource: ${self:custom.arnPrefix}${self:custom.ssmPath}
plugins:
  - serverless-iam-roles-per-function
```

Listing 8-7. An Example of Obtaining an SSM SecureString Parameter in a Lambda Function

```
const AWS = require('aws-sdk');
const ssm = new AWS.SSM();
const { PARAMETER_NAME } = process.env;
```

```
const params = {
    Name: PARAMETER_NAME,
    WithDecryption: true
};
module.exports.handler = (event, context, callback) => {
    return ssm
        .getParameter(params)
        .promise()
        .then((data) => {
            const apiKey = data.Parameter.Value;
            console.log(
                'apiKey:',
                apiKey.replace(/\w/g, '*'),
            );
            callback(null, {
                statusCode: 200,
                body: 'Success'
            });
        })
        .catch((err) => {
            console.error(err);
            callback(null, {
                statusCode: 500,
                body: 'Error'
            });
        });
};
```

We no longer have to maintain the Serverless configuration file and deploy it whenever the SSM parameter is updated. The Lambda function will dynamically obtain the latest SSM parameter value every time it executes. We should consider using the SSM SecureString parameter because the data is encrypted using an AWS-managed KMS key.

Scenario: Using AWS Key Management System (KMS)

We will explore how to use Key Management System (KMS) keys to encrypt our secrets.

We will create a CMK using the AWS Management Console and following the on-screen prompts; see Figure 8-5.

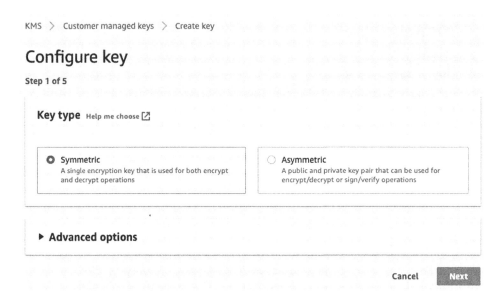

Figure 8-5. *An Example of Creating a Customer Managed Key*

We will use the Key ID listed in the KMS CMK section (see Figure 8-6) to encrypt our API key.

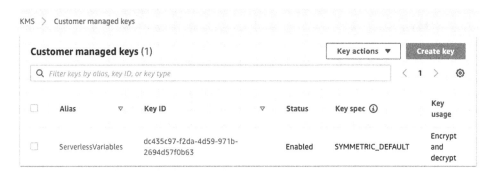

Figure 8-6. *An Example of a Customer Managed Key ID*

We will use the AWS CLI to encrypt the API key (see Listing 8-8), which returns a JSON object containing the ciphertext (see Listing 8-9).

Listing 8-8. An Example of Encrypting an API Key Using the AWS CLI

```
aws2 kms encrypt \
--key-id dc435c97-f2da-4d59-971b-2694d57f0b63 \
--plaintext 40d5263a-0952-4fa2-94c6-882b92523e5c \
--region us-east-1
```

Listing 8-9. An Example Output of the Encryption

```
{

    "CiphertextBlob": "AQICAHgC7mTtcEJQ1Y3mcIte25SbVsB/yZnL7UzGOfzWgHVJoAFS
    xCxpGJ6cyeLQl9J7s7+bAAAAgzCBgAYJKoZIhvcNAQcGoHMwcQIBADBsBgkqhkiG9w0BBw
    EwHgYJYIZIAWUDBAEuMBEEDP78crOWYO1h6POU8QIBEIA/VIZuslMvhwB9M8KE7ONKaqoY
    mQUgRwQivT63SZuA2BOifQg7uvbN2QgNEHo3VC0HfJKO+mS+bFXWHC1qJtiB",
    "KeyId": "arn:aws:kms:us-east-1:123456789012:key/dc435c97-f2da-4d59-
    971b-2694d57f0b63"
}
```

We can update the Serverless configuration file to use the ciphertext; see Listing 8-10. We added the appropriate IAM permissions to allow the Lambda function to access the KMS decryption and used the Serverless IAM Roles per Function plugin we discussed in Chapter 6.

Listing 8-10. Specifying the Ciphertext in the Serverless Configuration File

```
functions:
  chargeCC:
    handler: src/functions/chargeCC.handler
    events:
      - http:
          method: POST
          path: chargeCC
    environment:
      ENCRYPTED_API_KEY: |
```

AQICAHgC7mTtcEJQ1Y3mcIte25SbVsB/yZnL7UzGOfzWgHVJoAFSxCxpGJ6cyeLQl9J7s7+bAAA
AgzCBgAYJKoZIhvcNAQcGoHMwcQIBADBsBgkqhkiG9w0BBwEwHgYJYIZIAWUDBAEuMBEEDP78cr
OWYO1h6POU8QIBEIA/VIZuslMvhwB9M8KE7ONKaqoYmQUgRwQivT63SZuA2BOifQg7uvbN2QgNE
Ho3VCOHfJKO+mS+bFXWHC1qJtiB

```
    iamRoleStatements:
      - Effect: Allow
        Action: kms:Decrypt
        Resource: arn:aws:kms:${self:provider.region}:*:key/*
plugins:
  - serverless-iam-roles-per-function
```

We will decrypt the ciphertext using KMS during the Lambda function runtime; see Listing 8-11.

Listing 8-11. Decrypting the Ciphertext Environment Variable

```
const AWS = require('aws-sdk');
const kms = new AWS.KMS();
const { ENCRYPTED_API_KEY } = process.env;
const params = {
    CiphertextBlob: ENCRYPTED_API_KEY
};
module.exports.handler = (event, context, callback) => {
    return kms
        .decrypt(params)
        .promise()
        .then((data) => {
            const apiKey = data.Plaintext;
            console.log(
                'apiKey:',
                apiKey.replace(/\w/g, '*')
            );
```

```
        callback(null, {
            statusCode: 200,
            body: 'Success'
        });
    })
    .catch((err) => {
        console.error(err);
        callback(null, {
            statusCode: 500,
            body: 'Error'
        });
    });
};
```

We can integrate this KMS encryption and decryption approach with SSM by creating a parameter containing the ciphertext or integrate with Secrets Manager by creating a secret containing the ciphertext.

We might consider this approach as the most secure, yet it is arguably the most cumbersome and expensive. We first need to pay to create a CMK. We need to encrypt the API key. We need to store the encrypted API key in the Serverless configuration file and deploy it. The Lambda function needs to decrypt the API key. Whenever the CMK or API key is changed, the previous steps need to account for the change also.

Scenario: Using AWS Secrets Manager

We will explore how to use Secrets Manager to store our secrets as the ciphertext. We can use the AWS Management Console to save a new secret; see Figures 8-7 and 8-8.

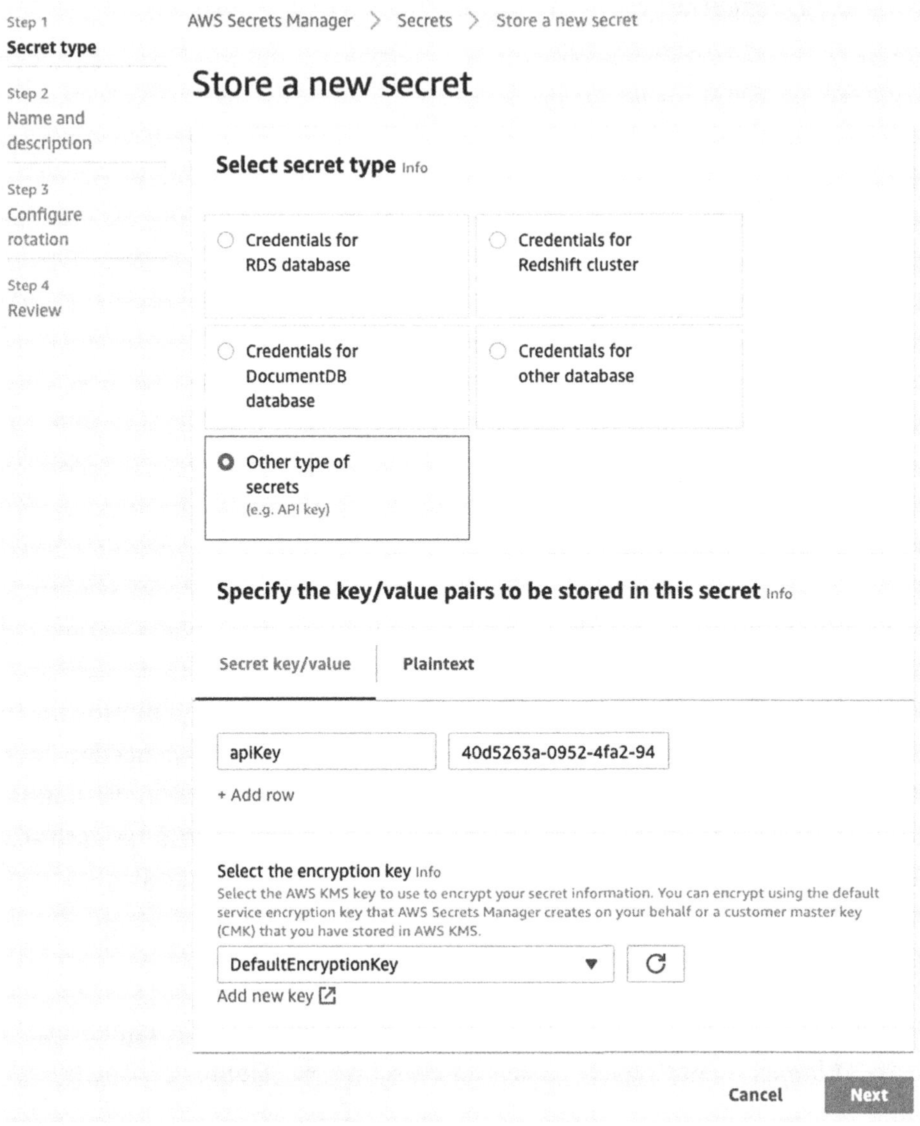

Figure 8-7. *An Example of Creating an AWS Secrets Manager Secret, Part 1*

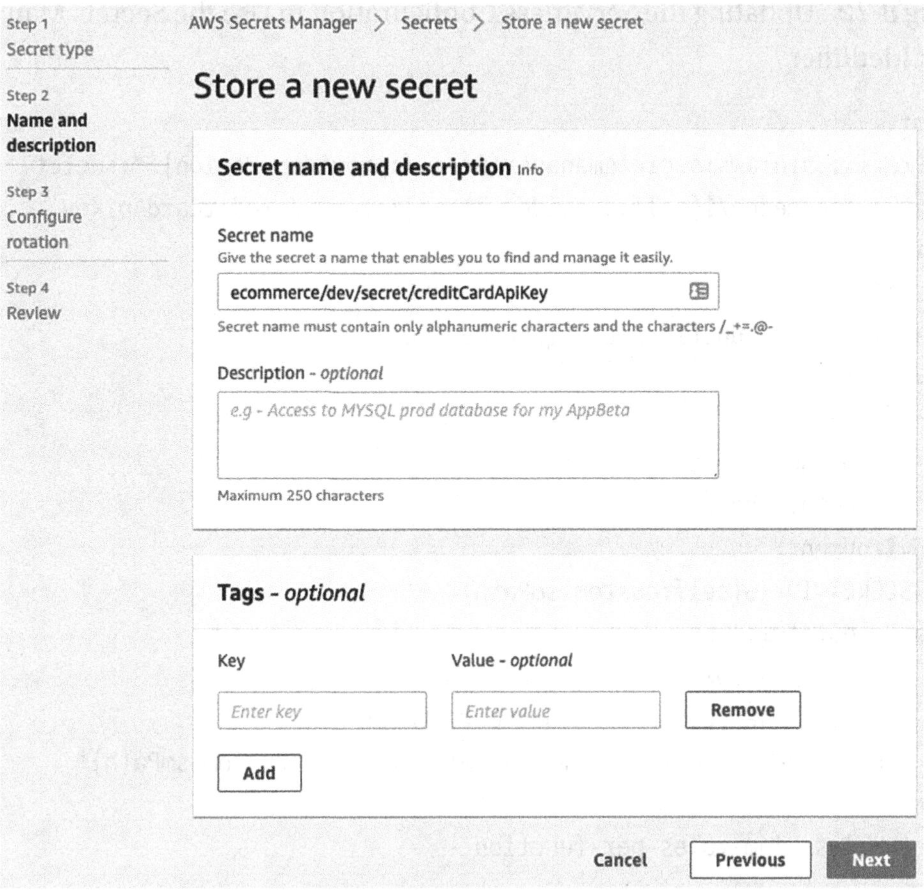

Figure 8-8. *An Example of Creating an AWS Secrets Manager Secret, Part 2*

The secret is stored in ciphertext when at rest and in motion and is converted to plaintext when in use by the correct KMS key.

We can update our Serverless configuration to reference the secret, but we will forego it because it passes the secret as plaintext in the Lambda function environment variables (as discussed in the SSM example). Therefore, we will focus on getting the secret during the Lambda function runtime; see Listings 8-12 and 8-13. We added the appropriate IAM permissions in Listing 8-12 to allow the Lambda function to access the KMS decryption and used the Serverless IAM Roles per Function plugin we discussed in Chapter 6.

Listing 8-12. Updating the Serverless Configuration to Use the Secrets Manager Secret Identifier

```
custom:
  arnPrefix: arn:aws:secretsmanager:${self:provider.region}:*:secret
  smPath: ecommerce/${self:provider.stage}/secret/creditCardApiKey
functions:
  chargeCC:
    handler: src/functions/chargeCC.handler
    events:
      - http:
          method: post
          path: chargeCC
    environment:
      SECRET_ID: ${self:custom.smPath}
    iamRoleStatements:
      - Effect: Allow
        Action: secretsmanager:GetSecretValue
        Resource: ${self:custom.arnPrefix}:${self:custom.smPath}*
plugins:
  - serverless-iam-roles-per-function
```

Listing 8-13. An Example of Obtaining a Secrets Manager Secret in a Lambda Function

```
const AWS = require('aws-sdk');
const secretsmanager = new AWS.SecretsManager();
const { SECRET_ID } = process.env;
const params = { SecretId: SECRET_ID };
module.exports.handler = (event, context, callback) => {
    return secretsmanager
        .getSecretValue(params)
        .promise()
        .then((data) => {
            const secret = JSON.parse(data.SecretString);
            const apiKey = secret.apiKey;
```

```
    console.log(
        'apiKey:',
        apiKey.replace(/\w/g, '*')
    );
    callback(null, {
        statusCode: 200,
        body: 'Success'
    });
})
.catch((err) => {
    console.error(err);
    callback(null, {
        statusCode: 500,
        body: 'Error'
    });
});
};
```

The Lambda function will dynamically obtain the latest secret value every time it executes.

From all the scenarios, this approach has an appropriate balance between security and convenience. We still use an encryption key, but the Secrets Manager performs the encryption for us. We do not store the KMS encrypted value in the Serverless configuration. Instead, we reference the Secrets Manager secret ID. Whenever we update the secret in Secrets Manager, we do not have to update the Serverless configuration nor redeploy it. This approach has the security benefits of using KMS encryption and the convenience of referencing an SSM parameter.

Azure

In the previous section, the AWS Secrets Manager had an appropriate balance between encryption and convenience. Therefore, we will focus on using the Azure Key Vault[7] feature that provides a similar capability.

---

[7]"What is Azure Key Vault?" Azure Key Vault documentation. Microsoft. `https://docs.microsoft.com/en-us/azure/key-vault/key-vault-overview`

The Azure Key Vault service provides secrets management, key management, certificate management, and hardware security modules. With secrets management, we specify the plaintext value, and the service encrypts the value when at rest and decrypts it when in use. Key management allows us to create encryption keys that we can use to encrypt and decrypt data. Certificate management will enable us to manage the certificates we use for network security. Hardware security modules will allow us to protect secrets using encryption hardware. We will focus on secrets management in this section.

We start by creating a new Key Vault; see Figure 8-9. We specify the subscription and the resource group where the Key Vault will exist. This example creates a new resource group to separate the Key Vault resource from other resources within the subscription.

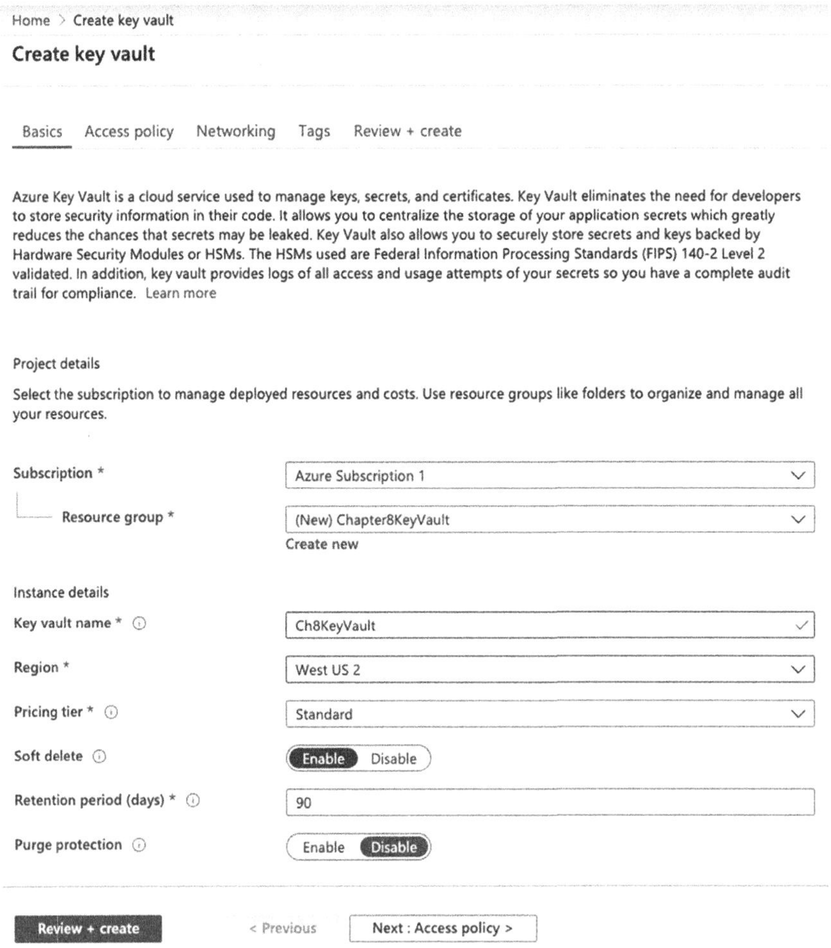

Figure 8-9. *An Example of Creating a New Azure Key Vault*

We create a new secret for the API key; see Figure 8-10.

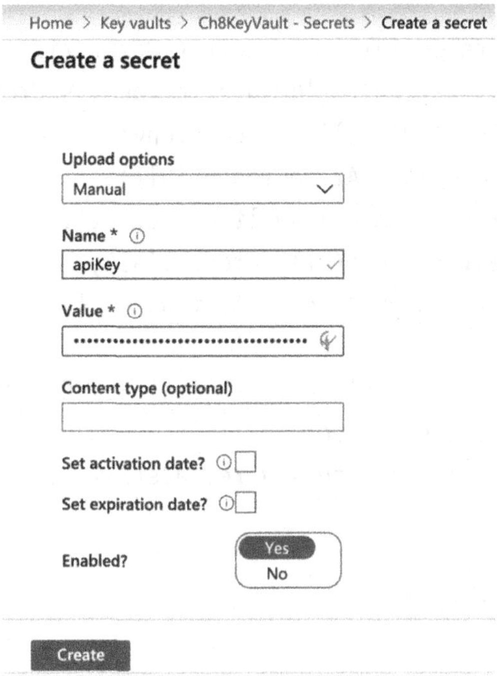

Figure 8-10. *An Example of Creating a New Secret in Azure Key Vault*

We now want to obtain the secret in the Azure Function. We define environment variables containing the Key Vault information in the Serverless configuration file; see Listing 8-14. We reference the environment variables when accessing the secret from Azure Key Vault; see Listing 8-15.

Listing 8-14. An Example of Defining the Secret Name in the Serverless Configuration

```
provider:
  name: azure
  region: West US 2
  runtime: nodejs10.x
  environment:
    KEY_VAULT: Ch8KeyVault
    SECRET_NAME: apiKey
```

Listing 8-15. An Example of Accessing the Key Vault Secret in the Azure
Function

```
const { DefaultAzureCredential } = require('@azure/identity');
const { SecretClient } = require('@azure/keyvault-secrets');
const { KEY_VAULT, SECRET_NAME } = process.env;
const credential = new DefaultAzureCredential();
const url = `https://${KEY_VAULT}.vault.azure.net`;
const client = new SecretClient(url, credential);
module.exports.handler = async (context, req) => {
    try {
        const secret = await client.getSecret(SECRET_NAME);
        let apiKey = secret.value;
        context.log('apiKey:', apiKey.replace(/\w/g, '*'));
        context.res = {
            status: 200,
            body: 'Success'
        };
    } catch (e) {
        context.log(e);
        context.res = {
            status: 500,
            body: 'Error'
        };
    }
};
```

After deploying the Serverless configuration, you might find the Azure Function
throws an error. The Azure Function currently has no permissions to access the secret.
We need to add an access policy in the Key Vault to allow the Azure Function's resource
group to get the secret; see Figure 8-11. The Serverless configuration automatically
creates the resource group for us.

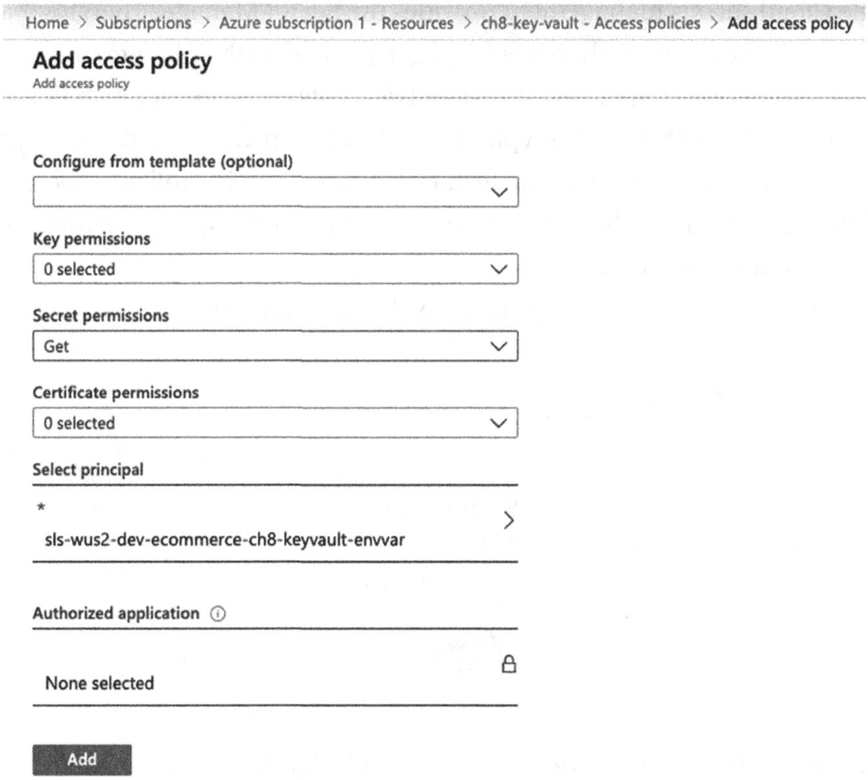

Figure 8-11. *An Example of Creating an Access Policy in Azure Key Vault*

The Azure Function will dynamically obtain the latest secret value every time it executes.

Google Cloud

Again, the AWS Secrets Manager had an appropriate balance between encryption and convenience. Therefore, we will focus on using the Google Cloud secrets management[8] feature that provides a similar capability.

---

[8]"Secrets Management." Google. `https://cloud.google.com/solutions/secrets-management`

Google Cloud secrets management provides the Secret Manager,[9] Berglas,[10] and HashiCorp Vault[11] services. With Secret Manager, we specify the plaintext value, and the service encrypts the value when at rest and decrypts when in use. With Berglas, we leverage Google Cloud KMS for encryption and decryption and store the encrypted data in Google Cloud Storage or Secret Manager. HashiCorp Vault is similar to Secret Manager and provides additional capabilities (e.g., identity-based access). We will focus on the Secret Manager in this section.

We start by enabling the Secret Manager API; see Figure 8-12.

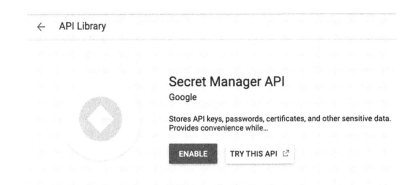

Figure 8-12. *An Example of Enabling the Secret Manager API*

We can now create a new secret for the API key; see Figure 8-13.

[9]"Secret Manager." Google. `https://cloud.google.com/secret-manager`
[10]"Berglas." GitHub. `https://github.com/GoogleCloudPlatform/berglas`
[11]"Vault." HashiCorp. `www.vaultproject.io`

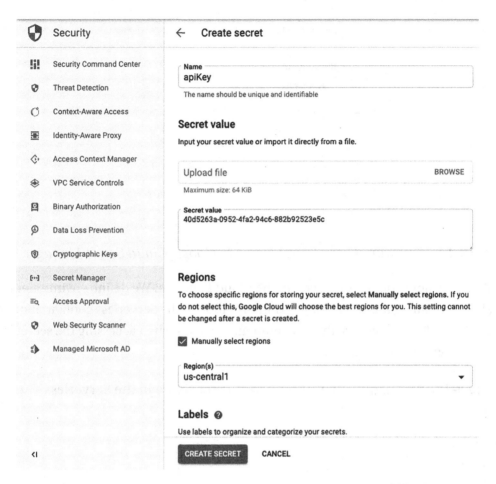

Figure 8-13. *An Example of Creating a New Secret in Google Cloud Secret Manager*

We view the secret details to obtain the secret name; see Figure 8-14. We will use the secret name in the Serverless configuration.

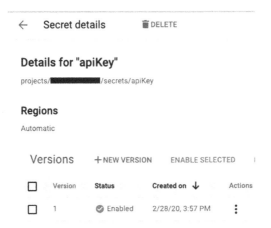

Figure 8-14. *An Example of a Secret Name in Google Cloud Secret Manager*

We now want to obtain the secret in the Cloud Function. We define environment variables containing the Secret Manager information in the Serverless configuration file; see Listing 8-16. We reference the environment variables when accessing the secret from Secret Manager; see Listing 8-17.

Listing 8-16. An Example of Defining the Secret Name in the Serverless Configuration

```
functions:
  first:
    handler: chargeCC
    events:
      - http: path
    environment:
      SECRET_NAME: projects/123456789012/secrets/apiKey/versions/latest
```

Listing 8-17. An Example of Accessing the Secret Manager Secret in the Cloud Function

```
const { SecretManagerServiceClient } = require(
    '@google-cloud/secret- manager');
const client = new SecretManagerServiceClient();
const { SECRET_NAME } = process.env;
exports.chargeCC = async (request, response) => {
```

```
try {
    const [version] = await client.accessSecretVersion({
        name: SECRET_NAME
    });
    const apiKey = version.payload.data.toString('utf8');
    console.log('apiKey:', apiKey.replace(/\w/g, '*'));
    response.status(200).send('Success');
} catch (e) {
    console.error(e);
    response.status(500).send('Error');
}
};
```

After deploying the Serverless configuration, you might find the Cloud Function throws an error. The Cloud Function currently has no permissions to access the secret. We need to add an IAM policy to allow the Cloud Function's service account to access the secret; Google Cloud automatically creates a default service account that Cloud Functions use.

We can obtain the service account by viewing the Cloud Function; see Figure 8-15.

Figure 8-15. *An Example of Obtaining the Cloud Function Service Account*

We create an IAM permission granting the service account permission to access the Secret Manager secret; see Figure 8-16. We give the service account the "Secret Manager Secret Access" permission.

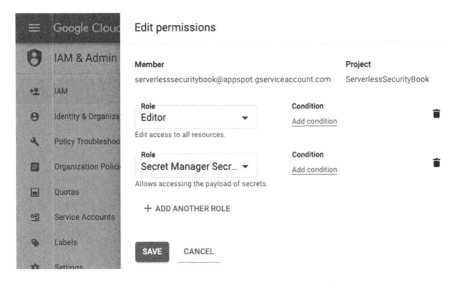

Figure 8-16. *An Example of Defining IAM Permissions for Secret Manager and Service Account*

The Cloud Function will dynamically obtain the latest secret value every time it executes.

Key Takeaways

We discussed how protecting secrets is essential because they might contain information that might have a business impact if accidentally disclosed. The first step to safeguarding secrets is removing that information from the function code. The next step is storing that information elsewhere and protecting it.

We found that putting the secrets in the Serverless configuration was insufficient in protecting them. We might save the Serverless configuration in a repository, but then the secret is no longer a secret. Therefore, we needed to find a different method for securely storing the secrets.

We explored three approaches in AWS to protect the secrets: SSM, KMS, and Secrets Manager. Using SSM allowed us to get the secret in multiple ways, but using the SecureString parameter and decrypting its value in the Lambda function code proved the best with this service. Using KMS allowed us to encrypt the secret, store it as an environment variable in the Serverless configuration, and decrypt it in the Lambda function code. Using Secrets Manager allowed us to securely store the secret when at rest using a CMK and decrypt it in the Lambda function. We selected the Secrets Manager approach as having the best balance between security and convenience.

We explored the Azure Key Vault secrets and Google Cloud Secret Manager because they have a comparable approach to that of the AWS Secrets Manager. We found both services allow us to securely store the secret when at rest and decrypt it in the function. We briefly discussed the other approaches Azure and Google Cloud provide.

With whatever approach we decide to use, it should provide the desired balance between security and convenience while meeting the customer and business requirements.

CHAPTER 9

Authentication and Authorization

In this chapter, we will define authentication and authorization. We will review different approaches for implementing both in our serverless application, discuss where those approaches might apply, and provide some security practices for each. Lastly, we will review services and capabilities that AWS, Azure, and Google Cloud provide to help us implement authentication and authorization.

Authentication and Authorization

Authentication and authorization are similar yet different. Authentication (AuthN) allows us to verify that the person/machine wanting access is who he/she/it claims to be. Authorization (AuthZ) determines whether the user is allowed to access a resource and perform an action. For example, a user will first authenticate with a username and password. After that, the user might only have the authorization to view and edit the account profile page but not view or edit any other pages. Authentication without authorization allows the user to perform any action, whereas authorization without authentication results in no control of accessing resources.

We want to use authentication to protect unwanted parties from accessing our serverless infrastructure. We might typically think of authentication like a username and password before establishing a user session. This paradigm varies slightly in a serverless environment because serverless functions do not retain state. After all, the computing resource is short-lived. In contrast, a traditional website has servers that remain online for a significant period. We also have little control over how the cloud provider manages serverless computing resources. This means features like caching and session management might no longer be available or difficult to establish. We want to adopt proven authentication mechanisms for serverless environments.

© Miguel A. Calles 2020
M. Calles, *Serverless Security*, https://doi.org/10.1007/978-1-4842-6100-2_9

We want to use authorization to protect certain authenticated parties from accessing protected capabilities in our serverless infrastructure. We might typically think of authorization as allowing administrator accounts to have access to more capabilities (e.g., creating and deleting accounts) and regular accounts to have access to specific capabilities (e.g., modifying the account profile). We will want to implement authorization for each serverless function and capability to ensure the function only executes with the proper privileges.

We will discuss general authentication and authorization techniques using methods available within AWS, Azure, and Google Cloud.

The Importance of Authentication and Authorization

The OWASP Top Ten[1] and the Interpretation for Serverless[2] include broken authentication[3] as the second most critical security risk to web applications and serverless technologies. Broken authentication is a scenario where a resource (e.g., a function) is accessible without authentication, or the authentication is bypassed or spoofed. Failure to adequately implement authentication could have undesired consequences.

Let's assume we have a function that processes customer refunds. The billing department requested to have a process where returns are authorized by sending an email to a specific email address. The email address triggers the serverless function that processes refunds. The email address serves as the authentication. The authentication process becomes broken when someone learns the email address and the format of the email content used to provide the refund information. Another common situation might be using a messaging platform (e.g., Slack[4]) that integrates a webhook that triggers a serverless function.[5]

---

[1]"OWASP Top Ten 2017." OWASP. 2017. `https://owasp.org/www-project-top-ten/ OWASP_Top_Ten_2017/`

[2]"OWASP Top 10 (2017): Interpretation for Serverless." OWASP. 2017. `https://github.com/ OWASP/Serverless-Top-10-Project/raw/master/OWASP-Top-10-Serverless- Interpretation-en.pdf`

[3]"A2:2017-Broken Authentication." OWASP Top Ten 2017. OWASP. 2017. `https://owasp.org/ www-project-top-ten/OWASP_Top_Ten_2017/Top_10-2017_A2-Broken_Authentication.html`

[4]Slack is a registered trademark of Slack Technologies, Inc.

[5]"Creating an AWS Lambda Function and API Endpoint." Slack. `https://api.slack.com/ tutorials/aws-lambda`

Implementing authorization might provide a layer of protection when someone breaks the authentication. Let's suppose the serverless function performs authorization by checking the sender's email address and the refund amount. Receiving an email from the incorrect email address will result in a rejection. Requesting a larger refund than the transaction amount might also result in a rejection. Implementing authorization in our serverless systems limits the extent of damage after broken authentication.

General Principles

We will review the different methods for authentication and authorization, scenarios where they might best be applicable, and security practices to consider.

Username and Password

Having an individual provide a username and password is a typical way to authenticate. The serverless application offers a secure way to submit the username and password; see Listing 9-1.

Listing 9-1. An Example of a Username and Password Submitted from a Web Login Form

```
POST /login HTTP/1.1
Host: myapp.com
Content-Type: application/x-www-form-urlencoded

username=myusername&password=mypassword
```

The application verifies those credentials against a user database or authentication system. The application will respond appropriately depending on successful or unsuccessful authentication.

Usernames and passwords are useful for authenticating persons rather than machines. A person will typically provide their username and password in a web login form, and the serverless application will use that data accordingly. Having a machine provide a username and password is undesirable because that data must be stored somewhere and becomes vulnerable to accidental disclosure.

When using usernames and passwords, we should consider the following security practices:

- Require strong passwords or passphrases.[6]

- Add two-step or multi-factor authentication, at a minimum, for specific actions (e.g., changing a username, email, password, or accessing or changing any sensitive data).

- Hash and salt your passwords before saving them in a database.

- Transmit the username and password using HTTPS.

Many of the authentication approaches we will discuss in the following sections will leverage usernames and passwords.

Application Programming Interface (API) Keys

API keys are static values used for authentication and authorization. Think of them as passwords that machines use to log in to another machine. We might use them for authorization by assigning different API keys to access different capabilities.

To use an API key for authentication or authorization, you can specify its value in the header or the content body of the HTTP(S) request. For example, the header could contain a UUID API key, while the JSON body contains a SHA-256 API key; see Listing 9-2.

Listing 9-2. An Example of Using API Keys in the HTTP Header and Body

```
POST /api/authentication HTTP/1.1
Host: ecommerce.com
key1: 4fff3782-999b-4666-90b3-4f04700da00e

{ "apikey": "2413FB3709B05939F04CF2E92F7D0897FC2596F9AD0B8A9EA855C7BFEBAAE892" }
```

We might use the API key in the header for authentication; any request with the correct API key will authenticate the request. We might use the API key in the body for authorization to grant or deny access depending on the value. We can use one API for both authentication and authorization or use multiple API keys; it depends on the use case and the desired level of security.

---

[6]"NIST Special Publication 800-63B: Digital Identity Guidelines." National Institute of Standards and Technology. June 2017. https://pages.nist.gov/800-63-3/sp800-63b.html

API keys are useful for machine-to-machine authentication and granting external access. Machine-to-machine authentication is where two servers, services, and so on exchange information. In serverless, it would be two serverless resources communicating between themselves. External access would be giving an external party (e.g., a customer) access to an API where it can query your system for information. There are numerous more scenarios we could explore. However, we will proceed to explore other authentication mechanisms.

When using API keys, we should consider the following security practices:

- Use a proven algorithm to generate API keys like Secure Hash Algorithm 2 (SHA-2)[7] or Universally Unique Identifier (UUID).[8]

- Avoid using weaker algorithms like MD5[9] and SHA-1[10] that someone can easily break.[11]

- Rotate (i.e., change) the API key periodically as frequent as every 60 to 90 days or, preferably, no longer than yearly.

- Use different API keys for different groups of functions or microservices, which might be one or multiple Serverless configurations.

- Store the API keys in a safe location.

- Encrypt keys when at rest or in transit. We can leverage the concepts for protecting secrets from Chapter 8.

Since API keys are static (unchanged) for long periods, the benefit of time sits with a malicious actor who is attempting to discover them. We must be prudent when and where we use the API keys and for what duration they remain active.

---

[7]"US Secure Hash Algorithms (SHA and HMAC-SHA)." D. Eastlake 3rd. Request for Comments: 4634. July 2006. https://tools.ietf.org/html/rfc4634

[8]"A Universally Unique IDentifier (UUID) URN Namespace." P. Leach. Request for Comments: 4122. IETF. July 2005. https://tools.ietf.org/html/rfc4122

[9]"The MD5 Message-Digest Algorithm." R. Rivest. Request for Comments: 1321. IETF. April 1992. https://tools.ietf.org/html/rfc1321

[10]"US Secure Hash Algorithm 1 (SHA)." D. Eastlake, 3rd. Request for Comments: 3174. IETF. September 2001. https://tools.ietf.org/html/rfc3174

[11]"How to Break MD5 and Other Hash Functions." Xiaoyun Wang and Hongbo Yu. Shandong University, Jinan 250100, China. http://merlot.usc.edu/csac-f06/papers/Wang05a.pdf

JavaScript Object Notation (JSON) Web Tokens (JWT)

We can use JSON Web Tokens[12] for authorization. They are used to represent "claims" between two parties. A claim contains information about one of the parties, usually the user, and its relationship to the other entity. A claim could contain the user's identifier, name, and additional information (e.g., user type). Both parties exchange the information by encoding the claims in a JSON object. The data is securely transmitted by signing the data with a Message Authentication Code (MAC)[13] and then encrypting it with a public-private key pair using a secure encryption algorithm (e.g., RSA or ECDSA).[14] The JWT information has three parts: the header, the payload that contains claims about the user, and the signature; see Listing 9-3.

Listing 9-3. An Example of the JSON Web Token (JWT) Parts

```
# Header (algorithm and type)
{
  "alg": "HS512",
  "typ": "JWT"
}
# Payload (data)
{
  "sub": "da618d53-4dbe-4871-8aab-a77ef4fa155d",
  "name": "Mike Streets"
}
#.Signature
HMACSHA512(
  base64UrlEncode(header) + "." +
  base64UrlEncode(payload),
  my-512-bit-secret
)
```

---

[12]"JSON Web Token (JWT)." M. Jones. Request for Comments: 7519. IETF. May 2015. `https://tools.ietf.org/html/rfc7519` and "Introduction to JSON Web Tokens." JWT.io. `https://jwt.io/introduction`

[13]"JSON Web Signature (JWS)." M. Jones. Request for Comments: 7515. IETF. May 2015. `https://tools.ietf.org/html/rfc7515`

[14]"JSON Web Encryption (JWE)." M. Jones. Request for Comments: 7516. IETF. May 2015. `https://tools.ietf.org/html/rfc7516`

The three parts are Base64-encoded,[15] signed with the signature, and joined together by periods; see Listing 9-4.[16]

Listing 9-4. An Example of an Encoded JWT

```
# All the characters are in one line.
# There is no text wrapping.
eyJhbGciOiJIUzUxMiIsInR5cCI6IkpXVCJ9.eyJzdWIiOiJkYTYxOGQ1MyOoZGJlLTQ4NzEtO
GFhYi1hNzdlZjRmYTE1NWQiLCJuYW1lIjoiTWlrZSBTdHJlZXRzIno.z-_xQHuNLP-dYx2SjWM
fRBkayDc5_LDXsahYyGYdhviH7JVORi8bdtb6sYAoYswmiaNvaUaILGzCuON8R1Q9Iw
```

If any part of the message is altered, the signature becomes invalid, and the data is no longer trust worthy.[17]

When a user successfully logs in to a system, the system will send the user a JWT. The user (or the web application) should securely store the JWT. The user will submit the JWT in a header to access protected pages; see Listing 9-5.

Listing 9-5. An Example of a JWT Authorization Header (All in One Line)

```
# All the characters are in one line.
# There is no text wrapping.
Authorization: Bearer eyJhbGciOiJIUzUxMiIsInR5cCI6IkpXVCJ9.eyJzdWIiOiJkYTY
xOGQ1MyOoZGJlLTQ4NzEtOGFhYi1hNzdlZjRmYTE1NWQiLCJuYW1lIjoiTWlrZSBTdHJlZXRzI
no.z-_xQHuNLP-dYx2SjWMfRBkayDc5_LDXsahYyGYdhviH7JVORi8bdtb6sYAoYswmiaNvaUa
ILGzCuON8R1Q9Iw
```

---

[15]"The Base16, Base32, and Base64 Data Encodings." S. Josefsson. Request for Comments: 4648. IETF. October 2006. https://tools.ietf.org/html/rfc4648

[16]I used the JWT.io Debugger to generate the encoded message. https://jwt.io/#debugger-io? token=eyJhbGciOiJIUzUxMiIsInR5cCI6IkpXVCJ9.eyJzdWIiOiJkYTYxOGQ1MyOoZGJlLTQ4NzEtO GFhYi1hNzdlZjRmYTE1NWQiLCJuYW1lIjoiTWlrZSBTdHJlZXRzIno.z-_xQHuNLP-dYx2SjWMfRBkay Dc5_LDXsahYyGYdhviH7JVORi8bdtb6sYAoYswmiaNvaUaILGzCuON8R1Q9Iw

[17]You will see the signing becoming invalid when you modify the encoded message. https:// jwt.io/#debugger-io?token=eyJhbGciOiJIUzUxMiIsInR5cCI6IkpXVCJ9.eyJzdWIiOiJkYTYxO GQ1MyOoZGJlLTQ4NzEtOGFhYi1hNzdlZjRmYTE1NWQiLCJuYW1lIjoiTWlrZSBTdHJlZXRzIno.z-_xQH uNLP-dYx2SjWMfRBkayDc5_LDXsahYyGYdhviH7JVORi8bdtb6sYAoYswmiaNvaUaILGzCuON8R1Q9Iw

JWT is useful for authorization and information exchange. As previously mentioned, a user first authenticates, the authentication server sends the JWT, and the user then uses the JWT to request access to protected APIs and web pages that verify the JWT to authorize access. JWT is useful in information exchange because the sender can use a public/private key pair to sign the token, and the recipient can use the key pair to verify the token.

When using JWT, we should consider the following security practices:

- Use browser session storage instead of local storage because of security concerns.[18]

- Avoid keeping the token longer than needed.

- Verify the JWT algorithm matches the desired algorithm and avoids accepting the "none" algorithm.[19]

- Use a secure key to prevent someone from modifying or creating tokens.[20]

- Validate all claims before authorizing access.[21]

- Expire tokens by including an "exp" claim in the payload.

- Use different types of tokens in different situations by using different values in the header's "typ" property.

JWT provides a simple, lightweight methodology to authorize users. Similarly to API keys, the benefit of time sits with a malicious actor who is attempting to discover a JWT. We must be prudent to limit how long a JWT is valid and increase the difficulty of someone being able to spoof it.

---

[18]"HTML 5 Security." OWASP Cheat Sheet Series Project. OWASP. `https://cheatsheetseries.owasp.org/cheatsheets/HTML5_Security_Cheat_Sheet.html#local-storage`

[19]"Hacking JSON Web Token (JWT)." Rudra Pratap. Medium. `https://medium.com/101-writeups/hacking-json-web-token-jwt-233fe6c862e6`

[20]"A Look at The Draft for JWT Best Current Practices." Sebastian Peyrott. Auth0 Blog. April 11, 2018. `https://auth0.com/blog/a-look-at-the-latest-draft-for-jwt-bcp/`

[21]"A Look at The Draft for JWT Best Current Practices."

Open Authorization (OAuth)

We can use Open Authorization (OAuth)[22,23] for authentication and authorization. OAuth allows us to delegate access to the authorizing server. For example, a user wants to print pictures from Share2Much (a fictitious social networking site) at Pics2Paper (a fictitious photo printing site). In the following example, suppose the social networking site supports OAuth 2.0.

Pics2Paper determines it will accept photos from Share2Much. Pics2Paper requests a client identifier (ID) and client secret from Share2Much. Share2Much provides the authentication URL where it will accept OAuth 2.0 requests. Pics2Paper will use the authentication URL when a user wants to print photos from Share2Much.

When the user wants to print photos, Pics2Paper will redirect the user to the Share2Much authorization URL with additional information: the redirect address (or URI), the client ID, and the request for the authorization code; see Listing 9-6.

Listing 9-6. An Example of OAuth 2.0 Authorization Request

```
GET /auth?response_type=code&client_id=0123456789&redirect_uri=https://
pics2paper.com/oauth/callback HTTP/1.1
Host: share2much.com
```

Share2Much receives the request and asks the user to log in; this is the authentication part. After a successful login, Share2Much will likely will ask the user to confirm whether Pics2Paper should have access to the photos; this is the authorization part. When the user grants the authorization, Share2Much creates an authorization code and redirects the user back to Pics2Paper; see Listing 9-7.

Listing 9-7. An Example of OAuth 2.0 Redirect with the Authorization Code

```
GET /oauth/callback&code=98765 HTTP/1.1
Host: pics2paper.com
```

Pics2Paper uses the authorization code to request the access token from Share2Much; see Listing 9-8.

---

[22]"The OAuth 1.0 Protocol." E. Hammer-Lahav, Ed. Request for Comments: 5849. IETF. April 2010. https://tools.ietf.org/html/rfc5849

[23]"The OAuth 2.0 Authorization Framework." D. Hardt, Ed. Request for Comments: 6749. IETF. October 2012. https://tools.ietf.org/html/rfc6749

Listing 9-8. An Example of Requesting an OAuth 2.0 Access Token

```
POST/oauth/token HTTP/1.1
Host: share2much.com

{
    "grant_type": "authorization-code",
    "client_id": "0123456789",
    "client_secret": "abcdefghijklmn",
    "code": "98765",
    "redirect_uri": "https://pics2paper.com/oauth/callback"
}
```

Share2Much will respond with the access token if the client ID, client secret, and authorization code match its records; see Listing 9-9.

Listing 9-9. An Example of Obtaining an OAuth 2.0 Access Token

```
HTTP/1.1 302 Found
Server: share2much.com

{
    "access_token": "pqrstuvwxyz",
    "refresh_token": "azbycxdweu"
}
```

The user can now access the photos from Share2Much and print them at Pics2Paper using the authorization from the social networking site.[24]

OAuth is useful when you want to get a user's data from another site. The serverless application might need information from the authorizing site. For example, the social networking site can provide information about the user's profile, connections, activity, and more, and it would be more efficient than having the user manually provide it.

---

[24]This YouTube video has a good step-by-step explanation of OAuth 2.0 authorization. "OAuth 2.0 – Part 4." David Rice. July 23, 2010. www.youtube.com/watch?v=OPvQcLzVGFo

When using OAuth, we should consider the following security practices:

- The authorization server should contain the specific redirect URIs it will accept, and the client should provide the redirect URI in its requests to the authorization server.[25]

- The redirect URI should avoid using open redirects that will redirect a user to an unintended website.[26]

- Avoid accepting the authorization code after receiving the initial authorization response.[27]

- Limit the authorization of the access token to the least privileges.[28]

- Expire the access token and request the user to reauthenticate with the authorization server.

OAuth can simplify obtaining user data by requesting it from the website that contains it. Similar to JWT, we should limit the life of the access token. We should also attempt to prevent a malicious attack from redirecting the user to a different site or accessing undesired functionality because the access token authorization has too many privileges.

OpenID Connect (OIDC)

OpenID Connect (OIDC) provides authentication and authorization by leveraging OAuth 2.0 and JWT.[29] A user will log in with an Identity Provider (IdP), which is the

---

[25]"OAuth 2.0 Security Best Current Practice: draft-ietf-oauth-security-topics-05." T. Lodderstedt, Ed. Internet-Draft. IETF. March 18, 2018. https://tools.ietf.org/id/draft-ietf-oauth-security-topics-05.html

[26]"OAuth 2.0 Security Best Current Practice: draft-ietf-oauth-security-topics-05." T. Lodderstedt, Ed. Internet-Draft. IETF. March 18, 2018. https://tools.ietf.org/id/draft-ietf-oauth-security-topics-05.html

[27]"OAuth 2.0 Security Best Current Practice: draft-ietf-oauth-security-topics-14." T. Lodderstedt. Internet-Draft. IETF. February 10, 2020. https://tools.ietf.org/html/draft-ietf-oauth-security-topics-14

[28]"OAuth 2.0 Security Best Current Practice: draft-ietf-oauth-security-topics-14." T. Lodderstedt. Internet-Draft. IETF. February 10, 2020. https://tools.ietf.org/html/draft-ietf-oauth-security-topics-14

[29]"OpenID Connect Core 1.0 incorporating errata set 1." N. Sakimura et al. OpenID. November 8, 2014. https://openid.net/specs/openid-connect-core-1_0.html

OAuth 2.0 authorization server. After a successful login, the user can use the IdP login session to "log in to" another website. The website configuration accepts login information from the IdP. For example, a user can log in to Share2Much by first logging in to the individual's Google account; Google is acting as the IdP.

Share2Much and the IdP (which is Google in this example) follow a similar setup, login, and authorization process, as described for OAuth 2.0. One difference is the IdP can provide an additional token, an identifier (ID) token. This token allows Share2Much to obtain information about the user's account and profile. The ID token is a JWT. Share2Much need not ask the user to log in to access it.

OIDC is useful when you want to use another resource to perform authentication. Our serverless application might not need to implement its authentication for technical and business reasons. Using a third-party login might be more secure than implementing custom authentication, and it enables the company to focus more resources on building the application.

When using OIDC, we should consider the following security practices:

- Use a reputable IdP.

- Expire the access token and a JWT after a predetermined length of time and request the user to reauthenticate with the IdP.

- If the application is linking an OIDC account, it should ask the user to reauthenticate before linking.[30]

- Configure the IdP or select an IdP that conforms to the desired password security policies.[31]

- Configure the IdP or choose an IdP that supports a two-step verification or multi-factor authentication.

OIDC can simplify authentication by having another service that performs that function. Similar to OAuth 2.0 and JWT, we should limit the life of the access token and ID token. We should select an IdP that has strong account security to reduce the risk of a malicious actor using the IdP to access our application.

---

[30]"OpenID Security Best Practices." PauAmma. OpenID Wiki. http://wiki.openid.net/w/ page/12995200/OpenID%20Security%20Best%20Practices

[31]"OpenID Security Best Practices." PauAmma. OpenID Wiki. http://wiki.openid.net/w/ page/12995200/OpenID%20Security%20Best%20Practices

Security Assertion Markup Language (SAML)

We can use Security Assertion Markup Language (SAML)[32] for authentication and authorization similar to how OIDC functions. SAML uses XML instead of JSON. The Share2Much site from the OIDC section also applies in this SAML example.

Share2Much determines it will accept logins from the IdP. Share2Much obtains XML metadata from the IdP that contains the signing certificate, the client ID, callback URI, and other configuration information; see Listing 9-10.

Listing 9-10. An Example SAML Identity Provider Metadata Document

```
<?xml version="1.0" encoding="UTF-8"?>
<md:EntityDescriptor entityID="http://idp.com/nc357exkzcJJ31fp5VB9"
xmlns:md="urn:oasis:names:tc:SAML:2.0:metadata">
    <md:IDPSSODescriptor WantAuthnRequestsSigned="false" protocolSupport
    Enumeration="urn:oasis:names:tc:SAML:2.0:protocol">
        <md:KeyDescriptor use="signing">
            <ds:KeyInfo xmlns:ds="http://www.w3.org/2000/09/xmldsig#">
                <ds:X509Data>
                    <ds:X509Certificate>MIIDpDCCAo...v7kaH
                    </ds:X509Certificate>
                </ds:X509Data>
            </ds:KeyInfo>
        </md:KeyDescriptor>
        <md:NameIDFormat> urn:oasis:names:tc:SAML:1.1:nameid-format:
        emailAddress</md:NameIDFormat>
        <NameIDFormat> urn:oasis:names:tc:SAML:2.0:nameid-format:
        persistent</NameIDFormat>
        <NameIDFormat> urn:oasis:names:tc:SAML:2.0:nameid-format:
        transient</NameIDFormat>
```

---

[32]"Security Assertion Markup Language (SAML) 2.0 Profile for OAuth 2.0 Client Authentication and Authorization Grants." B. Campbell. Request for Comments: 7522. IETF. May 2015. `https://tools.ietf.org/html/rfc7522`

```
        <md:SingleSignOnService Binding="urn:oasis:names:tc:SAML:2.0:
        bindings:HTTP-POST" Location="https://idp.com/app/
        share2much/1fpexBknc5zc957/sso/saml"/>
        <md:SingleSignOnService Binding="urn:oasis:names:tc:SAML:2.0:
        bindings:HTTP-Redirect" Location="https://idp.com/app/
        share2much/1fpexBknc5zc957/sso/saml"/>
    </md:IDPSSODescriptor>
</md:EntityDescriptor>
```

The IdP and Share2Much could be configured in different ways. One way is to have the user first log in to the IdP directly and click the Share2Much app. Another way is to have the user first visit Share2Much and try to log in with the IdP. The user is redirected to the IdP to log in and given access to Share2Much after a successful login. This is a similar process to OAuth 2.0 except the data is transmitted using XML documents.

SAML is useful when you want to use another resource to perform authentication; corporations and IdPs are using SAML heavily for Federated Identities and Single Sign-On (SSO) in their organizations.

When using SAML, we should consider the following security practices:

- Use a reputable IdP.

- When using SAML for SSO, the application should not accept username logins, password resets, and email address changes, but rather rely on the IdP.[33]

- Expire the access token after a predetermined length of time and request the user to reauthenticate with the IdP.

- Choose a robust X.509v3 certificate based on the SHA-2 algorithm to verify the SAML XML metadata.

- Send all SAML communications over TLS v1.2.[34]

---

[33]"Best Practices & FAQs." OneLogin Developers. https://developers.onelogin.com/saml/best-practices-and-faqs

[34]"SAML Security Best Practices." SecureAuth Documentation. https://docs.secureauth.com/display/KBA/SAML+Security+Best+Practices

- Sign the SAML authentication request to the IdP and configure the IdP to check the signing.[35]

- Configure the IdP or select an IdP that conforms to the desired password security policies.

SAML can simplify authentication, especially when an enterprise has many web applications. Similar to OIDC, we should limit the life of the access token. We should select an IdP that has strong account security to reduce the risk of a malicious actor using the IdP to access our application.

Amazon Web Services

AWS provides authentication and authorization with the following services: Amazon API Gateway, Amazon Cognition, AppSync, and IAM Identity Providers. Each service supports a different use case.

Amazon Gateway allows us to use different authentication and authorization methods:[36]

- Using resource policies to restrict access based on AWS account, source IP address, or whether the request originated from a Virtual Private Cloud (VPC)

- Using authorizers to verify the authorization before a Lambda function is triggered

- Using Amazon Cognito user pools for authorization and authentication

To authorize an AWS account to execute functions via the API Gateway, we can whitelist an AWS account using a resource policy; see Listing 9-11.

---

[35]"SAML Security Best Practices." SecureAuth Documentation. `https://docs.secureauth.com/display/KBA/SAML+Security+Best+Practices`

[36]"Controlling and Managing Access to a REST API in API Gateway." Amazon API Gateway Developer Guide. Amazon Web Services. `https://docs.aws.amazon.com/apigateway/latest/developerguide/apigateway-control-access-to-api.html`

Listing 9-11. An API Gateway AWS Account Whitelist Template

```
{
  "Version": "2012-10-17",
  "Statement": [{
    "Effect": "Allow",
    "Principal": {
      "AWS": [
        "arn:aws:iam::{{awsAcctId}}:root",
        "arn:aws:iam::{{awsAcctId}}:user/{{otherAwsUser}}",
        "arn:aws:iam::{{awsAcctId}}:role/{{otherAwsRole}}"
      ]
    },
    "Action": "execute-api:Invoke",
    "Resource": [
      "execute-api:/{{stage}}/{{httpVerb}}/{{resourcePath}}"
    ]
  }]
}
```

To authorize IP addresses to execute functions via the API Gateway, we can whitelist and blacklist IP addresses using a resource policy; see Listing 9-12.

Listing 9-12. An API Gateway IP Address Whitelist and Blacklist Template

```
{
  "Version": "2012-10-17",
  "Statement": [{
      "Effect": "Allow",
      "Principal": "*",
      "Action": "execute-api:Invoke",
      "Resource": [
        "execute-api:/{{stage}}/{{httpVerb}}/{{resourcePath}}"
      ]
    },
```

```
{
  "Effect": "Deny",
  "Principal": "*",
  "Action": "execute-api:Invoke",
  "Resource": [
    "execute-api:/{{stage}}/{{httpVerb}}/{{resourcePath}}"
  ],
  "Condition": {
    "IpAddress": {
      "aws:SourceIp": [
        "{{sourceIpOrCIDRBlock}}",
        "{{sourceIpOrCIDRBlock}}"
      ]
    }
  }
}
]
}
```

To authorize a VPC to execute functions via the API Gateway, we can whitelist a VPC using a resource policy; see Listing 9-13.

Listing 9-13. An API Gateway VPC Whitelist Template

```
{
  "Version": "2012-10-17",
  "Statement": [{
    "Effect": "Deny",
    "Principal": "*",
    "Action": "execute-api:Invoke",
    "Resource": [
      "execute-api:/{{stage}}/{{httpVerb}}/{{resourcePath}}"
    ],
    "Condition": {
      "StringNotEquals": {
        "aws:sourceVpc": "{{vpcID}}"
      }
```

```
    }
  },
  {
    "Effect": "Allow",
    "Principal": "*",
    "Action": "execute-api:Invoke",
    "Resource": [
      "execute-api:/{{stage}}/{{httpVerb}}/{{resourcePath}}"
    ]
  }
 ]
}
```

To use a JWT to authorize the execution of functions via the API Gateway, we create a custom authorizer Lambda function and configure the API Gateway to verify the JWT authorization before executing the target Lambda function. The authorizer Lambda function will verify the JWT; see Listing 9-14.

Listing 9-14. An Open Source Example Showing a Lambda JWT Custom Authorizer[37]

```
const jwt = require('jsonwebtoken');

console.log('Loading jwtAuthorizer');

exports.handler = function (event, context, callback) {
  console.log(
    'Received event',
    JSON.stringify(event, null, 2)
  );

  // remove the 'Bearer ' prefix from the auth token
  const token = event.authorizationToken.replace(/Bearer /g, '');

  // parse all API options from the event,
  // in case we need some of them
```

---

[37]Copyright 2017 Niko Kobler. The code is licensed under the MIT License. https://github.com/serverlessbuch/jwtAuthorizr/blob/master/index.js

```
  const apiOptions = getApiOptions(event);
  console.log(
    'API Options',
    JSON.stringify(apiOptions, null, 2)
  );

  // config data to check the content of the token and
  // public key to verify the signature of the token
  const config = {
    audience: process.env.TOKEN_AUDIENCE,
    issuer: process.env.TOKEN_ISSUER,
  };
  const secret = process.env.TOKEN_SECRET;

  // verify the token with publicKey and config and
  // return proper AWS policy document
  jwt.verify(token, secret, config, (err, verified) => {
    if (err) {
      console.error('JWT Error', err, err.stack);
      callback(
        null,
        denyPolicy('anonymous', event.methodArn),
      );
    } else {
      callback(
        null,
        allowPolicy(verified.sub, event.methodArn),
      );
    }
  });
};

const getApiOptions = function (event) {
  const apiOptions = {};
  const tmp = event.methodArn.split(':');
  const apiGatewayArnTmp = tmp[5].split('/');
```

```
  apiOptions.awsAccountId = tmp[4];
  apiOptions.region = tmp[3];
  apiOptions.restApiId = apiGatewayArnTmp[0];
  apiOptions.stageName = apiGatewayArnTmp[1];
  return apiOptions;
};

const denyPolicy = function (principalId, resource) {
  return generatePolicy(principalId, 'Deny', resource);
};

const allowPolicy = function (principalId, resource) {
  return generatePolicy(principalId, 'Allow', resource);
};

const generatePolicy = function (
  principalId,
  effect,
  resource
) {
  const authResponse = {};
  authResponse.principalId = principalId;
  if (effect && resource) {
    const policyDocument = {};
    // '2012-10-17' is the default version
    policyDocument.Version = '2012-10-17';
    policyDocument.Statement = [];
    const statementOne = {};
    // 'execute-api:Invoke' is the default action
    statementOne.Action = 'execute-api:Invoke';
    statementOne.Effect = effect;
    statementOne.Resource = resource;
    policyDocument.Statement[0] = statementOne;
    authResponse.policyDocument = policyDocument;
  }
  return authResponse;
};
```

We define the custom authorizer function in our Serverless configuration and require other functions to use it; see Listing 9-15.

Listing 9-15. An Example of Using a Custom Authorizer Function

```
functions:
  authorizer:
    handler: src/authorizer.handler
  protectedFunction:
    handler: src/protectedFunction.handler
    events:
      - http:
          path: protected
          method: post
          authorizer: ${self:custom.authorizerClient}
            name: authorizer
            resultTtlInSeconds: 0
            identitySource: method.request.header.ACCESS_TOKEN
```

AWS offers Amazon Cognito for authentication and authorization. Cognito supports OAuth 2.0, SAML, and OIDC. We can use Cognito User Pools, social IdPs[38] (e.g., Google, Facebook,[39] and Amazon), SAML IdPs[40] (e.g., Microsoft Active Directory and Shibboleth[41]), and OIDC IdPs[42] (e.g., Salesforce[43] and Ping Identity[44]). To create a user pool and require a function to use a user pool, we specify the user pool in our Serverless configuration; see Listing 9-16.

---

[38]"Adding Social Identity Providers to a User Pool." Amazon Cognito Developer Guide. Amazon Web Services. https://docs.aws.amazon.com/cognito/latest/developerguide/cognito-user-pools-social-idp.html

[39]Facebook is a registered trademark of Facebook, Inc.

[40]"Adding SAML Identity Providers to a User Pool." Amazon Cognito Developer Guide. Amazon Web Services. https://docs.aws.amazon.com/cognito/latest/developerguide/cognito-user-pools-saml-idp.html

[41]Shibboleth is a registered trademark of Internet2.

[42]"Adding OIDC Identity Providers to a User Pool." Amazon Cognito Developer Guide. Amazon Web Services. https://docs.aws.amazon.com/cognito/latest/developerguide/cognito-user-pools-oidc-idp.html

[43]Salesforce is a registered trademark of Salesforce.com, inc.

[44]Ping Identity is a registered trademark of Ping Identity Corporation.

Listing 9-16. An Example of Using an Amazon Cognito User Pool in a Serverless Configuration

```
functions:
  postAuthentication:
    handler: postAuthentication.handler
    events:
      - cognitoUserPool:
          pool: Chapter09UserPool
          trigger: PostAuthentication
```

If our application uses AppSync instead of API Gateway, AppSync supports custom API keys, AWS IAM, OIDC, and Amazon Cognito user pools for authentication and authorization.[45]

We can require all requests to use an API Gateway API key for authorization before triggering the functions. We can enable this functionality by updating the Serverless configuration to automatically create an API key and require the function to use the said API key; see Listing 9-17.[46]

Listing 9-17. An Example of Enabling API Keys in the API Gateway Serverless Configuration

```
provider:
  apiKeys:
    - authz # key name, API Gateway auto generates key value
functions:
  myFunction:
    handler: myFunction.handler
    events:
      - http:
          path: myFunctionNeedsAnApiKey.
          method: get
          private: true
```

[45]"Security." AppSync Developer Guide. Amazon Web Services. https://docs.aws.amazon.com/appsync/latest/devguide/security.html

[46]"API Gateway." Serverless Docs. https://serverless.com/framework/docs/providers/aws/events/apigateway/#setting-api-keys-for-your-rest-api

The HTTP request must contain the API key in the header for the API Gateway to authorize the Lambda function execution; see Listing 9-18.

Listing 9-18. An Example of Including the API Key in the HTTP Request

```
GET /login HTTP/1.1
Host: myapp.com
Content-Type: application/x-www-form-urlencoded
x-api-key: myAutoGeneratedApiKey
```

The different AWS authentication and authorization capabilities provide us with options to choose the appropriate methods that meet our technical and business requirements.

Azure

Azure provides authentication and authorization with the following services: Azure Functions, Azure API Management, and Azure App Service. Each service supports a different use case.

Azure Functions allow us to use authorization keys (similar to API keys) to authorize executing a function and the authorization level.[47] A function configured to use a function authorization level must have the matching API key in the HTTP request before it runs. A function set to use an admin authorization level must have the master admin key in the HTTP request before it runs, and it will have administrator-level privileges. We must use the admin authorization key with caution. A function can have an anonymous authorization level and will trigger without a key. We specify the desired authorization level in the Serverless configuration; see Listing 9-19.

Listing 9-19. An Example Serverless Configuration with the Different Azure Function Authorization Levels

```
anonymousAuthLevel:
  handler: src/handlers/anonymousAuthLevel.handler
  events:
```

---

[47]"Azure Functions HTTP trigger." Azure Functions documentation. Microsoft. https://docs.
microsoft.com/en-us/azure/azure-functions/functions-bindings-http-webhook-trigger
?tabs=javascript#authorization-keys

```
    - http: true
      x-azure-settings:
        methods:
          - GET
        authLevel: anonymous
  functionAuthLevel:
    handler: src/handlers/functionAuthLevel.handler
    events:
      - http: true
        x-azure-settings:
          methods:
            - GET
          authLevel: function
  adminAuthLevel:
    handler: src/handlers/adminAuthLevel.handler
    events:
      - http: true
        x-azure-settings:
          methods:
            - GET
          authLevel: admin
```

Azure API Management allows us to use an API gateway to redirect triggers to Azure Functions. We can use API Management policies to restrict how the functions are triggered.[48] We can use access restriction policies to verify a JWT, limit access by IP address, and set limits and quotas. We can use authentication policies to authenticate requests via multiple methods. We can use basic authentication (i.e., username and password). We can accept a client certificate. Or, we can use a back-end service (e.g., Microsoft Graph, Azure Resource Manager, Azure Key Vault, Azure Service Bus, Azure Blob storage, or Azure SQL) via an access token from Azure Active Directory. We can define the API Management access policies after we deploy the Serverless configuration; see Figures 9-1and 9-2.

---

[48]"API Management policies." API Management documentation. Microsoft. `https://docs.microsoft.com/en-us/azure/api-management/api-management-policies`

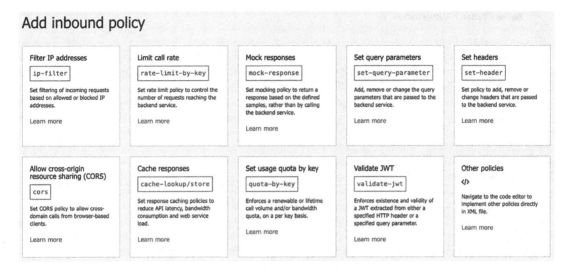

Figure 9-1. *An Example of Defining Azure API Management Access Policies*

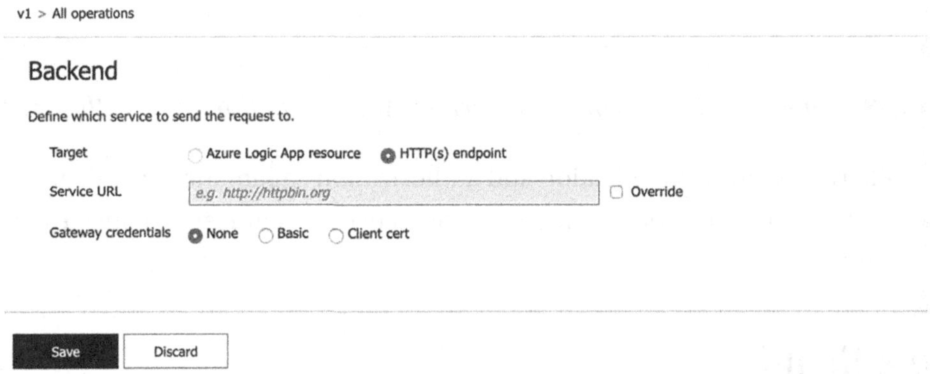

Figure 9-2. *An Example of Defining an Azure API Management Back-End Policy*

Azure App Service allows us to enable OAuth 2.0 or OIDC for authentication and authorization; see Figure 9-3. We can integrate our application with Azure Active Directory and social IdPs (i.e., Microsoft, Facebook, Google, and Twitter[49]). At the time of this writing, we need to manually configure the App Service authentication after we deploy the Serverless configuration.

---

[49]Twitter is a registered trademark of Twitter, Inc.

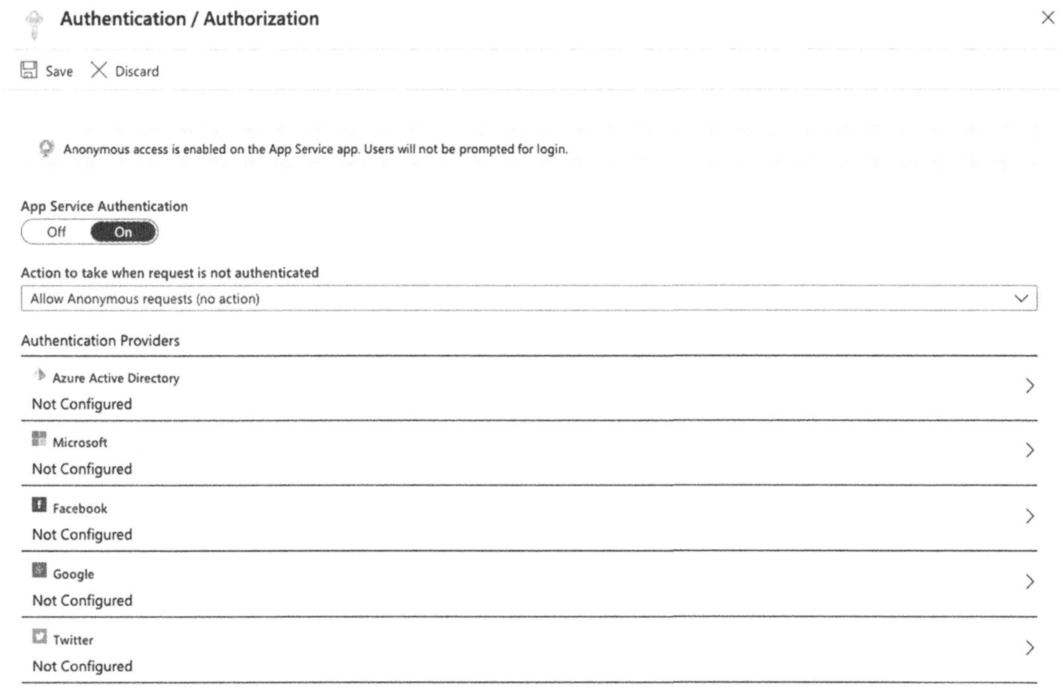

Figure 9-3. *An Example of Azure App Service Authentication and Authorization*

The different Azure authentication and authorization capabilities provide us with options to choose the appropriate methods that meet our technical and business requirements.

Google Cloud

Google Cloud provides authentication and authorization with the following capabilities and services: environment service accounts,[50] Google Cloud Endpoints, and Identity Platform. Each service supports a different use case.

We can use environment service accounts to allow Google Cloud Function to access other Google Cloud resources. We instantiate a client for the target Google Cloud resources (e.g., Google Cloud Storage) in the Cloud Function code; see Listing 9-20. We update the environment service account IAM permissions to grant access to target resources. See the Google Cloud Secret Manager code in Chapter 8 for a full example.

---

[50]"Authentication overview." Get started with Google Cloud. Google Cloud. `https://cloud.google.com/docs/authentication`

Listing 9-20. An Example of Instantiating a Google Cloud Storage Client in the Google Cloud Function Code

```
const {Storage} = require('@google-cloud/storage');
const storage = new Storage();
```

Google Cloud Endpoints allows us to use the following authentication and authorization solutions: API keys, Firebase authentication, Auth0,[51] Google ID token authentication, Okta,[52] custom OAuth 2.0 IdP, and service accounts (for authentication between Google Cloud services). We use Cloud Endpoints as an API gateway to trigger Cloud Functions. At the time of this writing, Cloud Endpoints are unsupported by the Serverless Framework and use the Google Cloud SDK.[53]

Google Cloud Identity allows us to use Google as a SAML IdP to integrate into an application. We configure our serverless web application to support SAML and accept logins from our Google Cloud Identity IdP.[54] At the time of this writing, the Serverless Framework does not support Cloud Identity.

The different Google Cloud authentication and authorization capabilities provide us with options to choose the appropriate methods that meet our technical and business requirements.

Key Takeaways

We started by describing the difference between authentication (AuthN) and authorization (AuthZ). Authentication helps our application determine the person or machine is who they claim. Authorization helps our application assess whether an authenticated person or machine can access a resource or perform an action. We reviewed different approaches for implementing authentication and authorization.

We can use usernames and passwords, API keys, and OpenID Connect and SAML to implement authentication in our application. We can apply one or more of these approaches. We typically will perform usernames and passwords, OpenID Connect, and

---

[51]Auth0 is a registered trademark of Auth0, Inc.

[52]Okta is a registered trademark of Okta, Inc.

[53]"Getting Started with Endpoints for Cloud Functions." Cloud Endpoints documentation. Google. https://cloud.google.com/endpoints/docs/openapi/get-started-cloud-functions

[54]"Set up your own custom SAML application." Cloud Identity Help. Google. https://support.google.com/cloudidentity/answer/6087519?hl=en&ref_topic=7558947

SAML to authenticate persons from the web browser. We use API keys to authenticate machine-to-machine interaction and typically not to authenticate a browser session. We want to authenticate when we have resources and actions we want to protect and restrict anonymous users from accessing.

We can use API keys, JWT, OpenID Connect, and SAML to implement authorization in our application. We can use the API key value to determine the level of authorization: read-only, limited, or escalated privileges. We use JWT to securely store the result of the authentication in the web browser and to notify the back-end functions that the user is authorized to perform actions. We can outsource implementing authentication by using OpenID Connect and SAML, which provide both authentication and authorization. Both will require the user to authenticate with an Identity Provider (IdP), after which the IdP will notify the application of the level of authorization. OpenID Connect creates its authorization access tokens using JWT, whereas SAML uses XML documents. Irrespective of the authorization method, our functions should verify the access tokens before executing the intended action.

AWS, Azure, and Google Cloud provide services and capabilities to help us implement authentication and authorization. We can use one or more of these and apply them ourselves or use third-party services.[55] We should make a considerable effort to implement and assess authentication and authorization in our serverless application because it is the most critical line of defense aside from the input validation in our application code.

---

[55]Only the third-party services that AWS, Azure, and Google Cloud reference in their documentation are mentioned.

CHAPTER 10

Protecting Sensitive Data

In this chapter, we will discuss some principles for protecting sensitive data. We will consider sensitive data to be information that are not secrets but might still result in damage when putting multiple pieces of data together. For example, driver's licenses, birthdays, medical history, and so on are sensitive data. We will learn how to apply these principles in the cloud provider services, the software used to build the application, and the application configuration.

Importance of Protecting Sensitive Data

The OWASP Top Ten[1] and the Interpretation for Serverless[2] include sensitive data exposure[3] and security misconfiguration[4] as top security risks, respectively. Sensitive data exposure is the risk of inadvertently disclosing important information (e.g., personally identifiable information [PII], credit card numbers, passwords, etc.). Having a risk realized is becoming more significant with the introduction of the European Union (EU) General Data Protection Regulation (GDPR) in 2018 and the US California Consumer Privacy Act (CCPA) in 2020. Security misconfiguration is the risk of improperly configuring or failing to maintain a security configuration in our application and its resources. Having insecure settings or outdated security settings might result in someone being able to break into our application and its resources.

---

[1]"OWASP Top Ten 2017." OWASP. 2017. https://owasp.org/www-project-top-ten/OWASP_Top_Ten_2017/

[2]"OWASP Top 10 (2017): Interpretation for Serverless." OWASP. 2017. https://github.com/OWASP/Serverless-Top-10-Project/raw/master/OWASP-Top-10-Serverless-Interpretation-en.pdf

[3]"A3:2017-Sensitive Data Exposure." OWASP Top Ten 2017. OWASP. https://owasp.org/www-project-top-ten/OWASP_Top_Ten_2017/Top_10-2017_A3-Sensitive_Data_Exposure

[4]"A6:2017-Security Misconfiguration." OWASP Top Ten 2017. OWASP. https://owasp.org/www-project-top-ten/OWASP_Top_Ten_2017/Top_10-2017_A6-Security_Misconfiguration

© Miguel A. Calles 2020
M. Calles, *Serverless Security*, https://doi.org/10.1007/978-1-4842-6100-2_10

Let's suppose our application stored credit card information as plaintext in our database. Our database might have proper security settings enabled, but it is running on a server with a known flaw. A malicious actor might exploit that flaw and download all the database content. Now that actor has access to all the credit card information.[5]

We could have encrypted our credit card numbers to protect that data. Still, we might have used a weak encryption technique or a short encryption key or failed to protect the key. With the advancements in computing and the discoveries in security research, specific algorithms have been found to be weak, putting encrypted data at risk. We should use newer and proven algorithms (e.g., AES, SHA, RSA, HMAC, etc.).[6] Even if we secure with encryption, we might still accidentally disclose that sensitive data when accessing it. If our application sends data over HTTP instead of HTTPS, we might transmit that sensitive data in the clear over the Internet where anyone can intercept it.

Given how we might introduce an insecure configuration or fail to maintain a secure configuration, we should assess what data to secure and determine how to secure it when at rest or in transit.

Protecting Sensitive Data

We will review the general principles for protecting sensitive data and how to apply them to the cloud provider services.

General Principles

There are many factors in securing our serverless application data, such as

- Default settings

- Default accounts

- Encryption

---

[5]"Financial companies leak 425GB in company, client data through open database." Charlie Osborne. ZDNet. March 17, 2020. `www.zdnet.com/article/financial-apps-leak-425gb-in-company-data-through-open-database`

[6]"CMVP Approved Security Functions: CMVP Validation Authority Updates to ISO/IEC 24759." NIST Special Publication 800-140C. National Institute of Standards and Technology. March 2020. `https://doi.org/10.6028/NIST.SP.800-140C`

- Logging

- And many others

In this chapter, we are going to review many of them.

Default Settings

Services, resources, and applications come with default settings. The default settings allow those items to work out of the box with little to no additional configuration. Sometimes, this means we have security configured to a less than ideal state. For example, we might inadvertently set our object storage with public access, which allows anyone on the Internet to access the data. We must consciously take action to configure every setting in the cloud provider services and resources we use. We want to configure settings in any application frameworks and software packages we use in our application code.

Default Accounts

A benefit of using serverless technologies is there are no servers to manage and no vendor-defined, default accounts. However, we are still vulnerable to introducing commonly known account credentials into our serverless application. Our serverless application might interface with a fully managed database server (although technically not serverless, it offloads the administrative and maintenance burden similarly to serverless technologies). When setting up the fully managed database server, we might use a common password known within the organization. Using this approach is effectively introducing a default account because anyone who knows this username and password combination can attempt to use it. The same applies to the application user accounts we create for developers and testers to evaluate the system. We might forget to disable or delete those accounts when we deploy our application to production. Furthermore, our development application is in the cloud, and anyone from the Internet can potentially access it with knowledge of the developer accounts. Whenever we have any type of account in our serverless application, we should use a unique username and password and record that information in a safe location or a password manager with limited access.

Encryption

We want to consider encrypting our data when it is at rest and in transit. The data we store in our storage or database might not be automatically encrypted. Fortunately, the data is automatically encrypted when it is in transit when transferred over HTTPS. This applies when we create serverless functions and deploy them using the Serverless Framework. However, our web application might still use HTTP when it makes requests to services other than serverless functions. Nowadays, we should avoid using HTTP connections unless we are developing on a local machine. Therefore, we still want to review how our application stores data and how it transmits to ensure we are using the proper protections.

Not all data needs protection. For example, we might consider driver license information sensitive but not necessarily the person's name. We must take more significant measures to protect sensitive data. We might want to leverage default encryption and manually encrypt sensitive data using encryption keys for added protection (see Chapter 8). The cloud providers offer settings to enable default encryption for data at rest, which reduces complexity and burden. This approach is useful because the default encryption protects us if someone steals the cloud provider's hardware containing the data. However, default encryption does not protect the content when someone utilizes the cloud provider's access methods. Having a manual encryption process protects the content because the data viewer must have access to the encryption key to decrypt the data.

Not only do we want to protect our data *where* appropriate, but we also want to ensure it is *adequately* protected. In former times, the industry relied heavily on MD5 for storing password hashes in a database. MD5 has proven to provide insufficient protection.[7] SHA-1 is another algorithm found to provide inadequate protection.[8] We should consider using more current algorithms, such as those defined in NIST Special Publication 800-140C.[9]

---

[7]"Updated Security Considerations for the MD5 Message-Digest and the HMAC-MD5 Algorithms." S. Turner. Request for Comments: 6151. IETF. March 2011. `https://tools.ietf.org/html/rfc6151`

[8]"Transitioning the Use of Cryptographic Algorithms and Key Lengths." E. Barker & A. Roginsky. NIST Special Publication 800-131A, Revision 2. National Institute of Standards and Technology. March 2019. `https://doi.org/10.6028/NIST.SP.800-131Ar2`

[9]"CMVP Approved Security Functions: CMVP Validation Authority Updates to ISO/IEC 24759." Kim Schaffer. NIST Special Publication 800-140C. March 2020. `https://doi.org/10.6028/NIST.SP.800-140C`

Key Management

In Chapter 8, we discussed using keys to protect our secrets. Not only do we need keys to protect secrets and data, but we also need a method to manage the keys. We should develop an approach to manage our secret keys as well.

The longer we use a secret key, the likelihood of someone discovering it or deciphering it increases. It behooves us to change (or rotate) the secret keys periodically. Key rotation allows us to reduce the risk of someone discovering the keys.

We should limit access to the secret keys. We increase the risk of inadvertently disclosing them with the increased number of individuals that have access to the secret keys. At a minimum, we should limit access to administrators. Still, we should consider limiting them to individuals who need to know them and a backup, such as an administrator not involved with the project.

The cloud providers have key management services. Furthermore, they might provide automatic rotation, provider-managed secret keys, and the ability to use custom secret keys. Using provider-managed secret keys allows us to implement secure encryption and decryption conveniently, and we should leverage IAM privileges to restrict access. We want to take advantage of any automatic rotation capabilities. Using custom secret keys places the burden of using secure encryption and rotation on us. Still, it gives us greater control to implement the desired level of security. We must weigh the business and technical requirements when defining the key management approach.

Data Lifetime

We should consider only keeping sensitive data as long as needed. We need to keep some sensitive data (e.g., password hashes) indefinitely. Still, others might only be short-lived (e.g., the credit card number and verification code) and can be deleted immediately. We might have to conform to privacy policies that limit how long we can store data. We can choose to store it in temporary storage (e.g., the temporary folder in the serverless function) or in permanent storage (e.g., a database) or not to store the data. The approach will depend on our requirements.

We should consider not storing the data whenever we have one-time transactions (e.g., a single credit card payment or a one-time password for two-step verification). After the application processes the payment or the user logs in, respectively, the application no longer needs that data.

We should consider using temporary storage when we convert data from one format to another. For example, we might want to download an encrypted file to the "/tmp" folder in the serverless function container, decrypt its contents, read the decrypted data, and delete the file. Although the decrypted data might be useful later, the function only needed the decrypted data to complete its process, and the data is not processed again.

We should consider using permanent storage when we need to use and process data more than once. We need to determine how long we keep the data. For example, we want to retain a user's geolocation data for the time specified by the privacy policy and any privacy laws and delete it after that. Another example, we might want to keep an encrypted credit card number if the customer enrolled in automatic payments.[10] The application might process both these types of data multiple times, and it makes sense to store them permanently. But, when their purpose is complete (e.g., the credit card expired, or the user cancels automatic payment), the application should delete the data.

We must be mindful of how we use global variables in our function code. Serverless functions run in containers but sometimes persist longer than we expect; this is true when frequently invoking the function. We should avoid declaring any global variables that are not constants because their values may contain sensitive data and persist into the next function invocation.

The cloud providers have features to assign lifetimes to data. The data is stored permanently by default, and enabling the lifetime (or expiration) features enables the cloud provider to automatically delete the data items after exceeding the data lifetime. We must be mindful of how we process data within a session, how it might persist into future sessions, and how we store it.

Caching

We should avoid caching sensitive data. Web browsers, cloud provider distribution networks, and API gateways support caching. Caching is useful in reducing response times when calling a resource that has the same data, but this means we can inadvertently serve the cached data to the unintended recipient. We should be selective on which type of data we choose to cache.

---

[10]This example is just for illustration in the event your application is a payment gateway. Otherwise, we should be using a payment gateway to process credit card payments and only storing the payment method's unique identifier in the database.

We should consider enabling caching for data that stays the same for long periods of time. For example, we might allow cache for media files stored in object storage or functions that return historical or static data. We should avoid caching any data that is dynamic (i.e., can change between function calls) or is sensitive because we might get outdated data or get unintended sensitive data, respectively.

Software Updates

A benefit of using serverless technologies is that the cloud provider fully manages the infrastructure and resources we use. We no longer have to maintain those items that make up our applications. There are still pieces of software we are responsible for keeping up to date (reference Chapter 3).

With the shared responsibility model, we are responsible for maintaining the application code and selecting the desired runtime. Since we chose Node.js as our serverless function runtime, we are responsible for deciding which version to use if the provider supports multiple runtimes. Since we selected any npm packages to use in our serverless function and web application code, we are responsible for keeping those packages up to date and without vulnerabilities. If we chose a framework to use in our web application, we are responsible for configuring it. Failure to keep the software up to date (or properly configured) might make our application vulnerable and result in accidentally disclosing sensitive information.

Logging

Our application might produce logs for different purposes. It might generate debug, informational, warning, or error log entries. These entries might be useful in helping us assess system health or in troubleshooting issues. We run the risk of accidentally logging sensitive data in the logs.

Logging sensitive data happens in various ways. A developer might temporarily log a sensitive entry while troubleshooting, and the temporary code modification gets accidentally committed to a code repository. The logs now consistently contain that data. The code might log any inputs and data transformations as informational log entries to assist with troubleshooting. Still, the code failed to omit the sensitive data before using the logging function. Regardless of why the application logs sensitive data, we need to take precautions in preventing it.

There are some best practices we can take to reduce the risk of logging sensitive data. We can avoid logging data to the web browser and instead send the logs to a dedicated logging location or platform to minimize what information a user sees. We can modify our logging function to check for sensitive data patterns and remove or obfuscate matches. We can disable logging debug entries and only log specific levels such as warnings and errors. We can also improve code review processes to check code logging. In the event our application does log sensitive data, we can choose to manually delete log entries or automatically delete log entries after exceeding their lifetime.

Source Code

We might also disclose sensitive data from our source code. The serverless functions have a copy of the required files needed to execute the function. Depending on how the settings used to deploy the function, the function's container might have more files than it needs. The excess files might include environment files that contain sensitive data. Alternatively, the code repository we use might contain sensitive data if the developer accidentally commits it. Anyone that obtains access to the source code repository now has access to sensitive data. Similarly, we might accidentally publish sensitive data to the npm repository. We must take measures to keep our serverless functions and source code repository (and npm) free of sensitive data.

We can use the "serverless-webpack" Serverless plugin to limit the files deployed to the serverless function.[11] This plugin allows us to package only the necessary files for the serverless function to execute correctly.

We can take advantage of features the repository provides to attempt to help prevent committing secrets. Repositories such as git and npm support ignore files that specify the files it will ignore when trying to save them to the repository. For example, if we add a file named ".env" into our ignore file, we are unable to save that file into the repository. Git provides hooks that allow us to run a script before performing an action (e.g., a commit). We can use a git pre-commit hook to check our files for sensitive data and prevent committing when sensitive data is present.

Whatever solutions we use, we want to reduce the risk of saving sensitive data to our serverless functions and repositories.

---

[11]"Serverless Webpack plugin." Nicola Peduzzi/Frank Schmid. GitHub. `https://github.com/serverless-heaven/serverless-webpack`

Security and Vulnerability Scanners

Finding security flaws and vulnerabilities manually can be an overwhelming task and a long one. Using software that automates the assessment not only saves us time but allows us to find issues we might miss. These tools (or services) are called security scanners and vulnerability scanners. These tools are commonly used in traditional server and desktop environments to find outdated software, vulnerabilities, and security misconfigurations. Some tools allow us to do the same in cloud environments.[12]

These tools perform automated checks when you authorize them to access your cloud provider account. They perform the following types of inspections:

- Finding public object storage

- Auditing IAM permissions and password policies

- Checking for activity in unused service provider regions

- Checking for changes to security settings

- Auditing configurations

- Checking for users without MFA enabled and expired access credentials

There are vendor-provided services (paid and free) and free and open source tools. Services offer periodic updates to their auditing rules and real-time auditing. We can obtain similar benefits using open source tools, but it might require more effort on our part. Whether we choose a service or prefer to run these tools manually, we should establish a repeatable process for checking our cloud provider environment and run the processes regularly.

Security Headers

Security headers are headers in the HTTP response. Various response headers define security settings that protect against known security issues in HTTP interactions.[13] We might associate these headers as being sent only in traditional server applications. However, they are still relevant in our serverless applications. Enabling these headers can help prevent redirecting and intercepting sensitive data.

---

[12]"How to Perform AWS Security Scanning and Configuration Monitoring?" Chandan Kumar. Geekflare. September 10, 2018. `https://geekflare.com/aws-vulnerability-scanner`

[13]"OWASP Secure Headers Project." OWASP. `https://owasp.org/www-project-secure-headers`

We typically use our serverless functions to act as the servers and serve the web application files from object storage. We receive an HTTP response by interacting with both services. Our serverless functions triggered by an HTTP event send HTTP headers, and the object storage service sends HTTP headers when accessing the web application files. We can define the headers we want to send in the serverless function code, the object storage settings, and possibly any web application framework we used to create our web application files. We should consider identifying which HTTP headers (and their values) we want to send to improve the security of our serverless applications.

Amazon Web Services (AWS)

We will discuss how the general principles apply to our serverless application in AWS.

Amazon Simple Storage Service (S3)

The Serverless Framework creates S3 buckets when we deploy the Serverless configuration. It establishes a bucket to store the deployment files. Optionally, we can choose to create buckets using the Serverless configuration. The default S3 settings vary.

When we deploy a Serverless configuration for the first time, the Serverless Framework creates a deployment bucket. By default, it enables AES-256 encryption, adds tags, adds an access control list that allows the bucket owner to read and write objects and permissions, and adds a bucket policy denying insecure transport. Furthermore, AWS encrypts external requests when using the AWS SDKs and published APIs,[14] and they maintain the software they use to support S3.[15] These settings are sufficient as long as we let the Serverless Framework add the files because it uploads them without public access. We should not add any other data to this bucket. Alternatively, we can manually create a deployment bucket and use it in the Serverless configuration; see Listing 10-1.

---

[14]"Infrastructure Security in Amazon S3." Amazon Simple Storage Service (S3) Developer Guide. Amazon Web Services. `https://docs.aws.amazon.com/AmazonS3/latest/dev/network-isolation.html`

[15]"Configuration and Vulnerability Analysis in Amazon S3." Amazon Simple Storage Service (S3) Developer Guide. Amazon Web Services. `https://docs.aws.amazon.com/AmazonS3/latest/dev/vulnerability-analysis-and-management.html`

Listing 10-1. An Example of Referencing a Deployment Bucket in the Serverless Configuration

```
provider:
  deploymentBucket:
   name: myDeploymentBucket
```

When we create an S3 bucket with the Serverless Framework, we add the S3 settings in the Serverless configuration. With the minimum settings, as shown in Listing 10-2, the Serverless Framework will only tag the data and add an access control list that allows the bucket owner to read and write objects and permissions.

Listing 10-2. The Minimum S3 Settings in a Serverless Configuration

```
resources:
  Resources:
   DataS3Bucket:
     Type: AWS::S3::Bucket
     Properties:
       BucketName: ${self:service}-${self:provider.stage}-data
```

We should consider adding all the security settings in the Serverless configuration. Even if we only want the default settings, defining them informs the Serverless Framework which settings to use when creating the S3 bucket; see Listing 10-3.[16] We can omit settings that do not require defining values because the Serverless Framework will set default values.

Listing 10-3. An Example of Updated S3 Settings in a Serverless Configuration

```
resources:
  Resources:
   DataS3Bucket:
     Type: AWS::S3::Bucket
     Properties:
       # see AWS CloudFormation reference
```

---

[16]"AWS::S3::Bucket." AWS CloudFormation. Amazon Web Services. https://docs.aws.amazon.com/AWSCloudFormation/latest/UserGuide/aws-properties-s3-bucket.html

```
# for a list of all the properties
# https://docs.aws.amazon.com/AWSCloudFormation/
# latest/UserGuide/aws-properties-s3-bucket.html
AccelerateConfiguration:
  AccelerationStatus: Enabled
AccessControl: Private
BucketEncryption:
  ServerSideEncryptionConfiguration:
    - ServerSideEncryptionByDefault:
        SSEAlgorithm: AES256
BucketName: ${self:service}-${self:provider.stage}-data
LifecycleConfiguration:
  Rules:
    - ExpirationInDays: 90
      Status: Enabled
PublicAccessBlockConfiguration:
  BlockPublicAcls: true
  BlockPublicPolicy: true
  IgnorePublicAcls: true
  RestrictPublicBuckets: true
VersioningConfiguration:
  Status: Enabled
```

These S3 settings provide us with the following:

- Faster uploads when supported

- Set the access control only to allow the bucket owner to modify the bucket

- Set the default encryption to AES-256

- Expire the data after 90 days and automatically delete it

- Block all public access

- Keep older versions of the data when updating the object

These settings address default settings, encryption, and sensitive data lifetime topics.

We can address the caching and security headers by adding the following settings into the Serverless configuration:

- WebsiteConfiguration

- CorsConfiguration

These settings were omitted earlier because they are optional settings, and their configuration varies on your business and technical requirements; there is no one-size-fits-all set of values.

AWS Lambda

The default Lambda settings do not address at-rest and in-transit data settings but are not necessarily insecure. They cannot be triggered without defining an event source to trigger them. They only send the response specified in the code, and it can be empty. They do not access external resources unless specified in the code. They have no sensitive data unless they exist in the environment variables or source code.

AWS addresses some of the security on our behalf. It automatically encrypts the data the Lambda receives,[17] and the API Gateway will automatically redirect any HTTP requests to HTTPS. Still, we must be careful to only use HTTPS requests to the API Gateway in our application code. Any event triggers are within the AWS internal network and sent over secure protocols.[18] They regularly maintain the software it uses to support Lambda.[19] Nevertheless, there are still some aspects we must configure.

We should configure the Lambda to use as much security as possible. The Lambda function code should always use HTTPS when making requests except when the target only accepts HTTP. We discussed protecting secrets with encryption and avoiding having sensitive data in environment variables (see Chapter 8). We should prevent logging sensitive data using npm logging packages (e.g., debug[20] and winston[21]) and avoid

---

[17]"Data Protection in AWS Lambda." AWS Lambda Developer Guide. Amazon Web Services. https://docs.aws.amazon.com/lambda/latest/dg/security-dataprotection.html

[18]"Infrastructure Security in AWS Lambda." AWS Lambda Developer Guide. Amazon Web Services. https://docs.aws.amazon.com/lambda/latest/dg/security-infrastructure.html

[19]"Configuration and Vulnerability Analysis in AWS Lambda." AWS Lambda Developer Guide. Amazon Web Services. https://docs.aws.amazon.com/lambda/latest/dg/security-configuration.html

[20]"debug." npm. www.npmjs.com/package/debug

[21]"winston." npm. www.npmjs.com/package/winston

logging sensitive data as described earlier. We can automatically delete logs saved to CloudWatch by defining the log retention period; see Listing 10-4. We can add security headers in our HTTP(S) responses as appropriate; see Listing 10-5.

Listing 10-4. An Example of Enabling CloudWatch Log Retention in the Serverless Configuration

```
provider:
  logRetentionInDays: 1
```

Listing 10-5. An Example of a Lambda Function Responding with Security Headers

```
'use strict';
const headers = {
    'Strict-Transport-Security': 'max-age=63072000;' +
        ' includeSubdomains; preload',
    'Content-Security-Policy':
        "default-src 'none'; img-src 'self';" +
        " script-src 'self'; style-src 'self';" +
        " object-src 'none'",
    'X-Content-Type-Options': 'nosniff',
    'X-Frame-Options': 'DENY',
    'X-XSS-Protection': '1; mode=block',
    'Referrer-Policy': 'same-origin'
};
module.exports.handler = (event, content, callback) => {
    callback(null, {
        statusCode: 200,
        headers
    });
};
```

We can also encrypt all environment variables for added protection; see Listing 10-6.

Listing 10-6. An Example of Enabling Environment Variable Encryption at Rest in the Serverless Configuration

```
custom:
  keyPrefix: arn:aws:kms:us-east-1:123456789012:key
  keyId: dc435c97-f2da-4d59-971b-2694d57f0b63
functions:
  myFunction:
    handler: myFunction.handler
    awsKmsKeyArn: ${self:custom.keyPrefix}/${self:custom.keyId}
    environment:
      SECRET_NAME: encryptedAtRestButNotInUse
```

We should take the appropriate measures to ensure our Lambda functions use HTTPS, have no sensitive data in code or environment variables, and send the appropriate response headers.

Amazon DynamoDB

When we create a DynamoDB table with the Serverless Framework, we add the DynamoDB settings in the Serverless configuration. With the minimum settings (see Listing 10-7), the Serverless Framework will enable default encryption using the AWS-managed encryption keys.[22] AWS security transmits DynamoDB data between services[23] and externally when using the AWS SDKs and published API calls.[24] Additionally, AWS security regularly maintains the software it uses to support DynamoDB.[25]

---

[22]"DynamoDB Encryption at Rest." Amazon DynamoDB. Amazon Web Services. https://docs.aws.amazon.com/amazondynamodb/latest/developerguide/EncryptionAtRest.html

[23]"Internetwork Traffic Privacy." Amazon DynamoDB Developer Guide. Amazon Web Services. https://docs.aws.amazon.com/amazondynamodb/latest/developerguide/inter-network-traffic-privacy.html

[24]"Infrastructure Security in Amazon DynamoDB." Amazon DynamoDB Developer Guide. Amazon Web Services. https://docs.aws.amazon.com/amazondynamodb/latest/developerguide/network-isolation.html

[25]"Configuration and Vulnerability Analysis in Amazon DynamoDB." DynamoDB Developer Guide. Amazon Web Services. https://docs.aws.amazon.com/amazondynamodb/latest/developerguide/configuration-vulnerability.html

Listing 10-7. The Minimum DynamoDB Settings in a Serverless Configuration

```
resources:
  Resources:
    DataTable:
      Type: AWS::DynamoDB::Table
      Properties:
       AttributeDefinitions:
          - AttributeName: Id
            AttributeType: S
       KeySchema:
          - AttributeName: Id
            KeyType: HASH
       ProvisionedThroughput:
          ReadCapacityUnits: 1
          WriteCapacityUnits: 1
       TableName: ${self:service}-${self:provider.region}-data
```

We can change the encryption to use a CMK and choose to expire data by adding a time-to-live (TTL) specification; see Listing 10-8. The TTL specification uses a specified database field for each entry and captures an expiration date and time. DynamoDB will automatically delete the entry when the current date and time is past the time value in that field.

Listing 10-8. An Example of Updated DynamoDB Settings in a Serverless Configuration

```
resources:
  Resources:
    DataTable:
      Type: AWS::DynamoDB::Table
      Properties:
        # see AWS CloudFormation reference
        # for a list of all the properties
        # https://docs.aws.amazon.com/AWSCloudFormation/
        # latest/UserGuide/aws-resource-dynamodb-table.html
        AttributeDefinitions:
```

```
    - AttributeName: Id
      AttributeType: S
  KeySchema:
    - AttributeName: Id
      KeyType: HASH
  ProvisionedThroughput:
    ReadCapacityUnits: 1
    WriteCapacityUnits: 1
   SSESpecification:
    KMSMasterKeyId: arn:aws:kms:us-east-1:123456789012:key/dc435c97-
    f2da-4d59-971b-2694d57f0b63
    SSEEnabled: true
    SSEType: KMS
  TableName: ${self:service}-${self:provider.region}-data
  TimeToLiveSpecification:
    AttributeName: Ttl
    Enabled: true
```

We should consider protecting sensitive data by encrypting it with a secret key or CMK before writing it to the database. This adds an additional layer of protection because any intercepted data is unusable without the secret key.

Amazon API Gateway

The API Gateway enables an HTTPS endpoint by default and redirects HTTP requests to the HTTPS endpoint. We can further protect sensitive data by enabling Cross-Origin Resource Sharing (CORS) and modifying the cache settings.

There are no CORS settings by default. We enable it for each HTTP(S) endpoint; see Listing 10-9. We can also set the cache policy to enable or disable the cache.

Listing 10-9. An Example of Enabling CORS in the Serverless Configuration

```
functions:
  myFunction:
    handler: myFunction.handler
    events:
      - http: # It will use HTTPS by default.
```

```
            path: myFunction
            method: get
            cors:
                origin: 'myservice.com'
                maxAge: 600
                allowCredentials: false
                cacheControl: |
                    max-age=600, s-maxage=600,
                    proxy-revalidate, private
    sensitiveData:
        handler: sensitiveData.handler
        events:
            - http:
                path: sensitiveData
                method: get
                cors:
                    origin: 'myservice.com'
                    maxAge: 600
                    allowCredentials: false
                    cacheControl: 'no-cache, no-store, no-transform'
```

We have the option of enabling API Gateway logging; see Listing 10-10. We should consider disabling the logging of full execution data because it will log the entire HTTP(S) request, which means it will log any sensitive data received within the request.

Listing 10-10. An Example of Enabling API Gateway Logging in the Serverless Configuration

```
provider:
    logs:
        restApi:
            accessLogging: true
            format: 'requestId: $context.requestId'
            executionLogging: true
            level: INFO
            fullExecutionData: false
```

We should configure API Gateway to use CORS in addition to not logging the entire HTTP(S) request to avoid sending sensitive data to the unintended recipients.

AWS Trusted Advisor

The Trusted Advisor service provides automated checks in five key areas across numerous AWS services and resources: cost optimization, performance, security, fault tolerance, and service limits.[26] It has free core security checks and service limit checks. These checks look at the following serverless technologies and settings:

- IAM S3 bucket permissions

- IAM users, groups, policies, and roles

- IAM instance profiles

- Server certificates

- DynamoDB read and write capacities

- Kinesis Streams shards

- SES daily sending quota

The free and paid tiers perform many other checks, provide architecture guidance, and many other benefits.[27]

Azure

Next, let's discuss how the general principles apply to our serverless application in Azure. The Azure capabilities discussed in the following are based on features available at the time of this writing.

Azure Functions

Similar to AWS Lambda functions, Azure Functions do not address at-rest and in-transit data settings. Still, they are not necessarily insecure, and Azure addresses some of the security

---

[26]"AWS Trusted Advisor." Amazon Web Services. `https://aws.amazon.com/premiumsupport/technology/trusted-advisor/`

[27]"Compare AWS Support Plans." AWS Support. Amazon Web Services. `https://aws.amazon.com/premiumsupport/plans/`

on our behalf. It automatically encrypts the data sent to the Azure Function and any Azure cloud services.[28] The API Management will return a "404 resource not found" response when using HTTP to trigger an Azure Function. They regularly maintain the software used to support Azure Functions,[29] but there are still some aspects we must configure.

We should employ the same security practices mentioned in the AWS section: make HTTPS requests, protect secrets (see Chapter 8), avoid logging sensitive data, and add security headers; see Listing 10-11.

Listing 10-11. An Example of an Azure Function Responding with Security Headers

```
'use strict';
const headers = {
    'Strict-Transport-Security': 'max-age=63072000;' +
        ' includeSubdomains; preload',
    'Content-Security-Policy':
        "default-src 'none'; img-src 'self';" +
        " script-src 'self'; style-src 'self';" +
        " object-src 'none'",
    'X-Content-Type-Options': 'nosniff',
    'X-Frame-Options': 'DENY',
    'X-XSS-Protection': '1; mode=block',
    'Referrer-Policy': 'same-origin'
};
module.exports.handler = async (context, req) => {
    context.res = {
        status: 200,
        headers
    };
};
```

[28]"Azure encryption overview." Azure security fundamentals documentation. Microsoft. https:// docs.microsoft.com/en-us/azure/security/fundamentals/encryption-overview

[29]"Azure infrastructure monitoring." Azure security fundamentals documentation. Microsoft. https://docs.microsoft.com/en-us/azure/security/fundamentals/ infrastructure-monitoring

When the Serverless Framework deploys the function, it uploads the function code as a zip without encryption. We have the option to store the function code in Azure Blob storage as a zip file, encrypt it using our customer master keys, and have the Azure Function use that Azure Blob storage zip file. This approach is available in the Serverless Framework; see Listing 10-12.[30]

Listing 10-12. An Example of Loading Azure Function Code from Storage in the Serverless Configuration

```
deploy:
  runFromBlobUrl: true
```

We should take the appropriate measures to ensure our Azure Functions use HTTPS, have no sensitive data in code or environment variables, and send the proper response headers.

Azure Blob Storage

The Serverless Framework creates an Azure Blob storage account when we deploy the Serverless configuration, but it does not support creating additional storage accounts; we need to create storage accounts manually. It creates a storage account to store the deployment files. By default, it enables 256-bit AES encryption using Microsoft-managed keys[31] and makes it private (i.e., no public access). It does not enable secure transfer, define CORS, soft delete, nor many other settings that Microsoft recommends.[32] We will need to enable any additional security settings outside of the Serverless Framework because it does not support them.

Azure Cosmos DB

The Serverless Framework does not support creating Azure Cosmos DB databases. We will need to create them manually. We should address Microsoft's security

---

[30]"Encryption at rest using customer master keys." Azure Functions documentation. Microsoft. https://docs.microsoft.com/en-us/azure/azure-functions/configure-encrypt-at rest-using-cmk

[31]"Azure Storage encryption for data at rest." Azure Storage Documentation. Microsoft. https://docs.microsoft.com/en-us/azure/storage/common/storage-service-encryption

[32]"Security recommendations for Blob storage." Azure Storage Documentation. Microsoft. https://docs.microsoft.com/en-us/azure/storage/blobs/security-recommendations

recommendations.[33] Fortunately, Microsoft enables encryption by default.[34] We have the option of using customer master keys instead of the Microsoft-managed keys. Furthermore, we can manually encrypt and decrypt the data using private keys. We must manually implement the desired level of security outside of the Serverless Framework and consider protecting sensitive data by encrypting it with a secret key or CMK before writing it to the database.

Azure API Management

The Serverless Framework supports creating APIs using API Management. It allows us to specify the protocols (e.g., HTTPS), enable CORS, and specify whether a request requires an API key, JWT validation, header validation, or IP validation; see Listing 10-13.

Listing 10-13. An Open Source Example of Enabling API Management Security Settings[35]

```
provider:
 apim:
   apis:
    - name: products-api
        subscriptionRequired: false
        displayName: Products API
        description: The Products REST API
        protocols:
           - https
        path: products
        tags:
           - tag1
        authorization: none
```

---

[33]"Security in Azure Cosmos DB - overview." Azure Cosmos DB documentation. Microsoft. `https://docs.microsoft.com/en-us/azure/cosmos-db/database-security`

[34]"Data encryption in Azure Cosmos DB." Azure Cosmos DB documentation. Microsoft. `https://docs.microsoft.com/en-us/azure/cosmos-db/database-encryption-at rest`

[35]Copyright 2016 Serverless. The code is licensed under the MIT License. `https://github.com/serverless/serverless-azure-functions/blob/master/docs/examples/apim.md`

```
backends:
  - name: products-backend
    url: api/products
cors:
    allowCredentials: false
    allowedOrigins:
      - "*"
    allowedMethods:
      - GET
      - POST
      - DELETE
    allowedHeaders:
      - "*"
    exposeHeaders:
      - "*"
```

We should enable HTTPS as the protocol and omit HTTP because HTTP is allowed by default. We should limit CORS to specific domains, methods, and headers. We should consider enabling subscription keys when appropriate.[36]

API Management has built-in security controls. It provides network isolation and tunneling, logging, authentication and authorization, encryption of data at rest using Microsoft-managed keys, and encryption of data in transit, and its software is kept up to date.[37]

Azure Security Center

Azure Security Center is an Azure service that helps improve our application's security posture. It provides security recommendations based on best security practices and common security misconfigurations.[38] We can use it to create and manage organization security policies that stem from Azure security controls. It provides capabilities that

---

[36]"Subscriptions in Azure API Management." API Management documentation. Microsoft. `https://docs.microsoft.com/en-us/azure/api-management/api-management-subscriptions`

[37]"Security controls for API Management." API Management documentation. Microsoft. `https://docs.microsoft.com/en-us/azure/api-management/api-management-security-controls`

[38]"What is Azure Security Center?" Azure Security Center documentation. Microsoft. `https://docs.microsoft.com/en-us/azure/security-center/security-center-intro`

detect and protect against security threats (e.g., brute-force attacks). The free tier provides continuous assessment and security recommendations and a security score for Azure App Services (which the Serverless Framework uses to deploy Azure Functions).[39] We might want to consider upgrading to the standard tier to enable the threat protection on the Azure App Service and Azure Storage accounts.

Google Cloud

Finally, we will discuss how the general principles apply to our serverless application in Google Cloud.

Cloud Functions

Similar to AWS Lambda functions, Google Cloud Functions do not address settings for data at rest or in transit. Still, they are not necessarily insecure, and Google Cloud addresses some of the security on our behalf. It automatically encrypts the data sent to the Cloud Function and any Google Cloud services.[40] Although Google Functions accept HTTPS requests, they also accept HTTP requests. We must be careful to only use HTTPS requests to the Cloud Functions in our application code. While they regularly maintain the software it uses to support Google Cloud,[41] there are still some aspects we must configure.

We should employ the same security practices we mentioned in the AWS section: make HTTPS requests, protect secrets (see Chapter 8), avoid logging sensitive data, and add security headers; see Listing 10-14.

Listing 10-14. An Example of a Google Function Responding with Security Headers

```
exports.http = (request, response) => {
    console.log('request', request);
    console.log()
```

---

[39]"Security Center pricing." Microsoft. `https://azure.microsoft.com/en-us/pricing/details/security-center/`

[40]"Encryption in Transit in Google Cloud." Google Cloud Encryption Whitepaper. Google Cloud. `https://cloud.google.com/security/encryption-in transit/resources/encryption-in transit-whitepaper.pdf`

[41]"Google Cloud Security Showcase." Google. `https://cloud.google.com/security/showcase`

```
response.set(
    'Access-Control-Allow-Origin',
    'https://mydomain.com',
);
response.set('Access-Control-Allow-Credentials', 'true');
response.set(
    'Strict-Transport-Security',
    'max-age=63072000; includeSubdomains; preload'
);
response.set(
'Content-Security-Policy',
"default-src 'none'; " +
"img-src 'self'; " +
"script-src 'self'; " +
"style-src 'self'; " +
"object-src 'none'");
response.set('X-Content-Type-Options', 'nosniff');
response.set('X-Frame-Options', 'DENY');
response.set('X-XSS-Protection', '1; mode=block');
response.set('Referrer-Policy', 'same-origin');
response.status(200).send();
};
```

Google Cloud Logging automatically has log retention periods as short as 30 days.[42] We can customize the logging retention period using the gcloud CLI; see Listing 10-15.[43]

Listing 10-15. An Example of Configuring Google Cloud Log Retention

```
gcloud beta logging buckets update _Default \
--location=global --retention-days=30
```

---

[42]"Quotas and limits." Management Tools. Google. https://cloud.google.com/logging/quotas

[43]"Storing logs." Management Tools. Google. https://cloud.google.com/logging/docs/ storage#custom-retention

We should take the appropriate measures to ensure our Google Cloud Functions use HTTPS, have no sensitive data in code and environment variables, send the appropriate response headers, and configure the log retention period.

Cloud Storage

The Serverless Framework creates a Cloud Storage bucket when we deploy the Serverless configuration. It creates a storage bucket to store the deployment files. By default, it enables encryption using a Google-managed key and configures secure access controls limited to the owners, editors, and viewers of the Google Cloud project. It does not enable the retention policies, lifecycle rules, and event-based holds (i.e., "do not delete") to prevent deletion or modification.[44] We will need to enable any additional security settings outside of the Serverless Framework because it does not support them at the time of this writing.

We can choose to deploy a Cloud Storage bucket with the desired security settings using the Serverless Framework. The Serverless Framework accepts the Google Cloud Deployment Manager configurations. The Google Cloud Documentation provides example deployment configurations.[45]

Cloud Database

As mentioned earlier, the Serverless Framework supports Google Cloud Deployment Manager configurations. We will need to use this approach to create a Google Cloud Firestore or Firebase Realtime Database database with the Serverless Framework. Google Cloud encrypts data at rest for Cloud Firestore.[46] We should consider protecting sensitive data by encrypting it with a secret key or CMK before writing it to any database.

---

[44]"Retention policies and Bucket Lock." Cloud Storage documentation. Google. `https://cloud.google.com/storage/docs/bucket-lock`

[45]"Example templates from the Cloud Foundation Toolkit." Google Cloud Deployment Manager documentation. Google. `https://cloud.google.com/deployment-manager/docs/reference/cloud-foundation-toolkit`

[46]"Server-side encryption." Cloud Firestore documentation. Google. `https://cloud.google.com/firestore/docs/server-side-encryption`

Security Command Center

Security Command Center is a Google Cloud service that helps improve our application's security posture. It can help protect sensitive data from accidental disclosure, audit logs, monitor access control settings, and discover web vulnerabilities.[47] This service is free but requires an organization (see Chapter 6). We might want to consider using the Security Command Center to improve our security posture.[48]

Key Takeaways

We discussed several principles to address sensitive data exposure and security misconfiguration as security risks. We can use encryption, key management, sensitive data lifetimes, software updates, security and vulnerability scanners, and security headers to improve our application security posture. We should modify default settings, change default accounts, limit caching, adjust logging, and protect our source control to reduce the risk of accidentally disclosing sensitive data. We must identify which data is sensitive, enumerate how it could be inadvertently disclosed, and determine the measures we need to implement to protect it. We concluded by reviewing how we might implement the principles in the AWS, Azure, and Google Cloud services.

---

[47]"Security Command Center." Google. https://cloud.google.com/security-command-center

[48]"Take command of your security in the cloud." Google Cloud Whitepaper. Google Cloud. December 2019. https://services.google.com/fh/files/misc/wp_take_command_of_your_security_in_the_cloud_rgb_v15c.pdf

CHAPTER 11

Monitoring, Auditing, and Alerting

In this chapter, we will discuss monitoring, auditing, and alerting. We will consider monitoring to be the process and tools we use to assess our application, auditing to be the process of looking for deviations from desired settings, and alerting to be the notification process when there are monitoring and auditing findings. We will review cloud provider services we can use to implement monitoring, auditing, and alerting.

The Importance of Monitoring, Auditing, and Alerting

The OWASP Top Ten[1] and the Interpretation for Serverless[2] include insufficient logging and monitoring[3] as a security risk. Logging allows the application to provide a record of its health by creating log records of different log levels. Debug logs provide us with more information and data than we would typically want during standard application logging. Information logs provide us with a record of the execution. We use warning logs to let us know when a process did not run normally but did not fail. Error logs inform us when a process fails to execute correctly, and it could not recover. Some logging tools have

---

[1] "OWASP Top Ten 2017." OWASP. 2017. https://owasp.org/www-project-top-ten/OWASP_Top_Ten_2017/

[2] "OWASP Top 10 (2017): Interpretation for Serverless." OWASP. 2017. https://github.com/OWASP/Serverless-Top-10-Project/raw/master/OWASP-Top-10-Serverless-Interpretation-en.pdf

[3] "A10:2017-Insufficient Logging & Monitoring." OWASP Top Ten 2017. OWASP Foundation. 2017. https://owasp.org/www-project-top-ten/OWASP_Top_Ten_2017/Top_10-2017_A10-Insufficient_Logging%252526Monitoring

© Miguel A. Calles 2020
M. Calles, *Serverless Security*, https://doi.org/10.1007/978-1-4842-6100-2_11

additional levels that provide more or less information than the levels we noted. Each log level is useful in monitoring.

The log levels are enabled depending on the development stage, and we can monitor them accordingly. We most likely enable debug logs in development stages and not in production stages. We can use debug logs to troubleshoot an application error because it provides amplifying information (e.g., variable values). Monitoring debug logs allows us to find potential issues before we release our code into the production stage. We can use information logs to assess how a system behaves under normal and optimal conditions. Monitoring information logs allows us to see patterns when a system operates correctly, and we can identify a degraded mode when the patterns start deviating. We can use warning logs to capture information about system degradation. Monitoring these logs allows us to determine when a software change introduced a defect or when a third-party service (e.g., a credit card merchant API) is having issues. We can use error logs to capture information that is preventing our application from functioning. Monitoring error logs allows us to respond to failures in our application by alerting the appropriate team. Our application in the production stage will likely record information, warning, and error logs.

Failure to produce any logs will prevent us from detecting failures and malicious activity. Let's suppose a malicious actor is trying numerous credit cards bought on the dark web. We might log these credit card processing failures as warnings or errors. Without capturing these logs, our monitoring solution is unable to notice an increased number of credit card failures and which parties are involved. Without alerting our support team, we are allowing the malicious actor to make purchases with stolen credit card numbers. We can potentially put the business under a financial risk and loss of credibility if the response teams fail to catch and stop this malicious activity promptly.

We want to audit our system to identify malicious activity outside the application. You can think of auditing as a type of monitoring that determines whether the application and infrastructure maintain the expected configuration. Failure to audit might allow a malicious actor to weaken the security posture or take over the application. Let's suppose we capture customer-uploaded images in a private storage bucket, but a malicious actor manages to get sufficient privileges to modify the bucket settings. That actor can change the storage bucket to have public access, and now all those private customer images are viewable by anyone on the Internet. Had auditing been in place, the change could have been detected before too many customer images were exposed on the Internet. Without regular or continuous auditing, we would be unable to detect the undesired change and revert the bucket settings to private and minimize the exposure.

Monitoring

Monitoring allows us to assess our serverless application. We can learn how it functions when all is working well. We can see patterns in function execution times, logging, storage consumption, API gateway status codes, database reads and writes, costs, and more. Monitoring our serverless application allows us to determine when it is experiencing degradation and failures. We will review the general principles and provider-specific capabilities that can assist us in monitoring our application.

General Principles

How we monitor our application will vary depending on its design, the business and security requirements, and the budget. Yet there are some general principles we should consider implementing in our monitoring solution.

Billing

We will discuss billing as the first item to monitor because the company's financial health can make or break an organization and whether that organization chooses to continue funding the development and operation of our serverless application. Therefore, we want to ensure we properly monitor billing in our cloud provider account.

Serverless applications are growing in popularity due to the potential for reduced costs when compared to typical server-based applications. The cloud providers typically bill for usage and storage or might include a free tier where we could potentially run our application at no cost. As our application grows in popularity and more users are using it, the costs may increase. We may also see cost increases for reasons other than an increasing user base. There are various reasons why the costs might increase: there might be an inefficient process that is running more often, the cloud provider changed its pricing methodology, a circular execution bug, or many other scenarios. We should aim to keep our serverless costs low and question increases in costs.

As an example, our application might be vulnerable to a Distributed Denial of Service (DDoS) attack where an attacker sends thousands of requests to a serverless function that takes a long time to execute. The serverless function takes the request inputs and makes a GraphQL query. The GraphQL configuration allows including additional queries within a query (which we will refer to as "nesting" queries). The attacker sends an input that causes the GraphQL query with several levels of nesting. It might take several seconds (even up to the maximum allowed execution time) for the GraphQL response to cause the function to send a return response.[4] This one function execution is costly. If the attacker can send numerous functions at once, it could cause our application to become unresponsive and increase our application costs. Monitoring costs allows us to find anomalies and to find ways to optimize our application in areas with high usage costs.[5]

HTTP Status Codes

We might be using an API gateway to trigger our serverless functions using HTTP events or object storage to host a serverless website. In either case, we should monitor any errors. We should monitor HTTP error codes in the 400s and 500s. Monitoring these status codes gives us insight into potential issues.

Each HTTP status code corresponds to an appropriate error, and seeing these codes in increasing quantities helps us determine what might be an issue. For example, an increase or significant spike in "401 Unauthorized" codes could indicate a malicious actor trying to brute force a protected endpoint, an error in our authentication method, or someone trying to discover new endpoints. Having numerous "500 Internal Server Error" codes might suggest the latest version of the software has a new bug, someone could be submitting invalid function inputs, or the function was not correctly configured or deployed. We might notice numerous "400 Not Found" codes, which might suggest someone was looking for protected pages. Monitoring the API gateway and object storage status codes could help us find and address issues before they become problematic and severe.

Log Aggregation

The application might store logs in various locations. Functions, object storage, the storage buckets, API gateways, and databases will store logs in their configured locations. The log storage might segregate the logs on a per-resource basis. Or, one action might

---

[4]I learned about this exploit at the OWASP AppSec California 2019 conference. "An Attacker's View of Serverless and GraphQL Apps." Abhay Bhargav. AppSec California 2019. OWASP. `www.youtube.com/watch?v=wCRkmeLYhYQ`

[5]In addition to monitoring, we could implement billing quotas to ensure our costs do not exceed a specified amount. Implementing quotas is a double-edged sword: we can limit excess usage like those from a DDoS attack, but can self-impose a DoS if our application has an unusually large spike in user activity.

generate logs in multiple locations, which makes seeing all the related logs somewhat troublesome. Using a log aggregation service allows us to see all the logs in one convenient view.

The cloud providers have some log aggregation capabilities, but we might want to consider using a third-party service too. Third-party services might have proprietary searching, filtering, and analysis capabilities. They might also support additional customization. Furthermore, they might integrate with alerting capabilities. We should select a log aggregation tool that gives us the log visibility and features we need to assess the application health, perform troubleshooting, and address business, security, and privacy requirements.

Outages

We should monitor planned outages. Planned outages are events the cloud provider schedules in advance to perform routine maintenance, make upgrades, and address security issues. Knowing when planned outages occur allows us to inform our application users and make any necessary plans to ensure the application is ready for a disruption of service. Failure to know the time frame of a planned outage might result in the response team receiving urgent notifications about an "unplanned" outage in our application.

We should also monitor for unplanned outages. As good and reliable as the cloud providers are, they do experience unexpected failures and degradation of service. The cloud provider will typically post an update on their status website and by other means. Accurately monitoring the provider status allows us to notify our application users about a disruption.

As speedily as the provider might send a service disruption status, it might be several moments since that the outage occurred. We should perform our own monitoring to assess the health of our application. Our monitoring should notice any change in behavior (e.g., numerous HTTP status errors, increased latencies, a growing number of function timeouts, etc.). It might detect a potential service outage earlier than the provider might, or it might catch a self-induced issue (i.e., not caused by the provider).

Utilization and Metrics

We should monitor the utilization and metrics to have a picture of how our application is performing. We can monitor our serverless functions, object storage, logging, API gateways, databases, and the other cloud provider services by monitoring their utilization and metrics.

We might typically associate utilization with the central processing unit (CPU) and memory, but these do apply to our serverless functions. The functions run in a container, which is a virtualized computer running a lightweight operating system. We have the option to select the memory allocated to each function, and the cloud provider determines the CPU allocation; typically, assigning more memory results in a higher CPU allocation. By monitoring the utilization patterns for each function, we can decide if we have allocated too little or too much memory. We can determine whether to optimize a function or increase the memory allocation if we find the CPU utilization is high. We might come to discover certain functions with high CPU utilization are vulnerable to exploits (e.g., Regular Expression Denial of Service attacks) designed to utilize as much CPU, memory, or time as possible. We may use the monitoring data to determine the optimal CPU-memory allocation for each function, which ultimately helps reduce our costs (higher allowances have higher prices). Monitoring the serverless function utilization allows us to tune our functions and observe any potential performance issues and detect Denial of Service attacks.

We can monitor the storage usage. Databases, object storage, and logging utilize the storage, which might have an impact on performance and cost. Queries and lookups might take longer when database tables have too much data. Keeping unused or old data in databases and object storage increases our costs, especially when we exceed any free-tier limits. We might move data into less expensive storage for archiving purposes if we need to satisfy any data retention requirements. We should monitor any related metrics to ensure we keep our storage sizes and costs as small as possible.

We monitor performance metrics to assess how the services our application uses are functioning. We can observe throttling and errors in our database performance, which might indicate the application is exceeding its read-write capacities.[6] We might see the throttling of stream records, which might indicate an usual volume of activity.[7]

---

[6]"DynamoDB Metrics and Dimensions." Amazon DynamoDB Developer Guide. Amazon Web Services. https://docs.aws.amazon.com/amazondynamodb/latest/developerguide/metrics-dimensions.html

[7]"Monitoring Kinesis Data Firehose Using CloudWatch metrics." Amazon Kinesis Data Firehose Developer Guide. Amazon Web Services. https://docs.aws.amazon.com/firehose/latest/dev/monitoring-with-cloudwatch-metrics.html

In addition to monitoring HTTP status codes, we can assess whether our API gateways are experiencing issues with caching and latencies.[8] Monitoring the metrics that give insights into the performance of the application allows us to respond when there are performance issues.

Third-Party Solutions

We might want to consider using a third-party solution instead of solely relying on those provided by our cloud provider. When our cloud provider is experiencing degradation, our monitoring solution might experience it as well. Having a third-party solution built independently from our cloud provider gives us increased reliability in our monitoring because any issues affecting our serverless application and infrastructure have no impact on our third-party solution. Additionally, third-party solutions may have additional features and integrations that our cloud providers might not provide.

Third-party solutions might be a service or a piece of software. We can use a service to avoid having to configure and maintain additional resources. A service might provide continuous or real-time monitoring features to ensure we see the most recent data. In contrast, a piece of software will require us to execute it manually or install and configure it to provide continuous or real-time features. We can adopt either approach or both depending on our business and technical requirements.

We might need to give third-party services access to our cloud provider environment. We should be cautious to grant least-privileged IAM policies and roles to the third-party entity. A data or Cybersecurity breach might give a malicious actor access to our AWS account. The malicious user might make undesired changes to our application and infrastructure if we used permissive IAM policies and roles that allow modifying and deleting resources.

We might need to give third-party software access as well. We run a risk similar to using a third-party service if someone gets access to the software or the credentials it uses. We should consider enabling and disabling the credentials before and after manually executing the software, respectively. If we develop a continuous monitoring solution, we should consider updating the credentials periodically; this applies to services as well. We should weigh the benefits and risks of using third-party software.

---

[8]"Amazon API Gateway dimensions and metrics." Amazon API Gateway Developer Guide. Amazon Web Services. https://docs.aws.amazon.com/apigateway/latest/developerguide/api-gateway-metrics-and-dimensions.html

Amazon Web Services (AWS)

We will discuss how we can leverage the different AWS features and capabilities to monitor our application and infrastructure.

Account Settings

We should update our alternate contacts to have billing, operations, and security contacts. We should use an email distribution list for each. Doing so allows the appropriate contacts to receive relevant notifications. We should update our billing preferences to receive free-tier usage alerts. This will enable us to respond if we are aiming to stay within the free tiers and keep costs low.

AWS Billing and Cost Management

The AWS Billing and Cost Management has different capabilities to help us monitor our usage and costs.[9] The service provides a dashboard, AWS Budgets, AWS Cost Explorer, AWS Cost and Usage Report, and AWS Cost Categories.

The dashboard provides a quick overview of the current incurred costs. We can quickly identify our most expensive services and assess whether we remain within the AWS Free Tier or exceed it.

AWS Budgets allows us to budget based on cost, usage, reservations, and savings plans. In a serverless environment, the cost and usage budgets are the most applicable. We might consider a reservation budget if we decide to use Elasticsearch[10] (an AWS-managed log aggregation service) to search the application logs.

We should configure notifications when the costs (actual or forecasted) and usage exceed the budgets. We can notify an email address and an SNS topic. An email distribution list or a ticketing system, which contains the appropriate billing contacts, should receive the notification.

AWS Cost Explorer allows us to group and filter usage costs. We can see patterns in usage costs and identify which services need cost optimization.

---

[9]"Monitoring your usage and costs." AWS Billing and Cost Management User Guide. Amazon Web Services. https://docs.aws.amazon.com/awsaccountbilling/latest/aboutv2/monitoring-costs.html

[10]Elasticsearch is a registered trademark of Elasticsearch BV.

AWS Cost and Usage Report allows us to create CSV exports of costs on an hourly or daily basis. We can use these CSV files to tailor our reports to conform to our business requirements. We should configure the report to provide additional details to identify trends in specific resources, even though it will increase the report size.

Amazon CloudWatch

CloudWatch provides multiple monitoring capabilities. CloudWatch Dashboards allows us to create customized dashboards with charts, counts, and query results. CloudWatch metrics allows us to monitor billing, usage, and metrics for services (e.g., DynamoDB, S3). CloudWatch Alarms allows us to notify via SNS when CloudWatch metrics exceeds and returns to a specified threshold. We can store our logs in CloudWatch Log Groups and query or forward those logs to a log aggregator. We also can query the log groups with CloudWatch Log Insights. CloudWatch Events allows us to configure an event source that triggers a Lambda function, SQS queue, SNS topic, Kinesis stream, and other targets that we can use to monitor the sources. CloudWatch ServiceLens takes advantage of AWS X-Ray to organize logs, metrics, X-Ray traces, and deployment canaries for a comprehensive monitoring solution for microservices. We can consider each Serverless configuration file as its microservices, for all intents and purposes, and using ServiceLens might be beneficial to enable. CloudWatch Synthetics allows us to monitor our application. We can have it check the availability of our API endpoints and perform a workflow to ensure the application is behaving as it should. We can get notified when an endpoint stops responding or a workflow fails to reach completion.

AWS X-Ray

AWS X-Ray allows us to link events and executions in our serverless environment. Our application has numerous individual parts, making it difficult to trace how they interconnect. Each Lambda function operates independently of each other, and multiple events can trigger them. Each DynamoDB table, API Gateway, SQS queue, SNS topic, and so on operate independently of each other as well. X-Ray allows us to follow the execution path by tracing the event. For example, a user request to a URL hosted by API Gateway will forward the request to a Lambda function. The function sends an event to an SNS topic. The topic forwards the message to an SQS queue, and the queue triggers another Lambda function. X-Ray allows us to trace that path. Furthermore, X-Ray will enable us to get a picture of the execution path via the service map. The tracing data and service map allows X-Ray to show latencies, error response codes, timestamps, and additional information.

AWS Personal Health Dashboard

The Personal Health Dashboard allows us to see when service degradations and outages affect the services our application uses. We can see a history of service issues and whether they affected our services.

Amazon Simple Storage Service (S3)

We can monitor our S3 buckets in multiple ways.[11] We can enable server access logs to capture log requests made to a bucket. We can use these logs to recognize patterns and anomalies. We can use the S3 management features. We enable the relevant CloudWatch metrics to monitor and visualize storage, requests, data transfer, and replication. We can allow analytics that automatically assesses access patterns and provide suggestions on the data lifecycle. We can use S3 to capture application logs in addition to CloudWatch Logs. S3 storage pricing is smaller than CloudWatch Logs. Using S3 to store logs allows us to store large-sized logs for extended periods and typically at lower costs.

Amazon Elasticsearch Service

Elasticsearch Service allows us to aggregate our application logs, CloudWatch metrics, and other relevant data. With relevant application data in one location, we can perform searches, queries, and monitoring. For example, we can correlate increased application error logs with error metrics to monitor for degraded application performance. We can use open source programs such as Kibana[12] to visualize the data and Logstash[13] to integrate with other tools.

---

[11]"Monitoring Amazon S3." Amazon Simple Storage Service Developer Guide. Amazon Web Services. `https://docs.aws.amazon.com/AmazonS3/latest/dev/monitoring-overview.html`

[12]Kibana is a registered trademark of Elasticsearch BV.

[13]Logstash is a registered trademark of Elasticsearch BV.

AWS Lambda

We can monitor AWS Lambda functions using the Lambda dashboard, CloudWatch metrics, and AWS X-Ray.[14]

The Lambda dashboard has prebuilt graphs we can view to monitor the overall performance of our Lambdas. These graphs can help us determine whether there is a performance issue (e.g., approaching the maximum allowed function invocations) for that AWS account. We cannot see issues with individual functions.

We can leverage CloudWatch metrics to monitor metrics for individual functions. We can use the function metrics to identify potential performance issues for each function. For example, we can monitor a Lambda function duration and update our Serverless configuration to limit the execution time to coincide with the typical duration time. We can also set up CloudWatch Alarms to notify us when metrics exceed specified thresholds.

We can leverage AWS X-Ray to trace the events that trigger a Lambda, the Lambda execution, and its following events, Lambda executions, or returns. Knowing the execution path allows us to pinpoint errors.

Amazon DynamoDB

We can monitor DynamoDB tables using the DynamoDB dashboard and CloudWatch metrics.[15] The dashboard provides us a status on CloudWatch Alarms and utilization of the DynamoDB capacity limits. We can use AWS CloudWatch metrics to monitor DynamoDB metrics. We can monitor these metrics with alarms to check when we exceed our capacities or see numerous errors, and we can adjust our provisioning appropriately.

---

[14]"Monitoring and troubleshooting Lambda applications." AWS Lambda Developer Guide. Amazon Web Services. `https://docs.aws.amazon.com/lambda/latest/dg/lambda-monitoring.html`

[15]"Monitoring Tools." Amazon DynamoDB Developer Guide. Amazon Web Services. `https://docs.aws.amazon.com/amazondynamodb/latest/developerguide/monitoring-automated-manual.html`

Azure

We will discuss how we can leverage the different Azure features and capabilities to monitor our application and infrastructure.

Account Settings

We should go to the Microsoft Account security settings and specify an alternate email address to receive security alerts. We should use an email distribution list for each. Doing so allows the appropriate contacts to receive relevant security notifications.

Azure Cost Management + Billing

Cost Management + Billing allows us to create a budget, perform a cost analysis, and optimize costs with recommendations from Azure Advisor. We can create a budget against a scope and configure an email alert when the costs exceed a percentage or amount threshold of the budget. The cost analysis graphs the costs per service, location, and subscription and compares it against the budgets. Advisor will provide us with recommendations by removing unused resources and enabling Blob storage lifecycle management to delete or archive old, unused data.

Azure Monitor

Azure Monitor allows us to centralize our logs and performance metrics in one location and monitor them. It collects Microsoft Active Directory (AD) audit logs, activity logs, resource logs, platform metrics, and any data reported via the Azure Data Collector API. These different data sources are grouped into metrics or logs. We can use metrics to access our application performance. The log data contains information about AD sign-in activity, service health, resource configuration changes, and resource operations logs. We can use the data sources in Azure Log Analytics to query the log data to find unusual behaviors, as described in the "General Principles" section. We can use them in Azure Application Insights to help us get an understanding of our application usage performance and any exceptions. We can use them in Azure Metrics Explorer to query our metrics. We can use them in Azure Dashboards to visualize our data. Finally, we can use them in Azure Workbooks to create interactive reports.

Azure Service Health

Azure Service Health allows us to see when service degradations and outages affect the services our application uses. Service Health provides us with a dashboard showing the service health and details of any disruption affecting our Azure resources.

Azure Sentinel

Azure Sentinel is a cloud-based security information and event management (SIEM) that uses artificial intelligence to analyze data from multiple Microsoft sources (e.g., Microsoft 365, Azure AD, and Microsoft Cloud App Security). We can use the REST API and built-in data connectors to ingest data from other sources. Azure Sentinel will generate alerts when it detects anomalies and potential security threats. We can create playbooks to automate our workflows in response to security alerts.

Google Cloud

We will discuss how we can leverage the different Google Cloud features and capabilities to monitor our application and infrastructure.

Account Settings

We should consider using a security email distribution list to get security-related notifications, and we should be cautious about who is on the distribution. If our Google account is personal, someone could potentially use that email address to recover a password. G Suite and Google Cloud Identity organizations provide additional features and help reduce that risk.

Billing and Cost Management

We can use Billing to review our costs. Billing provides a dashboard, reports, exports, cost breakdowns, price list, and the ability to create budgets. We can review our costs and identify which services and resources are the most costly and might need investigation and optimization. Budgets allow us to specify the desired monthly costs for the selected projects and services and to create notifications when the costs exceed certain thresholds. We can define a payment profile where we list an email distribution list that contains the appropriate billing contacts. Billing also provides us with recommendations for optimizing our costs.

IAM & Admin

We can update our "Privacy & Security" settings to specify email distribution lists for the European Union (EU) Representative Contact and Data Protection Officer in compliance with the EU General Data Protection Regulation legislation.

Google Cloud's Operations Suite

Google Cloud's operations suite provides services to help us monitor our application and infrastructure. We can send our logs to the Cloud Logging API, which passes them to the Logs Router. We specify rules in the Logs Router to determine which logs get accepted or discarded and which to include in exports. We can store the logs to the Logging storage, Cloud Storage, BigQuery, and Pub/Sub, which will send them to external systems. We can use Error Reporting to analyze our logs and notify us about errors. We can use Cloud Trace and Cloud Profiler to get latency statistics and resource consumption profiles, respectively, to help us find performance issues. Cloud Debugger allows us to investigate production issues without affecting the application. Cloud Monitoring will enable us to get health checks for our application endpoints to check that our application and its APIs are up and running. Cloud Monitoring also collects metadata, events, and metrics to visualize the data in a dashboard and send alerts. We can use Service Monitoring to detect issues in our App Engine serverless applications. We do this by defining service-level objects to monitor the appropriate App Engine operational and performance data, identify issues, generate service graphs, and create relevant alerts. We can take advantage of the different services to monitor low-level matters up to the entire application.

Auditing

Auditing allows us to check whether we correctly configured our serverless application and infrastructure. Over time, as the application evolves, we will notice changing settings and resources. Ideally, all the settings and resources will match what we expect. Realistically though, we may find there are unused resources still running, deprecated settings still enabled, and undesired modifications to security settings. With auditing, we can discover unusual behavior and potential weaknesses that might affect our security posture. We will review the general principles and provider-specific capabilities that can assist us in auditing our application and infrastructure.

General Principles

How we audit our application will vary depending on its design, the business and security requirements, and the budget. Yet, there are some general principles we can consider to implement in our auditing solution.

Authorization Attempts

We should consider monitoring failed authorization attempts in our serverless application and infrastructure. Our application should protect users by looking for suspicious activity and locking those user accounts because someone might be trying to take over our cloud provider account, which would put our business and application at risk.

Configuration Settings

Our application and infrastructure are configured based on specific settings. Some of these settings might potentially be benign if changed. But others could have serious implications. For example, application parameters that limit consecutive failed login attempts and require a minimum retry time between login attempts might have reduced security effectiveness if modified. Increasing the limit to an extremely large number and reducing the retry time to zero would allow someone to attempt a brute-force attack against login credentials. We should consider monitoring whether configuration settings match an approved baseline and when they are modified to ensure those changes pose no known or plausible security threat.

Infrastructure Changes

Although we are building and supporting a serverless application, the cloud provider does not limit us to having only serverless resources in our account. There may be unused resources enabled in our infrastructure. For example, a developer might have created a test resource and forgot to remove it, or a malicious user created a virtual machine to mine digital currency. It is also probable resources get modified or deleted. For example, someone might change our serverless database provisioning to a high value, resulting in a larger monthly bill, or a malicious user could delete user data records. We should consider monitoring when infrastructure is added, modified, or deleted. Additionally, check for the existence of new infrastructure and ensure its configuration matches a known baseline.

Privileges

In Chapter 6, we discussed Identity and Access Management (IAM) principles and how we might potentially implement them. The IAM policies and settings might start changing after we initially implement them. IAM privileges need updating as our application evolves, team members change, and development/business/security needs change. The changing landscape introduces the possibility that IAM privileges might need updating, or individuals might have access to resources they no longer need. We should consider auditing our IAM privileges to ensure we maintain the least privileges, assess what resources and permissions are in use, and remove access from users as appropriate.

Users and Credentials

We should consider auditing users and credentials that provide access to our cloud provider accounts. These entry points provide read, write, and delete privileges and might have detrimental effects if accessed by malicious users. We should check user accounts when a person joins or leaves the team and make sure we create and delete user accounts as appropriate. If a user has been inactive for a set period of time (e.g., 30 days), we should consider deactivating that user account. Users might have created credentials (e.g., access keys) that give another entry point to access the cloud provider account. We should review the last time they were used and their age. We should consider deactivating them when they were last used for a long period (e.g., two weeks) and were created more than a specified period (e.g., 90 days). This also applies to the credentials that our application uses. We should check the last time users changed their passwords and require a password change when it is older than a specified period (e.g., 90 days). We should check whether users have multi-factor authentication (MFA) enabled and, if not, require they enable it to add a layer of protection. Making sure we verify that our user accounts are up to date and credentials are short-lived helps reduce the risk of a malicious actor using either to access our cloud provider account.

Unusual Activity and Behaviors

Our application, users, and integrations follow typical behaviors. We would not expect a team colocated in the same region and working during a day shift to do massive workloads during the middle of the night from different locations. We should be suspicious of access from a country or region where our team members do not reside. We should be concerned when seeing API calls to disable security, monitoring, auditing, and alerting settings. We should, therefore, audit for unusual activity to identify activity that might have negative impacts on our business and application.

This topic might logically fit in the monitoring section because we would have to monitor this activity so we can respond to this promptly. However, this topic is in auditing because auditing is a general practice for checking compliance, whereas monitoring is responding to events. Security monitoring allows us to respond to security threats, but it can be argued we cannot identify a threat without some audit checks. Furthermore, the monitoring section focuses mostly on operational monitoring, whereas the auditing section focuses mainly on security compliance. Discussing a security monitoring topic seemed most appropriate in this section.

Known Vulnerabilities

We should audit our application code and resources for known vulnerabilities. As time progresses and our application evolves, the security communities might discover vulnerabilities that affect our application and infrastructure. Fortunately, using serverless resources offloads most of the vulnerability monitoring to the cloud provider. However, this does leave us with addressing any vulnerabilities in the configuration. Configuration settings that were once deemed secure might now be considered less secure. Our application code might use packages where security researchers have reported a known vulnerability. Failure to mitigate known vulnerabilities might leave our application and infrastructure vulnerable to the attack vectors mentioned in security findings. Therefore, auditing for security vulnerabilities will help us ensure we maintain a current security posture.

Third-Party Solutions

We might want to consider using a third-party solution that provides additional auditing capabilities to our cloud provider solution. Third-party solutions might support multiple auditing frameworks, requirement definitions, and industry best practices. They might provide other reporting formats and capabilities. They might integrate with our services that support our business and development processes. The third-party solutions and their additional features might be worth considering.

Third-party solutions might be services or a pieces of software. The benefits of a service are the features it provides and having reduced maintenance, but we risk storing security findings outside our cloud provider account. A data or Cybersecurity breach to the third-party services might expose our weaknesses to an outside party. We should consider addressing security findings as quickly as possible. Using a piece of software adds to our burden, but where we store the results is within our control. We can save the data using our internal processes or immediately purge the results after drafting a mitigation plan. We can adopt either approach or both depending on our business and technical requirements.

Our discussion about IAM privileges for our monitoring solution also applies to our auditing solution.

AWS

We will discuss how we can leverage the different AWS features and capabilities to audit our application and infrastructure.

AWS Config

We can use AWS Config to audit and monitor changes to our AWS resources. Config will identify our AWS resources and capture their current configuration. Whenever we add, modify, or delete a resource, Config will record the change in addition to who made it. We can create rules to define validation configurations for our resources. Config uses those rules to notify us when a resource fails to comply with its related Config rules. Config does support performing remediation to resolve findings. We can integrate Config with AWS CloudTrail to capture the API calls made to change a resource configuration. We should consider enabling Config to continuously audit and monitor our resources to ensure they maintain their desired configurations and comply with any business requirements and legal regulations.

AWS CloudTrail

CloudTrail allows us to audit and monitor data and management operations. It will capture API calls made to our serverless resources (e.g., S3, Lambda, and KMS) and record detailed information about the requests (e.g., IAM role, time, and IP address). It also captures actions for creating, modifying, and deleting resources and also records detailed information about the action. We should consider enabling CloudTrail in all AWS regions to identify any unusual activity and storing the audit records in S3 and CloudWatch for complying with business policies and legal regulations.

Amazon Macie

Amazon Macie is a service that analyzes, classifies, and protects our S3 data. Macie will use machine learning to analyze the S3 buckets for which we give it access. After analyzing the S3 objects, it will classify the data according to its sensitivity. It can monitor for suspicious user activity, such as a user downloading large quantities of sensitive data. We should consider using Macie when our application stores sensitive data in S3, and we need to protect that data as per legal regulations or business requirements.

AWS IAM Access Analyzer

IAM Access Analyzer is a feature of AWS IAM. When enabled, it provides continuous monitoring of our IAM permissions. Whenever we create or modify a policy, Access Analyzer evaluates the IAM permissions for IAM roles, S3 buckets, KMS keys, SQS queues, and Lambda functions. It reports findings for permissions and policies that might be a security concern and shows the last usage time for services. We can use these findings to adjust any policy changes that weaken our security posture and remove access to resources that our users are no longer using. We should consider using IAM Access Analyzer to help us achieve the least-privileged IAM policies and roles.

Amazon GuardDuty

GuardDuty provides us with continuous security monitoring by analyzing user activity and API request data from CloudTrail and Amazon VPC Flow and Domain Name System (DNS) logs. It identifies unusual and suspicious behavior and reports findings of possible threats. We can integrate GuardDuty with CloudWatch Events and Lambda to perform automated remediation of the security threat findings. We should consider using GuardDuty to respond to security threats quickly.

AWS Security Hub

Security Hub allows us to aggregate our security findings into one location. It works with Amazon GuardDuty, Amazon Inspector, Amazon Macie, and several AWS partner solutions. It reports results in a standardized format, grouped and prioritized for ease of review, analysis, and response. We can use CloudWatch Events, Lambda, and AWS Step Functions for automated remediation. We should consider using Security Hub to consolidate our security findings in one location so we can review and respond to security findings more efficiently.

Azure

We will discuss how we can leverage the different Azure features and capabilities to audit our application and infrastructure.

Azure Policy

Azure Policy helps us consolidate our policies and their compliance data. We can configure policies to audit findings (i.e., record compliance or noncompliance) or enforce them (i.e., allow or prevent configuration settings). We can manually review noncompliance findings or use bulk remediation to set the resources to be compliant automatically.

Azure Security Center

Azure Security Center audits your Azure resources. It checks the resources against best practices, common misconfigurations, security policies, and regulatory requirements. It consolidates the findings into a score and provides a list of recommendations to remediate the findings. Security Center also uses analytics and machine learning to detect potential threats and give you recommendations to address them. We can send the findings to Security Monitor for improved management.

Azure Advisor

Azure Advisor analyzes your Azure resources and usage data and provides recommendations to improve availability, security, performance, and cost. It consolidates the list of recommendations in one interface.

Google Cloud

We will discuss how we can leverage the different Google Cloud features and capabilities to audit our application and infrastructure.

Cloud Audit Logs

We can use Cloud Audit Logs, found in the IAM & Admin section, to detect unusual and suspicious activity. We can specify an audit configuration to capture audit logs when users perform data read, data write, and Google super admin[16] operations on our resources.

IAM & Admin

IAM allows us to enable Access Transparency when using an organization and have role-based support packages. Whereas Audit Logs capture the actions our team members perform, Access Transparency captures logs if and when Google personnel access our content.

Cloud Asset Inventory

Cloud Asset Inventory catalogs our resources and IAM policies by capturing metadata about them. We use the Cloud SDK CLI tool to work with that metadata. We can perform queries to search for our resources and IAM policies, export their metadata and history, and monitor changes. We can audit the current state of our resources and policies to make sure they are as we expect, and changes were made as intended. The monitoring allows us to get notified when someone modifies a resource and IAM policy. We can also analyze our IAM policies to audit who has access to what resources.

Data Catalog

Data Catalog allows us to discover our data and organizes it based on metadata. Data Catalog ingests data from BigQuery, Pub/Sub, and Cloud Storage and data outside Google Cloud via the Data Catalog API. We can search the metadata database to determine what type we have in our application. We might potentially find we have redundant data in multiple locations or have misplaced data in a location we did not expect.

---

[16]These users would be Google employees that use their privileges to access our account and data.

Cloud Data Loss Prevention (DLP)

Cloud DLP allows us to scan our data and classify it based on classification rules. We can run scans on Cloud Storage, BigQuery, and Datastore to identify whether they contain any sensitive data. We can send the results to BigQuery, Security Command Center, and Data Catalog for review and analysis. We might find we have sensitive data stored in locations where we do not expect. We can also send notifications via email or Pub/Sub to alert us of the results.

Security Command Center

Security Command Center centralizes our auditing functions by integrating with Cloud DLP and Cloud Audit Logs and generating compliance reports. It identifies security misconfigurations and vulnerabilities by identifying publicly exposed resources, insecure IAM configurations, firewalls with improper configurations, and compliance requirement findings. Security Command Center detects threats by monitoring Cloud Logging logs for unusual and suspicious activity and performing security scans for vulnerabilities in our web applications. The dashboard allows us to see all the findings in one location and apply the recommended remediations specified by the findings.

Alerting

Alerting allows us to receive notifications from our monitoring and auditing solutions. I chose to discuss alerting separately from monitoring and auditing to highlight that monitoring/auditing themselves may not notify us about the results. Monitoring and auditing may be performed either manually or automatically. A manual solution may not require alerting, whereas an automatic solution should require alerting because a person may not review the results within a reasonable time frame. Therefore, we should consider alerting as a different pillar and configure alerts to provide timely and relevant notifications to the response team. We will review the general principles and provider-specific capabilities that can assist us in alerting us.

General Principles

How we configure alerting will vary depending on the application's design, the business and security requirements, and the budget. Yet, there are some general principles we can consider to implement in our alerting solution.

Security-Related Notifications

Your organization should have a team that can respond to security-related events. Whether you have dedicated security teams or only developers, having individuals assigned to respond to security events allows your organization to respond more effectively. Your organization should have an email distribution list that includes individuals responsible for responding to security events.

After establishing the security email distribution list, we should set up our provider account and any third-party monitoring and alerting tools to send security-related notifications to that email list. This allows the security team to respond appropriately. The types of notifications this list might receive include upcoming deprecations, known vulnerabilities, and unusual and suspicious activities.

Operational Notifications

In addition to having a security email distribution list, we should have an email distribution list to catch all notifications and alerts. Whether an error happens in the system or we were notified of an upcoming outage, we should have a dedicated team to respond to these notifications. Without having this team, our application might stop functioning due to numerous errors or a planned outage, for example.

In addition to using an email distribution list, we can use provider and third-party tools. The providers have notification capabilities that can alert email addresses and mobile phones or trigger our serverless functions that perform custom notifications. Third parties allow us to add additional notification options (e.g., SMSs, phone calls, mobile app push notifications, instant message notifications) that might better support the processes, workflows, and preferences our organizations might have. Whether we use the cloud provider tools or a third-party system, we should configure the notifications to alert the correct individuals with the appropriate level of information and promptly.

Verbosity

The notification verbosity is sometimes an art to configure. The level of verbosity defines how many notifications to send, the types of notifications, how often to send them, and how much information to include. Having too much verbosity may result in recipients ignoring alerts. Conversely, too little could mean not sending a notification when one is much needed.

The response team will initially respond to notifications, but over time they become less responsive if they are receiving too many notifications or the severity (or importance) of the notifications seems irrelevant or unimportant. The story of "The Boy Who Cried Wolf" provides a relatable lesson in notification verbosity.[17] We need to ensure we send notifications when we want our response team to take action, and those notifications should include the proper level of urgency. This way, we avoid waking up a team member in the middle of the night for a lower urgency notification.

Let's not confuse notification verbosity with verbosity in our logs and audit records. We should have more verbosity in logs and audit records to make sure we have ample information that can ultimately result in notifications. We cannot send error notifications if our application is not logging errors or logging insufficient error logs. We cannot detect malicious activity if our auditing is not capturing different types of records. We cannot send notifications when our application behavior is deviating from standard patterns if we are not creating logs at different log levels. The more verbose our logs and audit records, the more we will achieve a higher probability of sending relevant notifications when the patterns start to deviate but, we must be careful not to log sensitive information as discussed in the previous chapter.

Notification Destinations

We should evaluate where we want our alert notifications to go. We can configure sending our alerts to message queues, individual email addresses, email distribution lists, third-party services, or a combination of any of these. We should configure a destination that allows the response team to receive timely notifications and

---

[17]This story is about a boy who pretended and cried, "Wolf! Wolf!" Others came to his rescue only to find no wolf. This happened multiple times. Eventually, everyone stopped listening to him. One day a real wolf came, but nobody came to his rescue. You may read this story at the Library of Congress. "The Shepherd Boy & the Wolf." The Aesop for Children. Circa 620–560 BCE. www.read.gov/aesop/043.html

acknowledge receipt. Failure to receive timely notifications might result in a service outage or a security incident. Failure to acknowledge receipt may result in the recipient forgetting to address the notification or thinking another team member will look into it. Depending on the severity of the alert, it might be worthwhile to consider manually sending follow-up notifications to the user base and stakeholders when the issue or finding is still unresolved after a reasonable time. Wherever we decide to send the alert notifications, we should ensure they are being reviewed and addressed.

Third-Party Solutions

Similar to our discussion about third-party monitoring and auditing solutions, third-party alerting solutions might provide additional features. These solutions might integrate with phone and text messaging systems, ticketing and support systems, mobile apps, instant messaging platforms, and others. We might be able to avoid the issue about IAM privileges by using webhooks, APIs, and other integrations that only need a way to trigger the alert and not need access to our cloud provider account. These systems might have reporting capabilities where we can assess how quickly our response team addresses notifications. These systems might even support the automatic notification closure when our application and infrastructure report a restoration. The case for having a third-party solution (whether a service or software) might be more compelling than using a cloud provider solution because we potentially get increased reliability in our notifications when our cloud provider is experiencing service degradation.

AWS

We will discuss how we can leverage the different AWS features and capabilities to alert us about our monitoring events and audit findings. The AWS monitoring and auditing services integrate with the following services in one way or another for sending alert notifications.

Amazon Simple Notification Service (SNS)

SNS allows us to receive notifications from DynamoDB, CloudWatch Alarms, CloudWatch Events, CloudTrail, Config, Elasticsearch, and so on. We can forward these notifications to a Lambda function, SQS queue, or a webhook to send the notification to the appropriate response team. We can use a Lambda function that sends an email to an email distribution list using Amazon Simple Email Service. We can use the SQS queue to store the SNS notification message and process it programmatically. We can use a webhook to send the notification to other applications or third-party services. Multiple Lambda functions, SQS queues, and webhooks can subscribe to the SNS topic. This allows us to have numerous ways to respond to alerts.

Amazon CloudWatch Alarms and Events and Event Bridge

Some services do not support sending alerts and notifications. CloudWatch Alarms and CloudWatch Events and Event Bridge help us bridge the gap. CloudWatch Alarms allow us to publish a message to an SNS topic when exceeding the threshold for a CloudWatch metric and when it returns to within range. This allows us to monitor our serverless resources continuously. CloudWatch Events and Event Bridge will enable us to trigger a Lambda function or Step Function state machine; publish a message to an SNS topic, SQS queue, or Kinesis team; run a Systems Manager operation; and so on from a CloudTrail API call. This allows us to respond to unusual activity that CloudTrail identifies. We can use CloudWatch Alarms and Events and Event Bridge to help us achieve continuous monitoring and auditing.

Azure

We will discuss how we can leverage the different Azure features and capabilities to alert us about our monitoring events and audit findings.

Azure Monitor

We can configure Azure Monitor to send alerts when our metrics exceed our metric thresholds. We will be able to see all the alerts in a centralized location where we can review, acknowledge, and query alerts. It will display the type of alert (metric or log), alert information, and the severity (information, warning, etc.). We also can query our alerts from Azure Resource Graph and an external system by using the Azure Alert Management REST API.

In addition to creating alerts, we can configure automated actions when we get an alert. The automated actions can call a webhook, launch an Azure Workbook, trigger an Azure Function, or start an Azure Logic Apps. Alerts enable us to improve our workflow.

We can integrate Azure Monitor with external monitoring and alerting systems (e.g., a security information and event management [SIEM] system). We can integrate with external systems by using Azure Event Hubs, Azure Partner integrations, or the Azure REST APIs.

Azure Service Health

Azure Service Health can automatically send us alerts via email, SMS, and push notification so we can respond to Azure service outages.

Google Cloud

We will discuss how we can leverage the different Google Cloud features and capabilities to alert us about our monitoring events and audit findings.

Google Cloud Operation's Suite

The services in Google Cloud Operation's suite support sending alerts via email, the Google Cloud Console Mobile App, SMS, Pub/Sub, and webhook. We can use webhooks and Pub/Sub topics to send alerts to third-party services.

Security Command Center

Security Command Center sends alerts via Gmail, SMSs, Pub/Sub, and Cloud Functions.

Cloud Pub/Sub

Many of the services we might use for monitoring and auditing support sending alerts to Pub/Sub topics. Some of these services include Budget alerts, Cloud Monitoring, Security Command Center, and Operation's suite. Pub/Sub will receive the alert, and it can distribute it to multiple targets (e.g., Cloud Functions, App Engine, and Firebase) where we can create user notifications and integrate into our workflows.

Cloud Functions

Whether our monitoring and auditing services support sending alerts to Cloud Functions or we trigger a Cloud Function from Pub/Sub, we can use them to send alerts. The Cloud Function can use an SDK, API, or any custom logic to send an alert to many types of notification capabilities and third-party solutions.

Key Takeaways

We established what monitoring, auditing, and alerting are and how they relate to each other. Monitoring allows us to assess how well our application is doing. By monitoring, we can detect performance issues and errors. Auditing allows us to identify potential security issues and noncompliance to legal regulations and business requirements. We discussed security monitoring in the auditing section because security issues are typically a result of a failure to comply with a security policy and best practices. We might liken security monitoring to having continuous auditing. Alerting allows us to receive notifications when our monitoring and auditing detect performance issues, suspicious activity, and noncompliance. We can configure alerts to send notifications via email, SMS, push notification, and third-party solutions (e.g., instant message and ticketing systems). The monitoring and auditing systems may or may not provide alerting capabilities, or they may allow us to forward findings to services that will start the alerting process. Monitoring, auditing, and alerting are related and essential in understanding how our application functions and to finding and addressing performance and security issues.

We discussed the general principles for each topic. These general principles provided items and practices to consider when implementing our monitoring, auditing, and alerting solutions. There are many additional factors to consider (like business and technical requirements, cost and schedule, and workflows), but the general principles are a starting point. We followed the general principles by reviewing the different AWS, Azure, and Google Cloud services we can utilize to implement our solution. Some services provide basic features, and others provide advanced capabilities (e.g., machine learnings and artificial intelligence). Whether choosing a basic or advanced service will depend on many factors. Ultimately, we want to make sure we detect when our application is experiencing issues and detect when our security posture is weakening to be able to send a notification to the appropriate persons.

CHAPTER 12

Additional Considerations

In this chapter, we will review additional topics for us to consider in our project. They are based on situations from projects using the Serverless Framework and Cybersecurity concepts. The topics we will review are in no particular order and were reserved for the penultimate[1] chapter to share additional thoughts without disrupting the main messages from the previous chapters.

Balancing Security and Other Requirements

We might find while working on our projects that sometimes there might be contention between security engineers, software developers, or end users. Developers and end users might perceive security requirements and processes as overbearing and burdensome. Security engineers might create overly burdensome and complex processes to reduce risk and address the concern that no one can be trusted. At some point, the developers and users will find ways to circumvent security policies. Rather than implement more security policies and processes, we should consider having a balanced approach.

As security engineers, our goal is to protect our application and business from security threats. We should avoid implementing any security that would cost the company more money than the cost of the attack/breach. For example, we should not spend $1 million to protect a $5 asset. Alternatively, we want to invest $1 million to address a security risk that would cost the business $1 billion if it were to happen. We should avoid implementing password security users might perceive too difficult. For example, we should not require passwords with a minimum of 64 mixed characters when requiring a minimum of 12 mix characters with multi-factor authentication enabled would achieve similar results. Alternatively, we might consider

---

[1]Second to last.

© Miguel A. Calles 2020
M. Calles, *Serverless Security*, https://doi.org/10.1007/978-1-4842-6100-2_12

adding passwordless authentication[2] to an application that stores no sensitive data (e.g., payment information, social security numbers, mailing addresses, etc.). Sometimes more security does not mean better, and simpler processes provide greater security.

Continuous Integration/Continuous Delivery

We should consider having a CI/CD pipeline to perform automated checks that someone might forget to run manually. CI/CD pipelines allow us to evaluate our source code and deploy it after completing all automated source code checks. We can require that the automated source code checks must pass before the source code is accepted, merged, and deployed. Some of the types of source code checks include unit tests, code coverage, static code analysis,[3] dynamic application security testing (DAST), and package and dependency vulnerability checks.[4] As good as checklists and manual inspections might be in helping us remember steps to take, individuals are still prone to forgetting to use them. When the automated checks pass and the source code is ready to deploy, the CI/CD pipeline should automatically deploy it to a nonproduction environment. Doing this helps test the deployment process. It provides us with an environment where we can perform interactive application security testing (IAST) by using the application and trying to find issues. Having a CI/CD pipeline provides us with a repeatable process and can improve our security posture with the proper automated checks.

We must remember to secure and maintain our CI/CD pipeline. Some CI/CD pipelines use a dedicated server, container orchestration software, or third-party solutions. We should keep our dedicated servers and containers up to date with the latest operating system updates, deployment software updates, and security settings. When we choose to deploy our source code, the CI/CD pipeline needs credentials to deploy to AWS, Azure, and Google Cloud. We must take measures to protect these credentials, as discussed in Chapter 8, and ensure they are least privileged as mentioned in Chapter 6. If a malicious user managed to get access to our CI/CD environment, that person could obtain any plaintext secrets (e.g., passwords and AWS access keys) and might trigger

---

[2]Passwordless authentication is a single-factor authentication approach where the user provides an email address or phone number. The user receives a one-time password (like a six-digit code or a secure link) that completes the login processes.

[3]Also known as linting and static application security testing (SAST).

[4]npm provides the npm audit feature to scan for known vulnerabilities in our dependencies.

delete processes that could remove our data and application. We should consider the CI/CD pipeline as an asset that needs protection from potential threats.

Source Control

Most likely, the majority of software projects use some type of source control software. What might not be common practice is how to secure the repositories we create in our source control software. We should set up our source control software and repositories with security in mind.

These security practices will help us protect our source code:

- Use end-to-end encryption (e.g., SSH) for data in transit.

- Limit access to the server or service through user accounts.

- Enable two-factor or multi-factor authentication when possible.

- Cryptographically sign commits with asymmetric keys.

- Keep the source control software (and any servers hosting it) up to date.

- Use hooks to verify the source code does not contain sensitive information before committing.[5]

- Consider encrypting the repository.

- Use ignore files to prevent committing unwanted files and files containing secrets (e.g., environment files).

Following these practices helps protect against a malicious actor obtaining or modifying our code.

Serverless Framework Plugins

The Serverless Framework plugins enhance how we use the Serverless Framework when deploying our application software. We might want to use plugins that optimize our

---

[5]One of my articles explains how to use pre-commit git hooks. "Removing Sensitive Data & Plaintext Secrets from GitHub." Miguel Calles. Secjuice. March 1, 2020. www.secjuice.com/github-complete-cleaning-sensitive-secrets

deployments, improve our security, add additional functionality, and so on. We can find these plugins at the Serverless Plugins Directory[6] or the Serverless GitHub page.[7]

When we find a plugin we are considering using, we should consider inspecting the source code. The majority of source code is open source, and we can check it freely. Although a plugin is open source, the author might be the only person that has inspected it. We might install a plugin that weakens our security posture. For example, there is a plugin that uses the JavaScript "eval" command, and it is possible to create a new file on the file system by injecting a command.[8] Understanding how the plugins work is essential because they assume the same privileges used to deploy the Serverless configuration. A rogue command coded into the plugin could potentially cause an undesired change.

We might want to build custom plugins. Having custom plugins reduces the risk of malicious code, assuming we use credible npm packages. We can use plugins without publishing to npm or the Serverless Plugins Directory by running them locally. Private plugins can be used in projects to enhance the application deployment and perform data checks against policies. Custom plugins are handy but do require a time investment.

Serverless Configuration Sizes

We should consider keeping our Serverless configurations small and use multiple configurations. We might want to have one Serverless configuration for each of the following items:

- Database

- Object storage

- Group of functions (or microservice)

- Application component

Keeping our Serverless configurations small reduces our security attack surface. For example, in a project, there could be a group of AWS Lambda functions accepting events

---

[6]"Serverless Framework Plugins." Serverless, Inc. `www.serverless.com/plugins`

[7]"Plugins." Serverless. GitHub. `https://github.com/serverless/plugins`

[8]"Insecure Serverless Plugins: Why You Should Inspect the Source Code." Miguel Calles. Secjuice. March 29, 2020. `www.secjuice.com/insecure-serverless-plugins-why-you-should-inspect-the-source-code`

from an Amazon API Gateway. One Lambda function managed to have flawed logic that sent numerous requests to its API Gateway. The flawed logic resulted in the API Gateway becoming overloaded and starting to throttle requests. Eventually, the API Gateway stopped accepting all requests, and none of the other functions could trigger. This is an example of accidentally performing a Denial of Service (DoS) attack against the API Gateway and denying access to all the functions. If the application has all its Lambda functions in the same Serverless configuration file, the entire application would have experienced the DoS.

Another example could be someone accidentally deleting a database when trying to delete the functions. Putting the database and functions into separate Serverless configurations prevents inadvertently modifying the database when adding, modifying or removing the functions. Separating the resources allows us to be mindful when altering the Serverless configuration files.

Optimizing Functions

We discussed monitoring our functions in Chapter 11. We can use the monitoring data and test results when initially developing the function to optimize the function. We should attempt to optimize our functions when we first create them and periodically after that.

Having inefficient functions may have speed, cost, and security implications. Having functions with inefficient code, large package sizes, and lengthy synchronous executions might result in long function execution time and latent responses in the application. The longer it takes a function to execute, the more costly it becomes. Also, improper CPU and memory sizing might result in longer execution time if inadequately sized or increased costs if overprovisioned. If we manage to send an input that results in longer execution time, we can potentially create a DoS attack by sending numerous inputs to that same function. We should take steps to optimize our functions to ensure they execute as efficiently as possible.

Some steps we can take to optimize our functions include

- Limit the scope of work in the function to a particular task.

- Functions should only accept input from one event source instead of multiple.

- Functions should limit interactions to one resource and one action (e.g., only write data to one database table).

- Generate test data or use monitoring data to find the optimal amount of CPU and memory.

- Set the shortest execution timeout that allows the function to finish executing.

- Reduce the function package size by using packaging tools (e.g., webpack[9]).

- Avoid using global variables in the function code and writing to temporary file systems because the data persists between function executions and may result in unexpected behavior.

Keeping functions small and optimized improves the application speed, reduces cost, and makes the application more resilient to DoS attacks.

Fault Trees

We should plan for outages. We mentioned DoS attacks earlier and service outages in Chapter 11. We can also experience outages from third-party integrations, unexpected changes in our function inputs, expired SSL certificates, and various other ways. Developing a fault tree can help us identify potential failures, and we can use that to develop mitigations.

These are some example failure scenarios and how we might mitigate them:

- The timer service that triggers our functions used to send bills to our customers becomes non-operational. We could set up a backup timer service in a different region within the same cloud provider, set up a backup timer service with a different cloud provider, or set up a small server to act as a backup timer service.

---

[9]webpack is a registered trademark of the OpenJS Foundation.

- Pricing data inputs suddenly changed their format to report price as a string instead of a number. We could configure the input validation to be flexible and accept strings containing numbers and cast them to a number.

- A third-party integration stops providing data or starts rejecting inputs. We could keep track of which data records and system events we have not yet processed and attempt to process them again when the third-party integration is functional.

We should do the best we can to plan for failures and determine how those failures might affect our application and security posture.

Key Takeaways

We explored some additional considerations based on situations from projects using serverless environments. We started by discussing that we should balance security with the other requirements. We want to avoid implementing security that exceeds the business value and creates a burden for the developer and end users. We should remember that simple solutions might provide sufficient protection. We continued by addressing topics in development and how they affect our security postures, such as Continuous Integration/Continuous Delivery pipelines and source control. We shifted the conversation into optimizations and security concerns when defining a Serverless configuration file and using Serverless Framework plugins. Finally, we concluded by providing ways to optimize the serverless functions and discussing why we should use a fault tree to identify potential failures. These topics might be worthwhile to include in your security assessment.

## CHAPTER 13

Finalizing the Risk Assessment

In this chapter, we will discuss how to finalize the risk assessment we started in Chapter 2 to present it to our business stakeholders.

Collecting All the Findings

In Chapter 2, we discussed how to prepare a risk assessment. It is the first technical chapter because it laid the foundation for addressing security in our serverless application. Reviewing the documentation, inspecting the source code, understanding the architecture, becoming acquainted with the application, and quantifying the threats prepared us in performing the risk assessment. Without understanding the uniqueness of the application and project, we would merely be suggesting good practices instead of addressing the specific security concerns that affect it. The subsequent chapters provided information about security topics that we can assess against the application.

We might have found potential security issues based on each chapter. Let's suppose we had a team of five security engineers that each used two chapters to assist them with their investigation. Each engineer identified ten findings per chapter. Collectively, this team found 100 security findings. We will want to consolidate all these findings in a manageable format. We can group the findings into logical groups. In Table 2-5, we used the asset type as one way to group findings. We can also group them by microservice, system functionality, or security topic (like the chapter names). Having all findings grouped will facilitate in scoring them from the most severe to the least.

© Miguel A. Calles 2020
M. Calles, *Serverless Security*, https://doi.org/10.1007/978-1-4842-6100-2_13

Scoring the Findings

After grouping and organizing all findings, we can identify the severity within each group. Let's suppose we organized by microservice. In the payment processing microservice, we might categorize one finding as having a high severity and the rest with low severity. We discovered that sending a negative payment amount into our function triggers an unexpected refund, and we deemed that as high severity because it would result in revenue loss. In the notification microservice, we discovered a finding that allows a function to send a payment reminder email to the incorrect recipients. We might deem this finding as the most severe finding within that microservice. We then continue to assess each microservice. By the end, we will have identified the most to least severe findings within each microservice.

We can proceed to compare the most severe findings between microservices. Continuing with the previous hypothetical situation, we may determine the most severe findings are the following: issuing unexpected refunds in the payment processing microservice and sending incorrect billing notifications in the notifications microservice. We might suggest that issuing unexpected refunds is more severe because it results in lost revenue. In contrast, we can address sending an incorrect billing notification by sending an apology email or answering customers' questions. We should probably consider lowering the severity of the second finding. Reducing this notification finding would result in potentially decreasing the other notification findings to maintain the relative severities within the microservice. After making these comparisons between each of the groupings, we would have a pretty good laddering of the findings.

Assessing the Business Impact

We should use the findings and populate the risk assessment, as we did in Table 2-5. The table will help us succinctly describe the threat, mitigation, and risk level. The severity is not a risk level, but it helps define it. The risk matrix from Table 2-6 helps us calculate the risk level by using likelihood and impact. The impact and severity are synonymous. With the risk level defined, we can start quantifying the business impact.

We should add a new column to the risk assessment table to specify the business impact. We should communicate it in terms meaningful to the business. We should compare the costs of someone exploiting the risk vs. the cost of implementing any protections and mitigations.

Let's suppose we have two functions: one which places orders and a second which issues refunds. Then, suppose our top two risks are these functions being susceptible to Denial of Service (DoS) attacks. We might capture these two risks in our risk assessment similar to Table 13-1.

Table 13-1. *Sample Updated Risk Assessment*

Microservice	Threat	Mitigation	Risk	Business Impact
Order processing	Cannot receive new orders	Add rate limiting and test with simulated DoS attacks	High	$50K in revenue lost per hour. $50K for DoS testing. Forty hours to add rate limiting. Two months to deliver
Payment processing	Issuing unexpected refunds for orders within three months	Improve input validation and require approval to issue refunds	High	$100M lost in refunds. Sixty hours to add input validation and business approvals. Two weeks to deliver

Let's suppose we believe the order processing and payment processing are very similar in risk. We will estimate it will take a total of three months to deliver the risk based on the business impact stated earlier. If we experience a DoS attack for three months continuously, the revenue lost would be slightly over $100 million at the rate of $50,000 per hour. The total monetary loss is effectively the same for both threats. We identified the order processing threat higher because we believe it requires less skill to launch a DoS attack than sending a well-crafted input to refund all the transactions within the past three months. We present our findings as best as we can and make a compelling case to the business stakeholders.

The stakeholders will ultimately decide what risks to address and those to accept (i.e., not fix at this time). They will also define the priorities in which to address the risks. For example, the stakeholders might prioritize the payment processing risk over the order processing risk. They might decide it is better to solve a top risk within two weeks rather than waiting two months to address any risks. Furthermore, although the likelihood of the payment processing risk is lower than the other, the business would realize a greater financial impact because it is unlikely a DoS attack would last three months continuously. We should work with the stakeholders and the implementation team to develop a schedule to meet the priorities and budget the stakeholders allocate.

Key Takeaways

Preparing the final risk assessment, in theory, should be relatively straightforward. By this point, you (and your team) would have done your due diligence in investigating the different security aspects for your serverless application. This book highlighted some methods; covered security topics; reviewed AWS, Azure, and Google Cloud services we can leverage; and provided recommendations. The security field, capabilities, and threats are always evolving. The chapters in this book aimed to provide you with an overview of serverless security that will guide you in your assessment and remediation. By using this book, you will have a comprehensive risk assessment to provide for your stakeholders. You will leverage your (and your team's) experience and knowledge and the knowledge of the business and technical requirements to perform your evaluation and to develop the mitigations. Your goal should be to present it effectively to the stakeholders. They should be informed about the business impacts the security risks pose. Having this information will enable them to make informed decisions and determine which risks to address, the budget to allocate, and notional delivery dates.

APPENDIX A

List of Acronyms

This appendix contains the acronyms used throughout the book.

Acronym	Definition
AD	Active Directory
AES	Advanced Encryption Standard
ALB	Application Load Balancers
AMQP	Advanced Message Queueing Protocol
API	Application Programming Interface
ARN	Amazon Resource Name
AuthN	Authentication
AuthZ	Authorization
AWS	Amazon Web Services
blob	Binary Large Object
CaaS	Container as a Service
CCPA	California Consumer Privacy Act
CD	Continuous Delivery
CDN	Content Delivery Network
CERT	Computer Emergency Response Team
CI	Continuous Integration
CIA	Confidentiality, Integrity, and Availability
CLI	Command-Line Interface

(continued)

© Miguel A. Calles 2020
M. Calles, *Serverless Security*, https://doi.org/10.1007/978-1-4842-6100-2

Acronym	Definition
CMK	Customer Master Key
CORS	Continuously Operating Reference Station
CPU	Central Processing Unit
CRON	Command Run On
CSA	Cloud Security Alliance
CVE	Common Vulnerabilities and Exposures
DAST	Dynamic Application Security Testing
DDoS	Distributed Denial of Service
DLP	Data Loss Prevention
DNS	Domain Name System
DoS	Denial of Service
ECDSA	Elliptic Curve Digital Signature Algorithm
EOL	End of Life
EU	European Union
FaaS	Function as a Service
FBI	Federal Bureau of Investigation
GCP	Google Cloud Platform
GDPR	General Data Protection Regulation
HMAC	Hash-based Message Authentication Code
HTTP	HyperText Transfer Protocol
HTTP(S)	HyperText Transfer Protocol or HyperText Transfer Protocol Secure
HTTPS	HyperText Transfer Protocol Secure
IaaS	Infrastructure as a Service
IAM	Identity and Access Management
IAST	Interactive Application Security Testing
IC3	Internet Crime Complaint Center

(continued)

Acronym	Definition
ID	Identifier
IdP	Identity Provider
IoT	Internet of Things
IT	Information Technology
JS	JavaScript
JSON	JavaScript Object Notation
JWE	JSON Web Encryption
JWS	JSON Web Signature
JWT	JavaScript Object Notation Web Token
KMS	Key Management System
MAC	Message Authentication Code
MFA	Multi-Factor Authentication
NCSC	National Computer Security Conference
NLB	Network Load Balancer
NoSQL	Not Only Structured Query Language
NVD	National Vulnerability Database
OAuth	Open Authorization
OIDC	OpenID Connect
OS	Operating System
OU	Organizational Unit
OWASP	Open Web Application Security Project
PaaS	Platform as a Service
PII	Personally Identifiable Information
PoLP	Principle of Least Privilege
RAIDs	Redundant Arrays of Independent Disks
RBAC	Role-Based Access Control

(continued)

Acronym	Definition
ReDoS	Regular Expression Denial of Service
REST	Representational State Transfer
RSA	Rivest-Shamir-Adleman
S3	Simple Storage Service
SaaS	Software as a Service
SAML	Security Assertion Markup Language
SAST	Static Application Security Testing
SDK	Software Development Kit
SEI	Software Engineering Institute
SES	Simple Email Service
SHA	Secure Hash Algorithm
SHA-2	Secure Hash Algorithm 2
sls	Serverless
SMS	Simple Messaging Service
SNS	Simple Notification Service
SQL	Structured Query Language
SQS	Simple Queue Service
SSH	Secure Shell
SSM	Systems Manager
SSO	Single Sign-On
URI	Uniform Resource Identifier
URL	Uniform Resource Locator
US	United States
UUID	Universally Unique Identifier
VPC	Virtual Private Cloud

(continued)

Acronym	Definition
XML	Extensible Markup Language
XSS	Cross-Site Scripting
YAML	Yet Another Markup Language
YML	Yet Another Markup Language

APPENDIX B

Setup Instructions

In this appendix, you will learn how to set up items you will need to work with serverless.

Installing Software

We mentioned in Chapter 2 that we would focus on the Node.js and the Serverless Framework.

To Install Node.js and npm

1. Go to `https://nodejs.org/en/download/`.

2. Download the installer for your OS and Node.js version (version 10 or later at the time of this writing).

3. Open the installer file and follow the prompts.

4. Open a terminal.

5. Type the following command and confirm it returns a version number:

    `node -v`

6. Type the following command and confirm it returns a version number:

    `npm -v`

© Miguel A. Calles 2020
M. Calles, *Serverless Security*, https://doi.org/10.1007/978-1-4842-6100-2

To Install the Serverless Framework

1. Open a terminal.

2. Configure your global npm package directory by typing the following commands:

    ```
    mkdir ~/.npm-packages
    npm config set prefix "${HOME}/.npm-packages"
    ```

3. Install the Serverless Framework globally by typing the following command:

    ```
    npm install -g serverless
    ```

4. Read the Serverless Framework "getting started" document at https://serverless.com/framework/docs/getting-started/ to learn more.

To Set Up Python (Required by the AWS CLI)

1. Go to www.python.org/downloads/.

2. Download the installer for your OS and Node.js version (version 3.5 or later at the time of this writing).

3. Open the installer file and follow the prompts.

4. Open a terminal.

5. Type the following command and confirm it returns a version number:

    ```
    python3 –version
    ```

To Set Up the Amazon Web Services (AWS) Command-Line Interface (CLI)

1.   Determine whether you need AWS CLI version 1 or 2. (If you are unsure, try installing version 2.)

2.   To install version 1:

     a. Install Python 3.

     b. Type the following commands:

         ```
         python3 -m pip install awscli --upgrade --user
         ```

     c. Visit the AWS CLI version 1 installation instruction at `https://docs.aws.amazon.com/cli/latest/userguide/install-cliv1.html` to learn more.

3.   To install version 2:

     a. Visit `https://docs.aws.amazon.com/cli/latest/userguide/install-cliv2.html`.

     b. Follow its instructions.

To Set Up the Microsoft Azure CLI

1.   Visit `https://docs.microsoft.com/en-us/cli/azure/install-azure-cli`.

2.   Follow its instructions.

To Set Up the Google Cloud Software Development Kit (SDK) and CLI

1.   Visit `https://cloud.google.com/sdk/docs`.

2.   Follow its instructions.

Configuring the Cloud Provider in the Serverless Framework

The Serverless Framework provides proper documentation to help you configure your cloud provider.

To Configure AWS

1. Visit www.serverless.com/framework/docs/providers/aws/ guide/credentials/.

2. Follow its instructions.

To Configure Azure

1. Visit www.serverless.com/framework/docs/providers/azure/ guide/credentials/.

2. Follow its instructions.

To Configure Google Cloud

1. Visit www.serverless.com/framework/docs/providers/google/ guide/credentials/.

2. Follow its instructions.

APPENDIX C

Exercises Review

In this appendix, we will review the exercises.

EXERCISE 2-1: PERFORMING A DOCUMENT REVIEW

Instructions:

Review each diagram to understand how the application works and identify how they relate.

Create a document highlighting areas of concern. Include a list of follow-up questions to inquire of the team.

Answer:

Some areas of concerns we could have highlighted include

- What was the rationale for the supplier server having access to our Amazon VPC?

- Can the supplier server perform unexpected triggers to Lambda functions within the Amazon VPC?

- How does the mobile application perform authentication to the API?

- How does the API verify the mobile application's authorization?

- How do we authenticate into the third-party APIs?

- Are the account Lambda functions and DynamoDB table outside from the Amazon VPC which the supplier uses?

- Is the mobile app able to query account DynamoDB table for data from other accounts?

© Miguel A. Calles 2020
M. Calles, *Serverless Security*, https://doi.org/10.1007/978-1-4842-6100-2

- Is the mobile app for both the seller and the buyer?

- What is the difference between the seller and the supplier?

- How does the seller list merchandise when the supplier does the fulfillment?

- Can the seller add merchandise to the inventory that the supplier cannot fulfill?

There are probably many more questions we could have added to our list.

EXERCISE 3-1: CHOOSING A RUNTIME

Instructions:

Assess all the results and recommend the package(s) the developers should use.

Answer:

At the time of this writing, the Node.js 8 versions had more known vulnerabilities than Node.js 10. The latest Node.js 8 version also had more known vulnerabilities than the latest Node.js 10 version. We should recommend Node.js 10 based on the number of vulnerabilities. Furthermore, the end-of-life date for Node.js 8 was December 31, 2019, and Node.js 10 is still supported, which is another reason to choose Node.js 10.

At the time of this writing, the most recent release of Python 2 and Python 3 had a very similar number of known vulnerabilities. Based on this alone, we would allow both. We should determine their release schedule and look for any end-of-life notices. We would have learned the end-of-life was January 1, 2020, for Python 2 and March 18, 2019, for Python 3.4. We would have discovered the final release was November 1, 2019, for Python 3.5. Lastly, we would have identified that Python 3.6 has active support until December 2021. We would suggest Python 3.6 or higher but would allow Python 3.5 until the announcement of the end-of-life date.

EXERCISE 3-2: ASSESSING PACKAGES

Instructions:

Assess all the results and recommend the package(s) the developers should use.

Answer:

At the time of this writing, we would have observed the following results:

1. "got" package

   - 30 nodes and 37 links in the dependency graph

   - No vulnerabilities per Snyk and npm audit

   - Outdated npm package

   - Has "request" as a peer dependency

2. "http-request" package

   - Nine nodes and eight links in the dependency graph

   - No vulnerabilities per Snyk and npm audit

   - Outdated npm package in the dependency graph

3. "request" package

   - 48 nodes and 60 links in the dependency graph

   - One vulnerability per Snyk

   - Seven moderate and three high vulnerabilities per npm audit

   - Outdated npm package

4. "request-promise" package

   - Eight nodes and seven links in the dependency graph

   - No vulnerabilities per Snyk and npm audit

   - Outdated npm package

   - Has "request" as a peer dependency

Based on these findings, we would avoid using "request" because it has the largest dependency graph and the most vulnerabilities. Furthermore, the request package became deprecated on February 11, 2020. We would recommend "http-request" due to the smaller dependency graph and having no known vulnerabilities.

Index

A

Access key, 139
Active Directory (AD)
    administrative roles, 141, 142
    application registrations, 141, 149–151
    assigning subscriptions, 185
    groups, 141, 143
    JSON role definition, 146–148
    role definitions, 144–148
    scope, 151, 152
    users, 141, 143, 144
Alerting
    AWS features/capabilities, 309
    Azure features/capabilities, 310
    general principles
        notification destinations, 308
        operational notifications, 307
        security-related notifications, 307
        third-party solutions, 309
        verbosity, 308
    Google Cloud features/capabilities, 311
Alexa smart home, 73
Amazon API Gateway, 73
Amazon CloudWatch, 73
Amazon Cognito, 74
Amazon DynamoDB, 74
Amazon Kinesis, 74
Amazon Lex, 74
Amazon Resource Names (ARNs), 133
Amazon Simple Storage Service (S3), 54, 75

Amazon Web Services (AWS), 16, 39
    CloudFormation, 75
    CodeCommit, 75
    configuration settings
        lambda layers, 121
        packaging defining, 121
        resources, 122
    EventBridge, 76
    general permissions model
        implementation
        CI/CD pipelines and
            CloudFormation roles, 168
        organization level, 165
        project and development stage
            levels, 165
        resource level, 169, 171
        role level, 166
        users, 166, 168
    interfaces, SDK, 77
    IoT, 76
    lambda event triggers, 73–76
    lambda runtime options, 40
    securing account
        alternate contacts, 191
        IAM password policy, 193
        one-time password, 193
        security status, 192
        updating information, 190
    setting up, 333
    users, permissions, 136–139

Q

R

Printed in the United States
By Bookmasters